In the name of justice

DATE DUE

IN THE NAME OF
JUSTICE

LEADING EXPERTS REEXAMINE THE CLASSIC ARTICLE
"THE AIMS OF THE CRIMINAL LAW"

IN THE NAME OF
JUSTICE

LEADING EXPERTS REEXAMINE THE CLASSIC ARTICLE
"THE AIMS OF THE CRIMINAL LAW"

EDITED BY TIMOTHY LYNCH

CATO
INSTITUTE
WASHINGTON, D.C.

Library of Congress Cataloging-in-Publication Data

In the name of justice : leading experts reexamine the classic article "The aims of the criminal law" / edited by Timothy Lynch.
   p. cm.
  Includes bibliographical references and index.
  ISBN 978-1-933995-22-9 (alk. paper)
  1. Criminal justice, Administration of—United States. 2. Criminal law—United States. 3. Criminal law. 4. Hart, Henry Melvin. Aims of the criminal law. I. Lynch, Timothy. II. Title.

KF9223.I58 2009
345.73'05--dc22   2008055110

Cover design by Jon Meyers.

Chapter 7 from *Tyranny of the Status Quo.*
Copyright © 1984 by Milton Friedman and Rose D. Friedman, reprinted by permission of Houghton Mifflin Harcourt Publishing Company.

Printed in the United States of America.

CATO INSTITUTE
1000 Massachusetts Ave., N.W.
Washington, D.C. 20001
www.cato.org

Contents

Introduction:

First Principles of American Criminal Justice

*Timothy Lynch**

A common question that pollsters ask Americans is whether they believe the country is on the "right track." The response is supposed to convey a rough assessment as to how well policymakers are perceived to be handling domestic and foreign policy challenges. If I were asked to give such a rough assessment about the criminal justice system today, I would say that it is on the "wrong track."

A recent government report says that America now has *7 million people* under criminal justice "supervision," which is the highest number ever.[1] The number of criminal offenses on the books has exploded even as the number of trials has dwindled.[2] The first principles of American justice seem to be falling by the wayside. Given these trends, it is an appropriate time to return to fundamentals so as to get a better handle on what is happening and why. The best place to begin is with Henry Hart's classic exposition, "The Aims of the Criminal Law."

Although Hart's article was written in 1958, it continues to be frequently cited in law journals because it contains a succinct and thoughtful discussion of criminal justice fundamentals. More than any other legal scholar, Hart challenges readers to consider the most basic question: What do we mean by "crime"? Is a crime anything lawmakers say it is? If not, what is a crime exactly? One may not always agree with Hart's conclusions, but he left us with a useful framework to examine many of the most important issues in our criminal justice system.

* The author wishes to thank Brandi Dunn, who provided superb administrative support, not only in helping him on this introductory chapter, but in helping to bring all of the chapters together into this handsome edited collection.

For his many insights, we owe Hart a debt of gratitude. And what better way to pay tribute to a teacher than to make his work even more accessible to people interested in the field of criminal law? So, we at the Cato Institute are pleased to republish Hart's classic article in this volume. To generate further discussion and debate about his ideas, we invited leading thinkers to offer comments on Hart's article. How have Hart's ideas held up over time? Did he miss anything important?

It is our hope that this book will prompt scholars, policymakers, and others to reflect on the proper role of the criminal sanction in a free society.

*   *   *

The American Constitution sets forth a philosophical foundation for our criminal justice system. My thesis is that the United States has been drifting away from that foundation. To prove this idea, I will briefly juxtapose the first principles of the criminal justice system against the current state of our law. Readers should know in advance that I will not be defending the first principles, such as the jury trial or the constitutional principle of federalism, at length. The importance of these principles, procedures, and safeguards—for purposes of this article—will be considered self-evident.[3] Henry Hart covered a lot of ground in his essay, but he did not attempt to survey the deterioration of constitutional safeguards. Much of the erosion, to be sure, transpired after his article appeared. But some of the damage was already well under way. Whatever may have been the reason for that omission, readers must understand that lost ground to better appreciate the way in which our system operates today. My purpose is to draw attention to the overall scope of that problem, to briefly discuss first principles for a free society more generally, and to assist policymakers who are ready to shift to a new paradigm of criminal justice.

Against that background, then, let me begin.

The Original Constitutional Understanding of "Crimes"

Most discussions about crime are surprisingly vague on the concept itself. The criminal law field is essentially divided between two positions: utilitarians and retributionists. Utilitarians hold that the criminal law should *prevent* anti-social behavior. Because people respond to incentives and disincentives, criminal penalties, if cali-brated sensibly, can minimize criminal infractions.[4] Retributionists hold that adults are responsible moral agents and that the criminal law should *punish* those who choose to commit offenses.[5] Whatever may be the merits and demerits of that philosophical debate, Hart called attention to the fact that the American Constitution is *not* ideologically neutral with respect to the content of the substantive criminal law.

Indeed, one of Hart's sharpest criticisms is directed at the Supreme Court over its failure to grapple with the original *constitutional under-standing* of the term "crime." It is a mistake to assume that the Constitution does not shape how the government may use the crimi-nal sanction. First, consider the numerous safeguards that are replete in the constitutional text. The Constitution prohibits unreasonable searches, excessive bail, and cruel and unusual punishment. To peo-ple accused of crimes, the Constitution guarantees a speedy, public, and impartial jury trial. The accused also has the right to the assis-tance of counsel, to confront witnesses, and to call their own wit-nesses. Clearly, the text of the Constitution sought to limit and circumscribe the application of the criminal law. And yet, if legisla-tors have carte blanch to define crimes and to withhold or abolish certain legal defenses, then the Constitution's procedural protections will prove mightily ineffectual. As Hart pointedly observed, "What sense does it make to insist upon procedural safeguards in criminal prosecutions if anything whatever can be made a crime in the first place?"[6]

Second, for William Blackstone and other criminal law experts of the 18th century, the term "crime" was not as general as the term "statute." Blackstone believed that "there should be no judgment of criminality without a finding of moral culpability."[7] When Justice William O. Douglas opined that the High Court does not "go with Blackstone in saying that 'a vicious will' is necessary to constitute a crime,"[8] Hart wanted to know the reasons for that conclusion. "Despite the unmistakable indications that the Constitution means something definite and something serious when it speaks of 'crime,' the Supreme Court of the United States has hardly got to first base in working out what that something is. From beginning to end, there is scarcely a single opinion by any member of the Court which confronts the question in a fashion which deserves intellectual respect."[9] Unfortunately, little progress has been made on this matter since Hart made that observation 50 years ago.[10]

If the original understanding of the words used by the Framers of the Constitution is the proper guidepost for a conscientious interpretation of the U.S. Constitution—and it is—then the question of what "crime" meant needs to be elucidated further by scholars, jurists, and policymakers.

Ignorance of the Law: A Perfectly Valid Defense

The sheer volume of modern law makes it impossible for an ordinary American household to stay informed. And yet, prosecutors vigorously defend the old legal maxim that "ignorance of the law is no excuse."[11] That maxim may have been appropriate for a society that simply criminalized inherently evil conduct, such as murder, rape, and theft, but it is wholly inappropriate in a labyrinthine regulatory regime that criminalizes activities that are morally neutral. As Hart noted, "In no respect is contemporary law subject to greater reproach than for its obtuseness to this fact."[12]

Carlton Wilson was prosecuted because he owned a firearm. Wilson's purchase of the firearm was perfectly legal, but, years later, he didn't know that he had to give it up after a judge issued a restraining order during his divorce proceedings. When Wilson protested that the judge never informed him of that obligation and that the restraining order itself said nothing about firearms, prosecutors shrugged, "ignorance of the law is no excuse."[13] Although the courts upheld Wilson's conviction, Judge Richard Posner dissented, "We want people to familiarize themselves with the laws bearing on their activities. But a reasonable opportunity doesn't mean being able to go to the local law library and read Title 18. It would be preposterous to suppose that someone from Wilson's milieu is able to take advantage of such an opportunity."[14] Posner noted that Wilson would serve more than three years in a federal penitentiary for an omission that he "could not have suspected was a crime or even a civil wrong."[15]

It is simply outrageous for the government to impose a legal duty on every citizen to "know" all of the mind-boggling rules and regulations that have been promulgated over the years.[16] Policymakers can and should discard the "ignorance-is-no-excuse" maxim by enacting a law that would require prosecutors to prove that regulatory violations are "willful" or, in the alternative, that would permit a good-faith belief in the legality of one's conduct to be pleaded and proved as a defense. The former rule is already in place for our complicated tax laws—but it should also shield unwary Americans from all of the laws and regulations as well.[17]

A Criminal Code with Clear and Objective Terms

Even if there were but a few crimes on the books, the terms of such laws need to be drafted with precision. There is precious little difference between a secret law and a published regulation that cannot be understood. History is filled with examples of oppressive governments that persecuted unpopular groups and innocent individuals by keeping the law's requirements from the people. For example, the Roman emperor Caligula posted new laws high on the columns of buildings so that ordinary citizens could not study the laws. Such abominable policies were discarded during the Age of Enlightenment, and a new set of principles—known generally as the "rule of law"—took hold. Those principles included the requirements of legality and specificity.

"Legality" means a regularized process, ideally rooted in moral principle, by which crimes are designated and prosecuted by the government. The Enlightenment philosophy was expressed by the maxim *nullum crimen sine lege* (there is no crime without a law). In other words, people can be punished only for conduct previously prohibited by law. That principle is clearly enunciated in the ex post facto clause of the U.S. Constitution (article I, section 9). But the purpose of the ex post facto clause can be subverted if the legislature can enact a criminal law that condemns conduct in general terms, such as "dangerous and harmful" behavior. Such a law would not give people fair warning of the prohibited conduct. To guard against the risk of arbitrary enforcement, the Supreme Court has said that the law must be clear:

> A criminal statute cannot rest upon an uncertain foundation. The crime, and the elements constituting it, must be so clearly expressed that the ordinary person can intelligently choose, in advance, what course it is lawful for him to pursue. Penal statutes prohibiting the doing of certain things, and providing a punishment for their violation, should not admit of

> such a double meaning that the citizen may act upon the one
> conception of its requirements and the courts upon another.[18]

The principles of legality and specificity operate together to reduce the likelihood of arbitrary and discriminatory application of the law by keeping policy matters away from police officers, administrative bureaucrats, prosecutors, judges, and members of juries, who would have to resolve ambiguities on an ad hoc and subjective basis.

Although the legality and specificity requirements are supposed to be among the first principles of American criminal law, a "regulatory" exception has crept into modern jurisprudence. The Supreme Court allows "greater leeway" in regulatory matters because the practicalities of modern governance supposedly limit "the specificity with which legislators can spell out prohibitions."[19] During the past 50 years, fuzzy legal standards, such as unreasonable, unusual, and excessive, have withstood constitutional challenge.

The Framers understood that democracy alone was no guarantor of justice. As James Madison noted, "It will be of little avail to the people that the laws are made by men of their own choice if the laws be so voluminous that they cannot be read, or so incoherent that they cannot be understood; if they be repealed or revised before they are promulgated, or undergo such incessant changes that no man, who knows what the law is today, can guess what it will be tomorrow."[20] Unfortunately, Madison's vision of unbridled lawmaking is an apt description of our modern regulatory state.[21] For example, the Environmental Protection Agency received so many queries about the meaning of the Resource Conservation and Recovery Act that it set up a special hotline for questions. Note, however, that the "EPA itself does not guarantee that its answers are correct, and reliance on wrong information given over the RCRA hotline is no defense to an enforcement action."[22] The situation is so obviously rotten that many prosecutors are acknowledging that there is simply too much uncertainty in criminal law. Former Massachusetts Attorney General Scott Harshbarger concedes, "One thing we haven't done well in government is make it very clear, with bright lines, what kinds of activity will subject you to . . . criminal or civil prosecution."[23]

The Supreme Court ought to revisit the precedents that created a regulatory exception to the requirement of specificity. Those precedents are making a mockery of the due process principles that have helped to secure procedural justice in ordinary criminal cases. Legal uncertainties should be resolved in favor of private individuals and organizations, not the state.

No Place for Strict Liability

The two basic premises that undergird Anglo-American criminal law are the requirements of *mens rea* (guilty mind) and *actus reus* (guilty act).[24] The first requirement says that for an act to constitute a crime there must be "bad intent." Dean Roscoe Pound of Harvard Law School writes, "Historically, our substantive criminal law is based upon a theory of punishing the vicious will. It postulates a free agent confronted with a choice between doing right and doing wrong and choosing freely to do wrong."[25] According to that view, a man could not be prosecuted for leaving an airport with the suitcases of another if he mistakenly believed that he owned the luggage. As the Utah Supreme Court noted in *State v. Blue* (1898), *mens rea* was considered an indispensable element of a criminal offense. "To prevent the punishment of the innocent, there has been ingrafted into our system of jurisprudence, as presumably in every other, the principle that the wrongful or criminal intent is the essence of crime, without which it cannot exist."[26]

By the same token, bad thoughts alone do not constitute a crime if there is no "bad act." If a police officer discovers a diary that someone accidentally dropped on the sidewalk, and the contents include references to wanting to steal the possessions of another, the author cannot be prosecuted for a crime. Even if an off-duty police officer overhears two men in a tavern discussing their hatred of the police and their desire to kill a cop, no lawful arrest can be made if the men do not take action to further their cop-killing scheme. The basic idea, of course, is that the government should not be in the business of punishing "bad thoughts."

When *mens rea* and *actus reus* were fundamental prerequisites for criminal activity, no person could be branded a "criminal" until a prosecutor could persuade a jury that the accused possessed "an evil-meaning mind with an evil-doing hand."[27] That understanding of crime—as a compound concept—was firmly entrenched in the English common law at the time of the American Revolution.

Over the years, however, the moral underpinnings of the Anglo-American view of criminal law fell into disfavor. The *mens rea* and *actus reus* requirements became viewed as burdensome restraints on well-meaning lawmakers who wanted to solve social problems through administrative regulations. As Professor Richard G. Singer observes, "Criminal law . . . has come to be seen as merely one more method used by society to achieve social control."[28]

The change began innocently enough. To protect young girls, statutory rape laws were enacted that flatly prohibited sexual intercourse with girls under the age of legal consent. Those groundbreaking laws applied even if the girl lied about her age and consented to the intercourse and if the man reasonably and in good faith believed the girl to be over the age of consent. Once the courts accepted that exception to the *mens rea* principle, legislators began to identify other activities that had to be stamped out—even at the cost of convicting innocent-minded people.

"Strict liability" criminal offenses exploded during the 20th century as legislators created hundreds of "public welfare offenses" relating to health and safety. Each time a person sought to prove an innocent state-of-mind, the Supreme Court responded that there is "wide latitude" in the legislative power to create offenses and "to exclude elements of knowledge and diligence from [their] definition."[29] Those strict liability rulings have been sharply criticized by legal commentators.[30] Hart, for example, argued that there could be no "justification for condemning and punishing a human being as a criminal when he has done nothing which is blameworthy."[31]

A dramatic illustration of the problem was presented in *Thorpe v. Florida* (1979).[32] John Thorpe was confronted by a thief who brandished a gun. Thorpe got into a scuffle with the thief and wrested the gun away from him. When the police arrived on the scene, Thorpe was arrested and prosecuted under a law that made it illegal for any felon to possess a firearm. Thorpe tried to challenge the application of that law by pointing to the extenuating circumstances of his case. The appellate court acknowledged the "harsh result," but noted that the law did not require a vicious will or criminal intent. Thus, self-defense was not "available as defense to the crime."[33]

Strict liability laws should be abolished because their very purpose is to divorce a person's intentions from his actions. But if the criminal sanction imports blame—and it does—it is a perversion to apply that sanction to self-defense and other acts that are not blameworthy.[34] Our criminal law should reflect the old Latin maxim, *actus not facit reum nisi mens sit rea* (an act does not make one guilty unless his mind is guilty).[35]

No Criminal Liability for the Acts of Another

Everyone agrees with the proposition that if a person commands, pays, or induces another to commit a crime on that person's behalf, the person should be treated as having committed the act.[36] Thus, if a husband hires a man to kill his wife, the husband is also guilty of murder. But it is another matter entirely to hold one person criminally responsible for the *unauthorized* acts of another. "Vicarious liability," the legal doctrine under which a person may be held responsible for the criminal acts of another, was once "repugnant to every instinct of the criminal jurist."[37] Alas, the modern trend in American criminal law is to embrace vicarious criminal liability.

Vicarious liability initially crept into regulations that were deemed necessary to control business enterprises. One of the key cases was *United States v. Park* (1975).[38] John Park was the president of Acme Markets Inc., a large national food chain. When the Food and Drug Administration found unsanitary conditions at a warehouse in April 1970, it sent Park a letter demanding corrective action. Park referred the matter to Acme's vice president for legal affairs. When Park was informed that the regional vice president was investigating the situation and would take corrective action, Park thought that was the end of the matter. But when unsanitary warehouse conditions were found on a subsequent inspection, prosecutors indicted both Acme and Park for violations of the Federal Food, Drug and Cosmetic Act. An appellate court overturned Park's conviction because it found that the trial court's legal instructions could have "left the jury with the erroneous impression that [Park] could be found guilty in the absence of 'wrongful action' on his part" and that proof of that element was constitutionally mandated by due process.[39] The Supreme Court, however, reversed the appellate ruling. Chief Justice Warren Burger opined that the legislature could impose criminal liability on "those who voluntarily assume positions of authority in business enterprises" because such people have a duty "to devise whatever measures [are] necessary to ensure compliance" with regulations.[40] Thus, under the rationale of *Park*, an honest executive can be branded a criminal if a low-level employee in a different city disobeys a supervisor's instructions and violates a regulation—even if the violation causes no harm whatsoever.[41]

Vicarious liability has not been confined to the commercial regulation context.[42] Tina Bennis lost her car to the police because of the actions of her husband. The police found him in the vehicle with a prostitute.[43] Pearlie Rucker was evicted from her apartment in a public housing complex because her daughter was involved with illicit drugs. To crack down on the drug trade, Congress enacted a law that was so strict that tenants could be evicted if one of their household members or guests used drugs. The eviction could proceed even if the drug activity took place outside the residence. Also under that federal law, it did not matter if the tenant was totally *unaware* of the drug activity.[44] Policymakers are also enacting laws to make parents *criminally* responsible when their children commit crimes.[45] Parents of wayward teens are now trapped by circumstances beyond their control. If a parent uses discipline that a prosecutor considers "too strong," the parent could face prosecution for child abuse. But parents can also go to prison for failing to rein in teenagers who commit crimes.

No Place for Corporate Criminal Liability

When corporate executives commit crimes, they can be arrested and jailed. "Corporate criminal liability" refers to holding the corporation itself liable for the acts of its employees. While enterprise liability is appropriate for purposes of civil liability, it "violates virtually every basic principle of criminal law, which generally limits liability to personal actions carried out with a culpable mental state and precludes the imposition of liability that is vicarious in the sense of imputing one person's act or state to another."[46] Artificial entities, such as corporations, are simply incapable of committing bad acts and forming the requisite "criminal intent" for criminal liability.

The doctrine of corporate criminal liability crept into U.S. law in 1909 in *New York Central and Hudson River Railroad v. United States*.[47] The rationale for the precedent—that criminal liability is the only means of effectively controlling commercial transactions—has proven to be unpersuasive to other courts. Many states reject the doctrine and continue to adhere to the common law rule, which requires criminal intent. George Mason University law professor

Jeffrey Parker observes, "Virtually every other modern legal system—East and West—rejects the concept of corporate criminal liability as inconsistent with the principles of criminal law."[48]

Furthermore, experience has shown that corporate criminal liability has no greater "deterrent effect" beyond that of corporate *civil* liability. So, some scholars have concluded that corporate crime legislation is mostly symbolic.[49] That is, whenever there is a public outcry in response to corporate wrongdoing, members of Congress enact more corporate crime legislation out of fear of an electoral setback. After the fanfare about the new legislation has passed, very little changes because of the infrequency of enforcement. Parker concludes that "there is no legitimate function to corporate criminal liability that cannot be served equally well, if not better, by civil enforcement."[50] He's right. Policymakers should excise the doctrine of corporate criminal liability from American law.[51]

A Limited Federal Role

The American Constitution created a federal government with limited powers. As James Madison noted in the *Federalist* no. 45, "The powers delegated by the proposed Constitution to the federal government are few and defined. Those which are to remain in the State governments are numerous and indefinite." Most of the federal government's "delegated powers" are specifically set forth in article I, section 8. The Tenth Amendment was appended to the Constitution to make it clear that the powers not delegated to the federal government "are reserved to the States respectively, or to the people."

Crime is a serious problem. But under the Constitution, it is a matter to be handled by state and local government. Unfortunately, as the years passed, Congress eventually assumed the power to enact a vast number of criminal laws pursuant to its power "to regulate Commerce with foreign Nations, and among the several States, and with the Indian Tribes."[52]

In recent years, Congress has federalized the crimes of gun possession within a school zone, carjacking, wife beating, and church arsons. All of those crimes and more have been rationalized under the Commerce Clause.[53] In *United States v. Lopez*, the Supreme Court finally struck down a federal criminal law, the Gun-Free School

Zone Act of 1990, because the connection between handgun possession and interstate commerce was simply too tenuous.[54] In a concurring opinion, Justice Clarence Thomas noted that if Congress had
been given authority over matters that simply "affect" interstate
commerce, much, if not all, of the enumerated powers set forth in
article I, section 8 would be unnecessary. Indeed, it is difficult to
dispute Justice Thomas' conclusion that an interpretation of the
commerce power that "makes the rest of §8 surplusage simply cannot be correct."[55]

Vices Are Not Crimes

An ideal criminal justice system would draw a sharp distinction
between vices and crimes. There are moral and practical reasons to
draw that distinction. It is wrong to initiate force against people in
an attempt to make them act "responsibly" in their personal lives.[56]
Social engineers may have good intentions about wanting to help
people avoid mistakes, but they are not justified in using raw power
against adults who are not persuaded by their arguments. People
must remember that, when a law is enacted, the police obtain the
power to snoop, search, and arrest. If a suspected violator resists
detection or arrest, the police can "beat them, stun-gun them, tear
gas them, seize their property, and shoot them."[57]

If the purpose of government is to secure the right to life, liberty,
and the pursuit of happiness, the state becomes *destructive* of that
end when it seeks to "protect" an adult from himself or herself.[58]
We would indignantly resist any attempt by a neighbor to break
into our home and tell us how to spend our time and money more
"wisely." The same holds true for politicians and bureaucrats.[59] As
Justice Louis Brandeis once noted, "Experience should teach us to
be most on our guard to protect liberty when the Government's
purposes are beneficent. Men born to freedom are naturally alert to
repel invasion of their liberty by evil-minded rulers. The greatest
dangers to liberty lurk in insidious encroachment by men of zeal,
well meaning but without understanding."[60]

Practical problems exist as well. First, the police, courts, and prisons are busy enough with the crimes that occur in their respective
jurisdictions. Murder, rape, assault, and theft should prompt swift
investigations and punishment. Those cases invariably suffer when
resources are directed toward vice "crimes."[61] Law enforcement

resources are limited. A police unit cannot follow up on leads for an unsolved rape if it must follow a lead about marijuana plants growing on secluded acreage.

Second, when the government attempts to police vice offenses, there are no complaining witnesses on which to base a case. People do not call the police to say they gambled in a game of dice, smoked a marijuana cigarette, or spent a night with a prostitute. Without complaining witnesses, the government typically turns to dubious tactics, such as wiretapping, informers, and paramilitary raids. And the collateral damage too often goes unexamined. Who remembers the innocent bystander who was struck and killed by a police car that was in pursuit of a bootlegger in the 1920s?[62] Today, during the drug war, innocent people die as the police break into homes in search of contraband.[63] The costs of those enforcement measures simply outweigh the benefits.[64]

Hart appears to have held a contrary view. He said the criminal law should be used to sharpen "the community's sense of right and wrong."[65] He seemed to believe that the criminal sanction could serve an educative function—"training for responsible citizenship."[66] His sole reservation seemed to be the practical one—that policymakers should not overreach and enact laws that would prove to be unenforceable.[67] Whether Hart simply glossed over the distinction between vices and crimes or failed to appreciate the significance of this issue is hard to say. In either event, this is the most significant shortcoming of his exposition on the role of the criminal sanction.

Jury Trials

The Constitution says that "the Trial of all Crimes, except in Cases of Impeachment; shall be by Jury...." Given that provision, most Americans can be forgiven for thinking that our criminal cases are adjudicated by lay juries in courtrooms. The ugly truth is that the U.S. system does not remotely resemble the system of jury trials contemplated by the country's fundamental charter. As Professor John Langbein has noted, "There is an astonishing discrepancy between what the constitutional texts promise and what the criminal justice system delivers."[68]

Jury trials are a rarity in the American criminal justice system. The vast majority of cases are not adjudicated at all—they are instead plea-bargained. No one can deny that the United States has essentially adopted a system of charge and sentence bargaining.[69] Still, one can argue that the rarity of jury trials does not necessarily prove that the exercise of the right to a jury trial is not "free." That is, one could argue that people just freely choose to waive their right to a trial. True enough, but *why* would thousands and thousands of criminal defendants enter a guilty plea and forgo their right against self-incrimination and a jury trial? The answer cannot be a matter of sheer happenstance. Fully 95 percent of federal criminal cases do not go to trial—and that high percentage has been the pattern for many years.[70] The truth is that government officials have deliberately engineered the system to "assure that the jury trial system established by the Constitution is seldom utilized."[71]

Plea-bargaining rests on the constitutional fiction that the government does not retaliate against individuals who wish to exercise their constitutional right to trial by jury.[72] Although the fictional nature of that proposition has been apparent to many for some time now, what is new is that more and more people are reaching the conclusion that the fiction is intolerable. For example, Chief Judge William G. Young of the Federal District Court in Massachusetts filed an opinion that was refreshingly candid about what is happening in the modern criminal justice system. "Criminal trial rates in the United States and in this District are plummeting due to the simple fact that today we punish people—punish them severely—simply for going to trial. It is the sheerest sophistry to pretend otherwise."[73] The Supreme Court let loose a runaway train when it sanctioned plea-bargaining. It is time to recognize that disastrous mistake and abolish plea-bargaining.[74]

Speedy Trials

The constitutional guarantee of a speedy trial, like the jury trial provision, has been under assault by the crushing caseloads that are clogging courthouses around the country. When a defense counsel seeks a delay in a case, the speedy trial guarantee is not implicated, but when the prosecution seeks repeated postponements, the courts are supposed to intervene on behalf of the person accused. It is bad enough when a person must live under the cloud of a criminal accusation, but it is much worse for a person who cannot raise enough money to make bail. Anyone who cannot make bail must remain in jail until the trial date. Our criminal justice system places those indigent people in an awful dilemma: plead guilty to the crime and get out of prison early or languish in prison until a trial date can be arranged. In a cruel twist, the indigent person who insists on his or her innocence—and who is eventually acquitted after a trial—may end up serving more time in jail than the person who was guilty of the crime but accepted a plea offer.[75]

Once again, despite the explicit guarantee set forth in the constitutional text, the courts have rationalized away the most blatant violations. For example, when Henry Bernard Spivey's speedy trial complaint reached the North Carolina Supreme Court in 2003, he had been in jail for *four years* without a trial.[76] The attorneys representing the state took the position that Spivey had not proven any "willful misconduct" by the government. And besides, the courthouse was clogged with cases, and there were staffing shortages. Under such circumstances, delays were inevitable. The state supreme court actually agreed with the prosecutors that there was no speedy trial violation!

Two justices dissented from the ruling. The dissenters pointed out that the idea behind the speedy trial guarantee goes all the way back to the Magna Carta. They said that the prosecutors in the case either did not recognize the problem that they were creating for themselves or they ignored it. Either way, a crowded court docket cannot justify a delay of *four years.* The justices said they doubted whether a single citizen in the state would find the delay acceptable if it concerned a spouse—or a son or daughter—who was waiting for a day in court. The dissenters also wondered about the ramifications of the ruling. What if the backlog of cases continued—or got even worse? In the year 2020, would seven-year delays become an accepted norm? The majority of the North Carolina Supreme Court did not respond to those questions.

The right to a speedy trial was included in the Bill of Rights for a reason—to prevent state agents from employing oppressive pretrial incarceration. If the rationale of the *Spivey* precedent is followed, this crucial constitutional safeguard will wither.

No Compulsory Self-Incrimination

Compulsory examination under oath may be the most notorious procedure associated with the English Star Chamber of the 15th to

17th centuries. Accused individuals had to swear on the Bible that they would answer all questions truthfully. Anyone who refused to take the oath could be cited for contempt and sent to prison. Henry VIII used the procedure against individuals who questioned the religious teachings of his ministers. Dissenters had to reveal their honest religious convictions under oath and risk torture and execution or to lie under oath and be, as they believed, eternally damned.

The Star Chamber was eventually abolished, of course, and the right against self-incrimination became a hallmark of the common law. After the American Revolution, the right was incorporated into the Bill of Rights and became binding in 1791. The Fifth Amendment states, "[N]or shall [any person] be compelled in any criminal case to be a witness against himself." Although this safeguard was originally regarded in England as a rule of testimonial evidence, the American judiciary took the principle further. In early American history, courts held that the Fifth Amendment guarantee protected individuals not only against compulsory courtroom testimony but also against the government's investigatory processes.[77]

The Supreme Court has held that corporate employees cannot invoke the right against self-incrimination to protect themselves from a criminal prosecution.[78] An accountant, for example, cannot resist a grand jury subpoena for the tax records of a corporation that is suspected of tax evasion—even if the records would incriminate the accountant personally. Lawmakers have exploited such tax-related precedents by requiring businesses to keep records of other activities and to make such records available to government agents. But as Justice Robert Jackson, among others, recognized, the Fifth Amendment is essentially nullified if the government can "require a citizen to keep an account of his deeds and misdeeds and turn over or exhibit the record on demand of government inspectors, who then can use it to convict him" of a crime.[79] Indeed, Justice Jackson noted sarcastically that government could simplify law enforcement by merely requiring every citizen "to keep a diary that would show where he was at all times, with whom he was, and what he was up to."[80]

The constitutional safeguard has also been compromised outside of the business and regulatory context. In the 1970s, the Supreme Court, over several dissents, approved myriad "stop and report" laws that require motor vehicle drivers to confess their infractions to the police.[81] More recently, the police have been given the power to forcibly extract a blood sample from a person suspected of driving under the influence of alcohol.[82]

Consent Forms for Consent Searches

If the police do not have a search warrant, they can still search a person's home, car, or belongings if they can secure that person's consent. By far, consent searches are the most common type of search employed by the authorities. Unfortunately, they are also the most frequently abused.[83] The reason is twofold: (a) most people are unaware of their right to withhold consent and (b) police agents systemically obscure the line between mere requests and lawful police commands.

So, for example, when a police officer uses his "command voice" and barks out, "Let's see what's in that backpack!" it is unclear whether he is making a request or issuing a command. Most people don't want to disobey, so they quickly comply. If contraband, such as, say, a marijuana cigarette is found, the person can be arrested, and the officer can testify that the search was lawful because the owner of the backpack "consented" to the search.

To minimize abuses, some cities require police officers to obtain a signature on a consent form before any search can take place.[84] This sensible policy should be followed in every jurisdiction by every police agency. The forms will remind citizens that they have a choice. Such forms can also help the police to demonstrate the probity of their conduct before skeptical judges and juries. This reform is certainly not a cure-all, but it will help to ensure that so-called consent searches are based on *bona fide* consent.

No Double Jeopardy

The Fifth Amendment's double jeopardy clause bars the government from subjecting any person to multiple prosecutions for the same offense. But the Supreme Court has interpreted that clause in a way that allows separate state and federal prosecutions for the same conduct. That legal doctrine, which is known as the "dual sovereign" exception to the double jeopardy principle, gives prosecutors the power to retry thousands of cases.

The double jeopardy principle has been recognized as one of the great bulwarks against government oppression. Without that protection, the government could use its vast resources to wear political dissidents and others down with repeated prosecutions. Multiple prosecutions also allow government attorneys to hone their trial tactics before new juries, which only increases the risk of an erroneous conviction. To guard against that danger, the Framers explicitly incorporated the immunity against double jeopardy into the Bill of Rights.

However, the Bill of Rights constrained only the federal government until the 1868 ratification of the Fourteenth Amendment, which extended the protections against state government actions. Because federal criminal prosecutions were few and far between for much of U.S. history, the question of how the double jeopardy principle fit into our federalist system remained a theoretical issue for many years. For example, American courts were vexed early on by whether the state and federal governments could make the same conduct a crime. As previously noted, the powers of the federal government are set forth in article I, section 8 of the Constitution, and the Tenth Amendment makes it clear that the "powers not delegated to the United States by the Constitution" are reserved to "the States respectively, or to the people." Early courts believed that, by virtue of the separation of powers and the creation of separate jurisdictions, "double trials would virtually never occur in our country." In the rare instances of concurrent jurisdiction, the courts expected the prosecutors to respect the double jeopardy principle. In *Jett v. The Commonwealth* (1867), for example, the Virginia Supreme Court stated, "We must suppose that the criminal laws will be administered, as they should be, in a spirit of justice and benignity to the citizen, and that those who are entrusted with their execution will interpose to protect offenders against double punishment, whenever their interposition is necessary to prevent injustice or oppression; and that if, in any case, they should fail to do so, the wrong will be addressed by the pardoning power."[85]

As long as the concurrent jurisdiction of the federal and state governments was limited, the potential for prosecutorial mischief was relatively minor. But the legal landscape was drastically altered after the turn of the century when the federal government expanded its criminal jurisdiction beyond "the unique areas of national concern listed among its constitutionally enumerated powers."[86] Attorney Daniel A. Braun writes, "The criminal codes of the states and the nation presently identify many of the same wrongs and share many of the same goals. For this reason, an individual who violates the criminal law of a state stands a considerable chance of violating a provision of the federal code as well."[87]

The Supreme Court has repeatedly upheld successive state and federal prosecutions. Its legal analysis typically emphasizes the law enforcement interests of government over the potential abuse of individual defendants. Justice Hugo Black, among others, insisted on viewing the legal issue "from the standpoint of the individual who is being prosecuted." In a biting dissent, Black observed, "If danger to the innocent is emphasized, the danger is surely no less when the power of State and Federal Governments is brought to bear on one man in two trials, than when one of these 'Sovereigns' proceeds alone."[88] The mischievous "dual sovereign" loophole in double jeopardy law should be closed immediately.[89]

Abolish Mandatory Minimum Sentences

Since the promulgation of the Model Penal Code by the American Law Institute in the 1950s, most crimes are generally defined by the legislature, and appropriate penalties are defined by statute. However, mandatory minimum sentences and rigid sentencing guidelines have shifted too much power to legislators who are not involved in particular cases. They turn judges into clerks and prevent judges from weighing all the facts and circumstances in setting appropriate sentences.[90]

In addition, mandatory minimums too often result in sentences that are grotesquely disproportionate to the gravity of the offenses.[91] Federal Judge J. Spencer Letts writes, "Under the statutory minimum, it can make no difference whether [the defendant] is a lifetime criminal or a first time offender. Indeed, under this sledgehammer approach, it could make no difference if the day before making his one slip in an otherwise unblemished life, the defendant had rescued fifteen children from a burning building, or had won the Congressional Medal of Honor while defending his country."[92]

Policymakers should repeal mandatory minimums and let judges perform their traditional function of weighing the facts and setting appropriate sentences. As Hart noted, "A society which entrusts its juries with power to bring in a verdict of acquittal in cases of undoubted guilt ought to be able to trust its judges to exercise the lesser discretion of leniency in sentencing."[93]

Keep Police Within, Not Above, the Law

Although government officials often proclaim that "no one is above the law" and that accountability in government is essential, police agents and government attorneys typically press for shocking privileges, or immunities, when actual cases arise.[94] When John Colaprete sued federal agents for unlawfully raiding his home and business and for stealing an expensive watch from his safe, government attorneys argued—and a court ruled—that the agents were immune from suit because it would be unfair to presume that police officers would know that stealing was against the law![95]

When an ordinary civilian is involved in a shooting, police detectives are anxious to question the people involved as soon as possible—preferably at the scene the same evening. But when police officers are involved in questionable shootings, they sometimes delay questioning for several days. Temple University Professor James Fyfe notes, "The cops in New York enjoy a degree of protection that doesn't exist in other places and is unwarranted."[96]

Most disturbing of all was the argument advanced by the Department of Justice when an agent from the Federal Bureau of Investigation was indicted for murder by an Idaho prosecutor. The Solicitor General of the United States urged the courts to dismiss the indictment because, "these federal law enforcement officials are privileged to do what would otherwise be unlawful if done by a private citizen."[97] Note that during a murder trial, the agent could argue self-defense, defense of others, or mistake. But the attorneys for the government contend that those legal defenses are not enough. As unbelievable as it may seem, they want sweeping immunity from murder statutes.

Policymakers at both the federal and state level should disavow such claims for special privileges. One would think that it would be desirable to hold police officers to a *higher* standard of conduct than ordinary civilians.

Retrials for *Brady* Violations

Prosecutorial misconduct, like police misconduct, is a reality. Most prosecutors have no interest in manufacturing evidence to frame innocent people. But in their zeal to convict people whom they believe are guilty, prosecutors too often withhold evidence from defense counsel, judges, and juries. In a landmark case, *Brady v. Maryland*, the Supreme Court ruled that evidence favorable to the accused must be turned over to defense counsel before the trial.[98] "It is not unusual for the prosecutor to have such favorable evidence in his possession in view of the acknowledged superiority of the government's investigative resources and its early access to crucial evidence. For example, the prosecutor might discover a police report of an interview with an eyewitness who stated that the defendant was not the perpetrator of the robbery; the police might tell the prosecutor that one of his key witnesses recently failed a lie detector test and then partially recanted his story; the prosecutor might learn that a laboratory test failed to link the defendant with the murder weapon and items of clothing worn by the killer; at the trial the prosecutor might hear his main witness embellish his testimony to such an extent that he is committing perjury."[99]

The *Brady* case established a sound and just rule, but the enforcement of that rule too often breaks down in practice. There are three reasons for this problem. First, as noted earlier, most cases never go to trial. Thus, as a practical matter, the prosecutor becomes "the de facto law after an arrest, deciding whether to charge the suspect with committing a crime, what charge to file from a range of possibilities, whether to offer a pre-trial deal, and, if so, the terms of the deal."[100] Second, prosecutors get to decide in the first instance whether certain evidence constitutes "*Brady* material." And in their zeal to win, prosecutors have an incentive to interpret the rule narrowly. Third, when *Brady* violations are discovered, the courts are reluctant to order retrials because of the objection that the outcome of the trial "would not have been any different." The upshot is that prosecutors do not face any significant sanctions.[101]

The best prosecutors have adopted an "open file" policy. As one prosecutor explained, "I say, give the defense everything. What's the downside, as long as you don't jeopardize an informant's life? It's an easy call for me."[102] A laudable policy—to be sure—but it is a mistake to rely on self-policing by prosecutors. A powerful impetus is needed to force prosecutors to follow through on their legal obligation. The best way to curb this form of prosecutorial misconduct would be to adopt a strict rule of retrials on the discovery of any *Brady* violation—however minor.[103] Prosecutors and trial judges detest retrials. Thus, the prospect of retrials will revitalize the *Brady* precedent, spur officials to meet their obligation, and improve the overall administration of justice.

Just Compensation for Police Actions

If the police must break down the door to a home to execute a search warrant, the government is not obligated to compensate the owner for the property damage. However, there are many other situations in which the police destroy the property of *innocent* people as they conduct various investigative activities. In those instances, the government should promptly come forward and compensate the innocent person or business. For example, the owner of a Sacramento convenience store had to spend $275,000 to repair damage and to replace merchandise after the police used tear gas to flush out a robbery suspect. A lawsuit was filed when the government refused to compensate the owner.

The store invoked the Fifth Amendment, which provides that "private property [shall not] be taken for public use without just compensation." And the Supreme Court has ruled that the purpose of that guarantee is to prevent state agents from "forcing some people alone to bear public burdens which, in all fairness and justice, should be borne by the public as a whole."[104] Despite that safeguard, the California Supreme Court ruled against the owner. A dissenting judge said the court's emphasis on the reasonableness of the employed police tactic missed the point. "The constitutional requirement of just compensation does not assume that the action was tortuous or otherwise improper. On the contrary, the provision declares that even if the government acted properly in the public interest, the cost of its action should not fall disproportionately on an individual owner."[105]

A closely related financial burden associated with law enforcement investigations concerns the costs of complying with subpoenas. Every day, *innocent* businesspeople are served with subpoenas that demand hotel records, bank records, phone records, credit card records, rental car records, and other transactional data. One telephone company received a subpoena from the Drug Enforcement

Administration that demanded all published and unlisted phone numbers and customer names in its service area. Much of that information could have been obtained from commercial databases. The DEA took the cheap and easy route—cheap and easy for itself, that is. The costs add up over the course of a year. The U.S. Telecom Association says that one of its member companies spent $3.7 million a year accommodating various law enforcement subpoenas.[106]

It is manifestly unfair for the government to foist the costs associated with police investigations on to innocent bystanders. These overweening, unfunded mandates must stop.[107]

Just Compensation for Prosecutorial Actions

If there is one reform that should garner support from across the political spectrum, it is the proposition that if the government makes a mistake and incarcerates the wrong person, the state has an obligation to compensate the victim. It is hard to believe that policymakers have long evaded that moral obligation—but they have.[108] For example, when Ray Kone was exonerated by a DNA test in 2002, he received $50, which was the usual exit payment to every prison convict. Sadly, Kone spent 10 years in the penitentiary before Arizona acknowledged its mistake.[109]

Anthony Robinson served 10 years in a Texas prison for a rape he did not commit. Robinson says it is important to remember that the state's mistake impacts not just the prisoners, but also their families. In Robinson's case, he laments not being available to care for his mother as she grew old.[110] Various "immunity doctrines and the very high bar for any civil remedy historically have made recovery for even the most abusive prosecution virtually impossible."[111] It is simply indefensible that most exonerated prisoners receive either paltry sums or nothing at all.

Federal Judge Frank Easterbrook has called for an even more sweeping reform. According to Easterbrook, any society professing the inestimable value of liberty should be prepared to reimburse the legal expenses of defendants who prevail *at or before trial*.[112] Judge Easterbrook's proposal makes sense. If the prosecution is confident about a particular defendant's guilt—and it ought to be if it filed charges—the government's losses should be minimal.

*　*　*

After reviewing the preceding list of deficiencies, one could easily come away with the mistaken impression that the American criminal justice system has been in a steady, downward spiral. But that is not so. The problems are quite serious, but a proper perspective needs to be maintained. First, the American criminal justice system, with all of its flaws, is still among the best in the world. Second, when some of the past problems have faded from the scene, people can easily forget the positive developments that have taken place over the years. For example, people no longer see trials conducted in a disorderly, mob-like atmosphere.[113] And the police are no longer permitted to shoot down unarmed, nondangerous, fleeing suspects.[114] Nevertheless, we must take a clear-eyed view of the country's wayward drift. The first principles of criminal justice that are plainly set forth in the Constitution are *not* outmoded relics from a bygone era. They are as important today as they were 200 years ago. But those safeguards are not self-executing. We must always remember that free societies do not just "happen." If we do not attend to our first principles, we will lose them and the free society that those principles were designed to secure.

1. The Aims of the Criminal Law

Henry M. Hart, Jr.*

I. Introduction

In trying to formulate the aims of the criminal law, it is important to be aware both of the reasons for making the effort and of the nature of the problem it poses.

The statement has been made, as if in complaint, that "there is hardly a penal code that can be said to have a single basic principle running through it."[1] But it needs to be clearly seen that this is simply a fact, and not a misfortune. A penal code that reflected only a single basic principle would be a very bad one. Social purposes can never be single or simple, or held unqualifiedly to the exclusion of all other social purposes; and an effort to make them so can result only in the sacrifice of other values which also are important. Thus, to take only one example, the purpose of preventing any particular kind of crime, or crimes generally, is qualified always by the purposes of avoiding the conviction of the innocent and of enhancing that sense of security throughout the society which is one of the prime functions of the manifold safeguards of American criminal procedure. And the same thing would be true even if the dominant purpose of the criminal law were thought to be the rehabilitation of offenders rather than the prevention of offenses.

Examination of the purposes commonly suggested for the criminal law will show that each of them is complex and that none may be thought of as wholly excluding the others. Suppose, for example, that the deterrence of offenses is taken to be the chief end. It will

---

* This article by Henry M. Hart, Jr., was originally published in *Law and Contemporary Problems* 25 (1958): 401. At the outset of the article, Professor Hart noted that "This paper is a revision of a mimeographed note originally prepared for first-year law students to serve as a supplement to other materials on the basic purposes of the criminal law. It will be seen that it still bears the marks of this origin both in the respect of being elementary and in the respect of not attempting a comprehensive examination of competing views of the criminal law."

1

still be necessary to recognize that the rehabilitation of offenders, the disablement of offenders, the sharpening of the community's sense of right and wrong, and the satisfaction of the community's sense of just retribution may all serve this end by contributing to an ultimate reduction in the number of crimes. Even socialized vengeance may be accorded a marginal role, if it is understood as the provision of an orderly alternative to mob violence.

The problem, accordingly, is one of the priority and relationship of purposes as well as of their legitimacy—of multivalued rather than of single-valued thinking.[2]

There is still another range of complications which are ignored if an effort is made to formulate any single "theory" or set of "principles" of criminal law. The purpose of having principles and theories is to help in organizing thought. In the law, the ultimate purpose of thought is to help in deciding upon a course of action. In the criminal law, as in all law, questions about the action to be taken do not present themselves for decision in an institutional vacuum. They arise rather in the context of some established and specific procedure of decision: in a constitutional convention; in a legislature; in a prosecuting attorney's office; in a court charged with the determination of guilt or innocence; in a sentencing court; before a parole board; and so on. This means that each agency of decision must take account always of its own place in the institutional system and of what is necessary to maintain the integrity and workability of the system as a whole. A complex of institutional ends must be served, in other words, as well as a complex of substantive social ends.[3]

The principal levels of decision in the criminal law are numerous. The institutional considerations involved at the various levels differ so markedly that it seems worthwhile to discuss the question of aims separately, from the point of view of each of the major agencies of decision.

II. The Perspective of Constitution Makers

We can get our broadest view of the aims of the criminal law if we look at them from the point of view of the makers of a constitution—of those who are seeking to establish sound foundations for a tolerable and durable social order. From this point of view, these aims can be most readily seen, as they need to be seen, in their relation to the aims of the good society generally.

In this setting, the basic question emerges: Why should the good society make use of the method of the criminal law at all?

A. What the Method of the Criminal Law Is

The question posed raises preliminarily an even more fundamental inquiry: What do we mean by "crime" and "criminal"? Or, put more accurately, what should we understand to be "the method of the criminal law," the use of which is in question? This latter way of formulating the preliminary inquiry is more accurate, because it pictures the criminal law as a process, a way of doing something, which is what it is. A great deal of intellectual energy has been misspent in an effort to develop a concept of crime as "a natural and social phenomenon"[4] abstracted from the functioning system of institutions which make use of the concept and give it impact and meaning.[5] But the criminal law, like all law, is concerned with the pursuit of human purposes through the forms and modes of social organization, and it needs always to be thought about in that context as a method or process of doing something.

What then are the characteristics of this method?

1. The method operates by means of a series of directions, or commands, formulated in general terms, telling people what they must or must not do. Mostly, the commands of the criminal law are "must-nots," or prohibitions, which can be satisfied by inaction. "Do not murder, rape, or rob." But some of them are "musts," or affirmative requirements, which can be satisfied only by taking a specifically, or relatively specifically, described kind of action. "Support your wife and children," and "File your income tax return."[6]

2. The commands are taken as valid and binding upon all those who fall within their terms when the time comes for complying with them, whether or not they have been formulated in advance in a single authoritative set of words.[7] They speak to members of the community, in other words, in the community's behalf, with all the power and prestige of the community behind them.

3. The commands are subject to one or more sanctions for disobedience which the community is prepared to enforce.

Thus far, it will be noticed, nothing has been said about the criminal law which is not true also of a large part of the noncriminal, or civil, law. The law of torts, the law of contracts, and almost every other branch of private law that can be mentioned operate, too, with general directions prohibiting or requiring described types of conduct, and the community's tribunals enforce these commands.[8] What, then, is distinctive about the method of the criminal law?

Can crimes be distinguished from civil wrongs on the ground that they constitute injuries to society generally which society is interested in preventing? The difficulty is that society is interested also in the due fulfillment of contracts and the avoidance of traffic accidents and most of the other stuff of civil litigation. The civil law is framed and interpreted and enforced with a constant eye to these social interests. Does the distinction lie in the fact that proceedings to enforce the criminal law are instituted by public officials rather than private complainants? The difficulty is that public officers may also bring many kinds of "civil" enforcement actions—for an injunction, for the recovery of a "civil" penalty, or even for the detention of the defendant by public authority.[9] Is the distinction, then, in the peculiar character of what is done to people who are adjudged to be criminals? The difficulty is that, with the possible exception of death, exactly the same kinds of unpleasant consequences, objectively considered, can be and are visited upon unsuccessful defendants in civil proceedings.[10]

If one were to judge from the notions apparently underlying many judicial opinions, and the overt language even of some of them, the solution of the puzzle is simply that a crime is anything which is *called* a crime,[11] and a criminal penalty is simply the penalty provided for doing anything which has been given that name. So vacant a concept is a betrayal of intellectual bankruptcy. Certainly, it poses no intelligible issue for a constitution-maker concerned to decide whether to make use of "the method of the criminal law." Moreover, it is false to popular understanding, and false also to the understanding embodied in existing constitutions. By implicit assumptions that are more impressive than any explicit assertions, these constitutions proclaim that a conviction for crime is a distinctive and serious matter—a something, and not a nothing.[12] What is that something?

4. What distinguishes a criminal from a civil sanction and all that distinguishes it, it is ventured, is the judgment of community condemnation which accompanies and justifies its imposition. As Professor Gardner wrote not long ago, in a distinct but cognate connection:[13]

4

> The essence of punishment for moral delinquency lies in the criminal conviction itself. One may lose more money on the stock market than in a court-room; a prisoner of war camp may well provide a harsher environment than a state prison; death on the field of battle has the same physical characteristics as death by sentence of law. It is the expression of the community's hatred, fear, or contempt for the convict which alone characterizes physical hardship as punishment.

If this is what a "criminal" penalty is, then we can say readily enough what a "crime" is. It is not simply anything which a legislature chooses to call a "crime." It is not simply antisocial conduct which public officers are given a responsibility to suppress. It is not simply any conduct to which a legislature chooses to attach a "criminal" penalty. It is conduct which, if duly shown to have taken place, will incur a formal and solemn pronouncement of the moral condemnation of the community.

5. The method of the criminal law, of course, involves something more than the threat (and, on due occasion, the expression) of community condemnation of antisocial conduct. It involves, in addition, the threat (and, on due occasion, the imposition) of unpleasant physical consequences, commonly called punishment. But if Professor Gardner is right, these added consequences take their character as punishment from the condemnation which precedes them and serves as the warrant for their infliction. Indeed, the condemnation plus the added consequences may well be considered, compendiously, as constituting the punishment. Otherwise, it would be necessary to think of a convicted criminal as going unpunished if the imposition or execution of his sentence is suspended.

In traditional thought and speech, the ideas of crime and punishment have been inseparable; the consequences of conviction for crime have been described as a matter of course as "punishment." The Constitution of the United States and its amendments, for example, use this word or its verb form in relation to criminal offenses no less than six times.[14] Today, "treatment" has become a fashionable euphemism for the older, ugly word. This bowdlerizing of the Constitution and of conventional speech may serve a useful purpose in discouraging unduly harsh sentences and emphasizing that punishment is not an end in itself. But to the extent that it dissociates the treatment of criminals from the social condemnation of their conduct which is implicit in their conviction, there is danger that it will confuse thought and do a disservice.

At least under existing law, there is a vital difference between the situation of a patient who has been committed to a mental hospital and the situation of an inmate of a state penitentiary. The core of the difference is precisely that the patient has not incurred the moral condemnation of his community, whereas the convict has.[15]

B. The Utility of the Method

We are in a position now to restate the basic question confronting our hypothetical constitution-makers. The question is whether to make use, in the projected social order, of the method of discouraging undesired conduct and encouraging desired conduct by means of the threat—and, when necessary, the fulfillment of the threat—of the community's condemnation of an actor's violation of law and of punishment, or treatment, of the actor as blameworthy for having committed the violation.

The question, like most legal questions, is one of alternatives. Perhaps the leading alternative, to judge from contemporary criticism of the penal law, would be to provide that people who behave badly should simply be treated as sick people to be cured, rather than as bad people to be condemned and punished. A constitutional guarantee to accomplish this could be readily drafted: "No person shall be subjected to condemnation or punishment for violation of law, but only to curative-rehabilitative treatment." Would the establishment of this new constitutional liberty be well-advised?

Paradoxically, this suggested guarantee, put forward here as an abandonment of the method of the criminal law, is not far removed from a point of view that has been widely urged in recent years as a proper rationale of existing law. Professors Hall and Glueck express this point of view in their recent casebook, more moderately than some of its other exponents. They recognize that "no general formula respecting the relative proportions of the various ingredients of the general punitive-corrective aim can be worked out." But they then go on to say:[16]

> It is the opinion of many of those who have studied both
> the causes of crime and the results of its treatment by means
> of the death penalty and the usual forms of incarceration,
> that for the vast majority of the general rule of delinquents

and criminals, the corrective theory, based upon a conception
of multiple causation and curative-rehabilitative treatment,
should clearly predominate in legislation and in judicial and
administrative practices. No other single theory is as closely
related to the actual conditions and mechanisms of crime
causation; no other gives as much promise of returning the
offender to society not with the negative vacuum of punish-
ment-induced fear but with the affirmative and constructive
equipment—physical, mental and moral—for law-abiding-
ness. Thus, in the long run, no other theory and practice
gives greater promise of protecting society.

This suggests the possibility of a modified version of the constitutional guarantee in question, directing that "The corrective theory
of crime and criminal justice, based upon a conception of multiple
causation and curative-rehabilitative treatment, shall predominate
in legislation and in judicial and administrative practices." Would
such a provision be workable? Would it be wise?

Any theory of criminal justice which emphasizes the criminal
rather than the crime encounters an initial and crucial difficulty
when it is sought to be applied at the stage of legislative enactment,
where the problem in the first instance is to define and grade the
crime. How *can* a conception of multiple causation and curative-
rehabilitative treatment predominate in the definition and grading
of crimes, let alone serve as the sole guide?[17] But even if it were
possible to gauge in advance the types of conduct to be forbidden
by the expected need for reformation of those who will thereafter
engage in them, would it be sensible to try to do so? Can the content
of the law's commands be rationally determined with an eye singly
or chiefly to the expected deficiencies of character of those who
will violate them? Obviously not. The interests of society in having
certain things not done or done are also involved.[18]

Precisely because of the difficulties of relating the content of the
law's commands to the need for reformation of those who violate
them, a curative-rehabilitative theory of criminal justice tends always
to depreciate, if not to deny, the significance of these general formula-
tions and to focus attention instead on the individual defendant at
the time of his apprehension, trial, and sentence. This has in it always
a double danger—to the individual and to society. The danger to
the individual is that he will be punished, or treated, for what he
is or is believed to be, rather than for what he has done. If his offense

is minor but the possibility of his reformation is thought to be slight, the other side of the coin of mercy can become cruelty.[19] The danger to society is that the effectiveness of the general commands of the criminal law as instruments for influencing behavior so as to avoid the necessity for enforcement proceedings will be weakened.

This brings us to the crux of the issue confronting our supposed constitution-makers. The commands of the criminal law are commands which the public interest requires people to comply with. This being so, will the public interest be adequately protected if the legislature is allowed only to say to people, "If you do not comply with any of these commands, you will merely be considered to be sick and subjected to officially-imposed rehabilitative treatment in an effort to cure you"? Can it be adequately protected if the legislature is required to say, "If you do not comply, your own personal need for cure and rehabilitation will be the predominating factor in determining what happens to you"? Or should the legislature be enabled to say, "If you violate any of these laws and the violation is culpable, your conduct will receive the formal and solemn condemnation of the community as morally blameworthy, and you will be subjected to whatever punishment, or treatment, is appropriate to vindicate the law and to further its various purposes"?

On the sheerly pragmatic ground of the need for equipping the proposed social order with adequate tools to discourage undesired conduct, a responsible constitution-maker assuredly would hesitate long before rejecting the third of these possibilities in favor of either of the first two. To be sure, the efficacy of criminal punishment as a deterrent has often been doubted. But it is to be observed that the doubts are usually expressed by those who are thinking from the retrospective, sanction-imposing point of view.[20] From this point of view, it is natural to be impressed by the undoubted fact that many people do become criminals, and will continue to do so, in spite of all the threats of condemnation and of treatment-in-consequence-of-condemnation that society can offer. But the people who do *not* commit crimes need to be taken into account, too. A constitution-maker, thinking from the prospective point of view of the primary, as distinguished from the remedial, law has especially to think of them, if he is to see his problem whole. So doing, he will be likely to regard the desire of the ordinary man to avoid the moral condemnation of his community, as well as the physical pains and inconveniences of punishment, as a powerful factor in influencing human behavior which can scarcely with safety be dispensed with.[21] Whether he is right or wrong in this conclusion, he will align himself, in reaching it, with the all but universal judgment, past and present, of mankind.

Moreover, there are other and larger considerations to be weighed in the balance. The case against a primarily rehabilitative theory of criminal justice is understated if it is rested solely on the need for the threat of criminal conviction as an instrument of deterrence of antisocial conduct. Deterrence, it is ventured, ought not to be thought of as the overriding and ultimate purpose of the criminal law, important though it is. For deterrence is negative, whereas the purposes of law are positive. And the practical fact must be faced that many crimes, as just recognized, are undeterrable. The grim negativism and the frequent seeming futility of the criminal law when it is considered simply as a means of preventing undesired behavior no doubt help to explain why sensitive people, working at close hand with criminals, tend so often to embrace the more hopeful and positive tenets of a curative-rehabilitative philosophy.

However, a different view is possible if an effort is made to fit the theory of criminal justice into a theory of social justice—to see the purposes of the criminal law in their relation to the purposes of law as a whole. Man is a social animal, and the function of law is to enable him to realize his potentialities as a human being through the forms and modes of social organization. It is important to consider how the criminal law serves this ultimate end.

Human beings, of course, realize their potentialities in part through enjoyment of the various satisfactions of human life, both tangible and intangible, which existing social resources and their own individual capacities make available to them. Yet, the social resources of the moment are always limited, and human capacities for enjoyment are limited also. Social resources for providing the satisfactions of life and human capacities for enjoying them, however, are always susceptible of enlargement, so far as we know, without eventual limit.[22] Man realizes his potentialities most significantly in the very process of developing these resources and capacities—by making himself a functioning and participating member of his community, contributing to it as well as drawing from it.

What is crucial in this process is the enlargement of each individual's capacity for effectual and responsible decision. For it is only through personal, self-reliant participation, by trial and error, in the problems of existence, both personal and social, that the capacity to participate effectively can grow. Man learns wisdom in choosing by being confronted with choices and by being made aware that he must abide the consequences of his choice. In the training of a child in the small circle of the family, this principle is familiar enough. It has the same validity in the training of an adult in the larger circle of the community.

Seen in this light, the criminal law has an obviously significant and, indeed, a fundamental role to play in the effort to create the good society. For it is the criminal law which defines the minimum conditions of man's responsibility to his fellows and holds him to that responsibility. The assertion of social responsibility has value in the treatment even of those who have become criminals.[23] It has far greater value as a stimulus to the great bulk of mankind to abide by the law and to take pride in so abiding.

This, then, is the critical weakness of the two alternative constitutional provisions that have been discussed—more serious by far than losing or damaging a useful, even if imperfect, instrument of deterrence. The provisions would undermine the foundation of a free society's effort to build up each individual's sense of responsibility as a guide and a stimulus to the constructive development of his capacity for effectual and fruitful decision.[24]

If the argument which has been made is accepted and it is concluded that explicit abandonment of the concept of moral condemnation of criminal conduct would be unsound, what then is to be said of the soundness of an interpretation of existing law which tries to achieve a similar result by indirection—treating the purpose of cure and rehabilitation as predominating, while sweeping under the rug the hard facts of the social need and the moral rightness of condemnation and of treatment which does not dilute the fact of condemnation?

C. Constitutional Limitations on the Use of the Method

It is evident that the view which the constitution-maker takes of the function of criminal law will be important in shaping his attitude on inclusion in the document of many of the traditional guarantees of fair procedure in criminal trials. Most of these, such, for example, as indictment by a grand jury or even trial by a petit jury, are largely or wholly irrelevant to the offender's need for, or his susceptibility to, curative-rehabilitative treatment.[25] Indeed, as already suggested,[26] even the basic concept that criminality must rest upon criminal conduct, duly proved to have taken place, would come into question under a purely rehabilitative theory. Present laws for the confinement and care of mentally-ill persons do not insist upon this requirement, and, if criminality were to be equated with sickness of personality generally, its rationale would not be readily apparent. But if what is in issue is the community's solemn condemnation of the accused as a defaulter in his obligations to the community, then the default to be condemned ought plainly to consist of overt conduct, and not simply of a condition of mind; and the fact of default should be proved with scrupulous care. The safeguards which now surround the procedure of proof of criminality or the essentials of them, in other words, will appear to be appropriate.

Should the constitution-makers go further and prescribe not only procedural safeguards, but substantive limitations on the kinds of conduct that can be declared criminal? For the most part, American constitution-makers have not done this.[27] They have relied, instead, primarily on the legislature's sense of justice. Secondarily, they have relied on the courts to understand what a crime is and, so, by appropriate invocation of the broad constitutional injunction of due process, to prevent an arbitrary application of the criminal sanction when the legislature's sense of justice has failed. Whether they have been wise in so doing is a question which can best be left to the reader's judgment, in the light of the examination which follows of the actual handling of the problems by legislatures and courts.

III. The Perspective of the Legislature

A legislature deals with crimes always in advance of their commission (assuming the existence of constitutional prohibitions or practices excluding ex post facto laws and bills of attainder). It deals with them not by condemnation and punishment, but only by threat of condemnation and punishment, *to be imposed always by other agencies*. It deals with them always by directions formulated in *general terms*. The primary parts of the directions have always to be interpreted and applied by the private persons—the potential offenders—to whom they are initially addressed. In the event of a breach or claim of breach, both the primary and the remedial parts must be interpreted and applied by the various officials—police, prosecuting attorneys, trial judges and jurors, appellate judges, and probation, prison, and parole authorities—responsible for their enforcement. The attitudes, capacities, and practical conditions of work of these officials often put severe limits upon the ability of the legislature to accomplish what it sets out to accomplish.

If the primary parts of a general direction are to work successfully in any particular instance, otherwise than by fortunate accident, four conditions have always to be satisfied: (1) the primary addressee who is supposed to conform his conduct to the direction must know (a) of its existence, and (b) of its content in relevant respects; (2) he must know about the circumstances of fact which make the abstract terms of the direction applicable in the particular instance; (3) he must be able to comply with it; and (4) he must be willing to do so.

The difficulties of satisfying these conditions vitally affect the fairness and often even the feasibility of the effort to control the behavior of large numbers of people by means of general directions, subject only to an after-the-event sanction. This is so even when the sanction is civil, such as a judgment for compensatory damages or restoration of benefits. But the difficulties are especially acute when the sanction is criminal. For then, something more is involved than the simple necessity of getting the direction complied with in a sufficient proportion of instances to keep it in good working order— that is, to maintain respect for it and to avoid arbitrary discrimination in singling out individual violators as subjects of enforcement pro-ceedings. If what was said in part two is correct, it is necessary to be able to say in good conscience in *each* instance in which a criminal sanction is imposed for a violation of law that the violation was blameworthy and, hence, deserving of the moral condemnation of the community.

This raises two closely related questions which lie at the heart of the problems of the criminal law: *First,* what *are* the ingredients of moral blameworthiness which warrant a judgment of community condemnation? *Second,* retracing the ground of part two, can the position be maintained that guilt in the sense of the criminal law is an individual matter and cannot justly be pronounced by the community if the individual's conduct affords no basis for a judg-ment of moral condemnation?

These questions present themselves in different guises in different types of criminal statutes. They can best be examined separately in relation to the various major types of purposes for which a legislature may seek to employ a criminal sanction.

A. *The Statement of the Minimum Obligations of Responsible Citizenship: The Control of Purposeful Conduct*

The core of a sound penal code in any view of the function of the criminal law is the statement of those minimum obligations of conduct which the conditions of community life impose upon every participating member if community life is to be maintained and to prosper—that is, of those obligations which result not from a discretionary and disputable judgment of the legislature, but from the objective facts of the interdependencies of the people who are living together in the community and of their awareness of the interdependencies.

In the mind of any legislator who recognizes this central and basic job as a distinct one and who is trying to do it faithfully and intelligently, a variety of aims will coalesce, to the point of becoming virtually indistinguishable. The inculcation of a sense of social responsibility throughout the society will be the dominant aim. But the stated obligations will, at the same time, represent desired standards of conduct and so will necessarily involve the aim of deterrence of undesired conduct. Since violators are to be condemned as defaulters in their duty to the community and treated accordingly, the aim can also be described as punitive. And if the conduct declared to be criminal does, indeed, evince a blameworthy lack of social responsibility, the declaration will also constitute an essential first step in identifying those members of the community whose behavior shows them to be in need of cure and rehabilitation, and this aim will likewise be included. So also, subordinately, will be the aim of temporary or permanent disablement of certain of the more serious offenders.

Returning now to the four conditions earlier stated for the successful operation of a general direction and to the problem of deciding when a failure of compliance due to a failure to satisfy one of the conditions is blameworthy, it will be seen that in this area of the criminal law, the difficulties are minimal, so long at least as the legislature is denouncing purposeful or knowing, as distinguished from reckless or merely negligent, conduct.[28]

If the legislature does a sound job of reflecting community attitudes and needs, actual knowledge of the wrongfulness of the prohibited conduct will usually exist. Thus, almost everyone is aware that murder and forcible rape and the obvious forms of theft are wrong. But in any event, knowledge of wrongfulness can fairly be assumed. For any member of the community who does these things without knowing that they are criminal is blameworthy, as much for his lack of knowledge as for his actual conduct. This seems to be the essential rationale of the maxim, *Ignorantia legis neminem excusat*, which has been so much misunderstood and abused in relation to regulatory crimes, involving conduct which is not intrinsically wrongful.[29]

Similarly, knowledge of the circumstances of fact which make the law's directions applicable will ordinarily exist when harms are inflicted or risks created of the elementary and obvious types sought to be prevented by these intrinsically wrongful crimes. But suppose that knowledge does not exist? The traditional criminal law, concerned almost exclusively with crimes of this kind, has ready to hand a solution in the traditional maxim that ignorance of fact excuses, as well as in cognate doctrines such as that of claim-of-right in the law of theft.[30] If the legislature can depend upon the courts to read these doctrines into its enactments, the requisite of blameworthiness as an element of criminality will be respected.

Obligations of conduct fixed by a fair appraisal of the minimum requirements for the maintenance and fostering of community life will, by hypothesis, be obligations which normal members of the community will be *able* to comply with, given the necessary awareness of the circumstances of fact calling for compliance. But suppose that in a particular case, this ability does not exist? Again, the traditional law provides materials for solution of the problem when inability negatives blameworthiness; and the only question is whether the legislature can count upon the courts to make use of the materials. The materials include doctrines with respect to duress, as well as doctrines providing for the exculpation of those individuals who because of mental disease or defect are to be deemed incapable of acting as responsible, participating members of society.[31]

There remains only the question of willingness to comply. In relation to directions which make a reasonably grounded appeal to the citizen's sense of responsibility as a citizen, this willingness is likely to be at a maximum. Individuals who are able but unwilling to comply with such directions are precisely the ones who ought to be condemned as criminals.

In the sphere of conduct which is intrinsically wrongful, the legislature's task is further simplified by its ability (or the ability which it is entitled to suppose it has) to rely upon the courts for the elaboration of detail and the solution of unanticipated or peripheral problems. Indeed, this was a body of law which was largely built up by English judges without benefit of acts of Parliament and which in this country required the intervention of the legislature, on its primary side, only to satisfy the theoretical and emotional appeal of the maxim, *Nullum crimen sine lege*. Despite the maxim, most American legislatures have been content to make use of familiar words and phrases of the common law, relying upon the courts to fill in their meaning, and even leaving whole areas of doctrine, such as criminal intent and various phases of justification, entirely to the courts. So long as the courts are faithful in their reflection of the community's understanding of what is morally blameworthy, judgments of conviction are not subject to the reproach of being, even in spirit, ex post facto.

B. The Statement of the Minimum Obligations of Responsible Citizenship: The Control of Reckless and Negligent Conduct

Special difficulties are presented when the criminal law undertakes to state an obligation of conduct in a way which requires an addressee, if he is to comply with it, to have a certain kind of general knowledge or experience, or to exercise a certain degree of skill and attention, or to make an appraisal of the probable consequences of what he does or omits to do with a certain degree of accuracy. When can a criminal sanction be properly authorized in cases in which the addressee fails in one or another of these respects and harm results or a risk is created because of his failure?[32]

For example, one who undertakes to practice as a physician does not know that flannels saturated with kerosene will tend to produce severe burns if applied directly to the flesh of a patient.[33] A foreman of a railroad section gang misreads a timetable and orders railroad tracks to be taken up for replacement just before a train is due.[34] The owner of a night club fails to realize that the means of egress would be inadequate if a fire were to break out when the club was

15

crowded.[35] Upon precisely what kind of showing can a legislature justly provide that such people are to be condemned and punished as criminals?

If the legislature requires that an awareness of the risk be brought home to the actor and that the risk be one which, by the general standards of the community, is plainly excessive, a direction for criminal punishment creates no difficulty of principle, however trying may be the problems of application. For judgment about whether a given risk can justifiably be taken to promote a given end depends upon the evaluations implicit in community standards of right and wrong to which each member of the community can justly be expected to conform his conduct. If an individual knowingly takes a risk of a kind which the community condemns as plainly unjustifiable, then he is morally blameworthy and can properly be adjudged a criminal. He is criminally reckless in the traditional sense articulated with precision by the draftsmen of the American Law Institute's Model Penal Code.[36]

This concept of criminal recklessness may well embrace not only situations in which the actor adverts directly to the possibility of the ultimate harm, but those in which he adverts only to his own deficiencies in appraising the possibility of harm or preventing it from coming to pass and to the possible consequences of *those* deficiencies. Thus, the doctor who swathes his patient with kerosene-soaked rags, without even suspecting what is going to happen, may, nevertheless, know that special knowledge and training is generally needed in order to treat patients safely and successfully and that he does not have that knowledge and training. In any such situation, if the actor knows of his deficiency and of the risk which such a deficiency creates, and if *that* risk is one which in community understanding is plainly unjustifiable, there is a basis for legislative condemnation of the conduct as criminally reckless.

Moreover, as considered more fully under the next subheading, if the actor knowingly goes counter to a valid legislative determination that the risk he is taking is excessive, even though he himself does not believe it to be, there is an independent basis for moral condemnation in this deliberate defiance of law.

The question remains whether simple unawareness of risk, without awareness of any deficiency preventing appreciation or avoidance of it and without any element of knowing disregard of a relevant

16

legislative decision, can justly be declared to be culpable. The answer would seem clearly to be no, at least in those situations in which the actor lacks the ability either to refrain from the conduct which creates the risk or to correct the deficiency which makes engaging in the conduct dangerous, for otherwise, the third of the requisites above stated for the successful operation of a general direction is impossible to satisfy.[37] But suppose the actor has this ability? Guilt would, then, seem to depend upon whether he has been put upon notice of his duty to use his ability to a degree which makes his unawareness of the duty, in the understanding of the community, genuinely blameworthy. In exceptional situations of elementary and obvious danger, the circumstances of fact of which the actor is conscious may be sufficient in themselves to give this notice. But this can be true only when the significance of the circumstances of fact would be apparent to one who shares the community's general sense of right and wrong. If this is not so—if appreciation of the significance of the facts depends upon knowledge of what happens to be written in the statute books—then, the problem becomes one of the nature and extent of the moral obligation to know what is so written, which is discussed under the next subheading.

Criminal punishment of merely negligent behavior is commonly justified not on the ground that violators can be said to be individually blameworthy, but on the ground that the threat of such punishment will help to teach people generally to be more careful. This proposes, as legitimate, an aim for the legislature which is drastically different from that of inculcating minimum standards of personal responsibility to society. The issues it raises are examined under the subheading after the next.[38]

C. The Regulation of Conduct Which Is Not Intrinsically Wrongful: Bases of Blameworthiness

The statute books of the forty-nine states and the United States are filled with enactments carrying a criminal sanction which are obviously motivated by other ends, primarily, than that of training for responsible citizenship. The legislature simply wants certain things done and certain other things not done because it believes that the doing or the not doing of them will secure some ultimate social advantage, and not at all because it thinks the immediate conduct involved is either rightful or wrongful in itself. It employs

17

the threat of criminal condemnation and punishment as an especially forceful way of saying that it really wants to be obeyed, or else simply from lack of enough imagination to think of a more appropriate sanction. Such enactments present problems which neither the courts nor the legislatures of this country have yet succeeded in thinking through.[39]

When a legislature undertakes to prohibit or require conduct theretofore untouched by the criminal law, what considerations *ought* to guide it in deciding whether to declare that noncompliance with its direction shall be a crime?

1. If the legislature can, in good conscience, conclude that the new direction embodies standards of behavior which have to be observed, under existing social conditions, if social life is to be maintained, then the use of a criminal sanction raises no difficulty. Obviously, there is room for growth, as conditions and attitudes in society change, in the central body of law earlier discussed which undertakes to state the minimum obligations of responsible citizenship. Obviously also, the legislature is an appropriate agency to settle debatable questions about the appropriate extent of growth, whether or not it is desirable for courts to have a share in the process.[40]

Statutes which make well-considered additions to the list of the citizen's basic obligations are not open to the objection of undue multiplication of crimes. Normal principles of culpability, moreover, can properly apply to such offenses, and should apply. Absent exceptional circumstances, in other words, ignorance of the criminality of the conduct (act or omission) which is forbidden ought not to be a defense. *Per contra*, ignorance of the facts ought to be. And, of course, the usual defenses based on inability to comply should be available.

2. If the legislature cannot, in good conscience, regard conduct which it wishes to forbid as wrongful in itself, then it has always the option of declaring the conduct to be criminal only when the actor knows of its criminality or recklessly disregards the possibility that it is criminal. For knowing or reckless disregard of legal obligation affords an independent basis of blameworthiness justifying the actor's condemnation as a criminal, even when his conduct was not intrinsically antisocial. It is convenient to use the word "wilful" to describe this mode of culpability, although the term is by no means regularly so limited in conventional usage.[41]

The inclusion in a new regulatory crime of the requirement of "wilfulness" avoids any difficulty of principle in the use of the criminal sanction—assuming that the requirement comprehends not only a culpable awareness (knowing or reckless) of the law, but a culpable awareness also of the facts making the law applicable, together with a sufficient ability to comply. The requirement, moreover, mitigates any objection on the score of undue multiplication of regulatory crimes, although it can hardly eliminate it entirely.[42]

3. Under what, if any, circumstances may a legislature properly direct the conviction as a criminal of a person whose conduct is not wrongful in itself and who neither knows nor recklessly disregards the possibility that he is violating the law?

To engage knowingly or recklessly in conduct which is wrongful in itself and which has, in fact, been condemned as a crime is either to fail to comprehend the community's accepted moral values or else squarely to challenge them. The maxim, *Ignorantia legis neminem excusat*, expresses the wholly defensible and, indeed, essential principle that the action, in either event, is blameworthy.[43] If, however, the criminal law adheres to this maxim when it moves from the condemnation of those things which are *mala in se* to the condemnation of those things which are merely *mala prohibita*, it necessarily shifts its ground from a demand that every responsible member of the community understand and respect the community's moral values to a demand that everyone know and understand what is written in the statute books. Such a demand is *toto coelo* different. In no respect is contemporary law subject to greater reproach than for its obtuseness to this fact.

Granting that blame may, in some circumstances, attach to an actor's antecedent failure to determine the legality of his conduct, it is, in any event, blame of a very distinctive kind.

a. The blame in such a case is largely unrelated, in gravity or any other respect, to the external conduct itself, or its consequences, for which the actor is purportedly convicted. Indeed, all such instances of conduct in ignorance of laws enjoining *mala prohibita* might well be thought of as constituting a single type of crime, if they constitute any kind of crime at all—the crime of ignorance of the statutes or of their interpretation. Knowledge of the facts and ability to comply may be formal requisites of criminality, but in the absence of knowledge of the law, they are irrelevant, and willingness to comply remains untested. The whole weight of the law's effort to achieve its purpose has to be carried, in the first instance, by the effort to get people to know and understand its requirements.[44]

19

b. In such cases, the essential crime, if that is what it is, is always a crime of omission. If the purported crime is itself one of omission, as in the failure to take out a license, then the offense is doubly negative. As Professor Graham Hughes has recently abundantly demonstrated,[45]

> . . . a penal policy of omissions and a criminal jurisprudence of offenses of omission are overdue, . . . [W]here inaction is evidently socially harmful, no good reason appears for shrinking from penal prohibition. Any penal policy, however, must be linked with a consciousness of the need to promulgate and publicize offenses of omission and a recognition by the judiciary that conventional attitudes to *mens rea*, particularly with respect to ignorance of the law, are not adequate tools to achieve justice for those accused of inaction.

Even when the nominal crime is one of commission rather than omission, the problem of promulgating and publicizing the offense, which Professor Hughes mentions, is likely to be serious if the nature of the affirmative conduct gives no warning of the possibility of an applicable criminal prohibition. But it is especially likely to be serious when the nominal crime is itself one of omisson, for mere inaction often gives no such warning whatever.[46]

c. The gist of a crime of statutory ignorance may lie not in the failure to inform oneself of the existence of an applicable statute, which is always in some sense a do-able thing if the statutes are published and there is a decent index to them, but in the failure to divine their meaning, which may be altogether non-do-able. All statutes are, of necessity, indeterminate in some of their applications. When a criminal enactment proscribes conduct which is *malum in se*, such as murder or manslaughter, however, the moral standards of the community are available always as a guide in the resolution of its indeterminacies, and there is a minimum of unfairness when doubt is resolved against a particular defendant. This guidance is missing when the proscribed conduct is merely *malum prohibitum.* The resolution of doubts must, thus, depend not upon a good human sense of moral values, but upon a sound grasp of technical doctrines and policies of statutory interpretation. Dean Pound has justly observed of American lawyers and judges that "we have no well-developed technique of developing legislative texts."[47] To condemn a layman as blameworthy for a default of technical judgment in a matter which causes trouble even for professional judges is, in many cases, so manifestly beyond reason that courts have developed various makeshift devices to avoid condemnation in particular situations.[48] And the draftsmen of the Model Penal Code have devised for such cases a generalized defense of limited scope.[49] Until the nature and dimensions of the problem have been more fully perceived, however, no genuinely satisfactory solution can be reached.

d. No doubt there are situations in which one who engages in a particular course of conduct assumes an obligation, in general community understanding, to know about the law applicable to that kind of conduct. Sometimes, this may be true in areas of statutory law affecting people generally, such as motor vehicle laws. It is most likely to be true of laws applicable to particular occupations. One cannot say categorically, therefore, that ignorance of a law creating a merely statutory crime never affords a basis for moral condemnation. What can be said, in general terms, is that (1) the criminal law as a device for getting people to know about statutes and interpret them correctly is a device of dubious and largely unproved effectiveness; (2) the indiscriminate use of the device dilutes the force of the threat of community condemnation as a means of influencing conduct in other situations where the basis for moral condemnation is clear; (3) the loss to society from this dilution is always unnecessary, since the legislature has always the alternatives of either permitting a good faith belief in the legality of one's conduct to be pleaded and proved as a defense,[50] or of providing a civil rather than a criminal sanction for nonwilful violations.

e. Under what, if any, circumstances may a legislature properly direct the conviction as a criminal of one who knows about the applicable law but who has been negligent, although not reckless, in ascertaining the facts which make the law applicable to his conduct— where the kind of conduct involved is morally neutral, both from the point of view of the actor and in actuality?

In the usual situation of assertedly criminal negligence earlier discussed,[51] the harm caused or threatened by failure of advertence is one which it would be morally wrongful to cause advertently. The assertion of a duty of attention is, thus, strengthened by the gravity of the risks actually involved. In the situation now under discussion, the facts are morally neutral, even to one who knows about them, save for the existence of an applicable statute. Thus,

21

the basis of blame, if any, is inattention to one's duty as a citizen to see that the law gets complied with in all the situations to which it is supposed to apply. For example, manufactured food becomes adulterated or misbranded within the meaning of a statute, but in a way which involves no danger to health.

Condemning a person for lack of ordinary care in ascertaining facts at least does not involve the offense to justice sometimes involved in the ignorance-of-interpretation-of-statute cases of condemning him for failure to do the impossible. But otherwise, most of the points just made about ignorance of regulatory law apply: (1) the basis of moral blame will usually be thin and may be virtually nonexistent; (2) the likelihood of substantial social gain in stimulating greater care is dubious; (3) the social cost is a weakening of the moral force and, hence, the effectiveness of the threat of criminal conviction; and (4) the cost is unnecessary, since the legislature has always the alternative of a civil sanction.

D. Strict Liability

A large body of modern law goes far beyond an insistence upon a duty of ordinary care in ascertaining facts, at the peril of being called a criminal. To an absolute duty to know about the existence of a regulatory statute and interpret it correctly, it adds an absolute duty to know about the facts. Thus, the porter who innocently carries the bag of a hotel guest not knowing that it contains a bottle of whisky is punished as a criminal for having transported intoxicating liquor.[52] The corporation president who signs a registration statement for a proposed securities issue not knowing that his accountants have made a mistake is guilty of the crime of making a "false" representation to the state blue-sky commissioner.[53] The president of a corporation whose employee introduces into interstate commerce a shipment of technically but harmlessly adulterated food is branded as a criminal solely because he was the president when the shipment was made.[54] And so on, ad almost infinitum.

In all such cases, it is possible, of course, that a basis of blameworthiness might have been found in the particular facts. Perhaps the company presidents actually were culpably careless in their supervision. Conceivably, even, the porter was culpably remiss in failing to ask the traveler about the contents of his bag, or at least in failing to shake it to see if he could hear a gurgle. But these possibilities are irrelevant. For the statutes in question, as interpreted, do not require any such defaults to be proved against a defendant, nor even permit him to show the absence of such a default in defense. The offenses fall within "the numerous class in which diligence, actual knowledge and bad motives are immaterial. . . ."[55] Thus, they squarely pose the question whether there can be any justification for condemning and punishing a human being as a criminal when he has done nothing which is blameworthy.

It is submitted that there can be no moral justification for this, and that there is not, indeed, even a rational, amoral justification.

1. People who do not know and cannot find out that they are supposed to comply with an applicable command are, by hypothesis, nondeterrable. So far as personal amenability to legal control is concerned, they stand in the same posture as the plainest lunatic under the *M'Naghten* test who "does not know the nature and quality of his act or, if he does know it, does not know that the act is wrong."

2. If it be said that most people will know of such commands and be able to comply with them, the answer, among others, is that nowhere else in the criminal law is the probable, or even the certain, guilt of nine men regarded as sufficient warrant for the conviction of a tenth. In the tradition of Anglo-American law, guilt of crime is personal. The main body of the criminal law, from the Constitution on down, makes sense on no other assumption.

3. If it be asserted that strict criminal liability is necessary in order to stimulate people to be diligent in learning the law and finding out when it applies, the answer, among others, is that this is wholly unproved and prima facie improbable. Studies to test the relative effectiveness of strict criminal liability and well-designed civil penalties are lacking and badly needed. Until such studies are forthcoming, however, judgment can only take into account (a) the inherent unlikelihood that people's behavior will be significantly affected by commands that are not brought definitely to their attention; (b) the long-understood tendency of disproportionate penalties to promote disrespect rather than respect for law, unless they are rigorously and uniformly enforced; (c) the inherent difficulties of rigorous and uniform enforcement of strict criminal liability and the impressive evidence that it is, in fact, spottily and unevenly enforced;[56] (d) the greater possibilities or flexible and imaginative adaptation of civil penalties to fit particular regulatory problems, the greater reasonableness of such penalties, and their more ready enforceability; and

(e) most important of all, the shocking damage that is done to social morale by open and official admission that crime can be respectable and criminality a matter of ill chance, rather than blameworthy choice.[57]

4. If it be urged that strict criminal liability is necessary in order to simplify the investigation and prosecution of violations of statutes designed to control mass conduct, the answer, among others, is that (a) maximizing compliance with law, rather than successful prosecution of violators, is the primary aim of any regulatory statute; (b) the convenience of investigators and prosecutors is not, in any event, the prime consideration in determining what conduct is criminal; (c) a prosecutor, as a matter of common knowledge, always assumes a heavier burden in trying to secure a criminal conviction than a civil judgment; (d) in most situations of attempted control of mass conduct, the technique of a first warning, followed by criminal prosecution only of knowing violators, has not only obvious, but proved superiority; and (e) the common-sense advantages of using the criminal sanction only against deliberate violators is confirmed by the policies which prosecutors themselves tend always to follow when they are free to make their own selection of cases to prosecute.[58]

5. Moral, rather than crassly utilitarian, considerations re-enter the picture when the claim is made, as it sometimes is, that strict liability operates, in fact, only against people who are really blameworthy, because prosecutors only pick out the really guilty ones for criminal prosecution.[59] This argument reasserts the traditional position that a criminal conviction imports moral condemnation. To this, it adds the arrogant assertion that it is proper to visit the moral condemnation of the community upon one of its members on the basis solely of the private judgment of his prosecutors. Such a circumvention of the safeguards with which the law surrounds other determinations of criminality seems not only irrational, but immoral as well.

6. But moral considerations in a still larger dimension are the ultimately controlling ones. In its conventional and traditional applications, a criminal conviction carries with it an ineradicable connotation of moral condemnation and personal guilt. Society makes an essentially parasitic, and hence illegitimate, use of this instrument when it uses it as a means of deterrence (or compulsion) of conduct which is morally neutral. This would be true even if a statute were

to be enacted proclaiming that no criminal conviction hereafter should ever be understood as casting any reflection on anybody. For statutes cannot change the meaning of words and make people stop thinking what they do think when they hear the words spoken. But it is doubly true—it is ten-fold, a hundred-fold, a thousand-fold true—when society continues to insist that some crimes *are* morally blameworthy and then tries to use the same epithet to describe conduct which is not.

7. To be sure, the traditional law recognizes gradations in the gravity of offenses, and so does the Constitution of the United States. But strict liability offenses have not been limited to the interpretively-developed constitutional category of "petty offenses," for which trial by jury is not required.[60] They include even some crimes which the Constitution expressly recognizes as "infamous."[61] Thus, the excuse of the Scotch servant girl for her illegitimate baby, that "It was only such a leetle one," is not open to modern legislatures. And since a crime remains a crime, just as a baby is unalterably a baby, it would not be a good excuse if it were. Especially is this so since the legislature could avoid the taint of illegitimacy, much more surely than the servant girl, by simply saying that the "crime" is not a crime, but only a civil violation.[62]

E. The Problem of Providing for Treatment

In determining that described conduct shall constitute a crime, a legislature makes necessarily the first and the major decision about the appropriate sanction for a violation of its direction. For it decides then that community condemnation shall be visited upon adjudged violators. But there remain hosts of questions about the degree of the condemnation and the nature of the authorized punishment, or treatment-in-consequence-of-violation.

Entangled with the problems of the appropriate aims to be pursued which are involved in these questions are problems of the appropriate assignment of powers to make decisions in carrying out the aims. To what extent should the legislature undertake to give binding directions about treatment which will foreclose the exercise of any later discretion? To what extent should it depend, instead, upon the judgment and discretion either of the sentencing court or of the correctional authorities who will become responsible for defendants after they are sentenced?

It is axiomatic that each agency of decision ought to make those decisions which its position in the institutional structure best fits it to make. But this, as will be seen, depends in part upon the criteria which are to guide decision.

1. The traditional criminal law recognizes different grades of offenses, such as felony and misdemeanor, and modern statutes recognize different degrees within the grades. If the criminal law were concerned centrally with reforming criminals, this would scarcely be appropriate: a confirmed petty thief may have much greater need of reformation than a once-in-a-lifetime manslaughter-er. If the thesis of this paper is accepted, however, it follows that grading is not only proper, but essential; that the legislature is the appropriate institution to do the grading; that the grading should be done with primary regard for the relative blameworthiness of offenses (a factor which, of course, will take into account the relative extent of the harm characteristically done or threatened to individuals and, thus, to the social order by each type of offense); and that the grading should be determinative of the relative severity of the treatment authorized for each offense.

2. Given such a ranking of offenses, the question remains: how far up or down the scale of possible severity or lenity of treatment should the whole array be moved? Are comparatively severe punishments to be favored or comparatively lenient ones? Here is a question of public policy which is pre-eminently for the legislature. On this question, its cardinal aims should be its cardinal guide. Punishments should be severe enough to impress not only upon the defendant's mind, but upon the public mind, the gravity of society's condemnation of irresponsible behavior. But the ultimate aim of condemning irresponsibility is training for responsibility. The treatment of criminals, therefore, should encourage, rather than foreclose, the development of their sense of responsibility. Allowance for the possibility of reformation, or formation, of character in the generality of cases becomes at this point, in other words, an overriding consideration. This consideration will point inexorably in the direction of eliminating capital punishment and minimizing both the occasions and the length of incarceration.

3. Should the legislature prescribe a single definite and unvarying form of treatment for each type of offense? The almost universal judgment of modern legal systems is that, ordinarily at least, it

should not.[63] Two types of considerations seem to underlie this judgment. The first is the need of making the treatment fit the crime. Statutory definitions of offenses are, of necessity, highly general categories covering a host of variant circumstances which are relevant to the blameworthiness of particular crimes. All the circumstances which are relevant in a particular case cannot be known until the case has been tried. The second type of consideration is the need of making the treatment fit the criminal, so as to take into account not only the kind of thing he did, but the kind of person he is. Only in this way can room be allowed for the effective play, on the basis of individualized judgment, of the criminal law's subordinate aims of reforming offenders or of disabling them where a special period of disablement seems to be needed. Both types of considerations indicate that discretion should be left to trial courts or correctional authorities, with respect both to the type of treatment—fine, imprisonment, probation, or the like—and to its extent or duration.

4. Should the legislature fix the maximum punishment, or the maximum severity of the treatment authorized, for particular types of crimes? Basic considerations of liberty as well as the logic of the aims of the criminal law dictate that it should. Men should not be put to death or imprisoned for a crime unless the legislature has sanctioned the penalty of death or imprisonment for that crime. Even with respect to penalties of an authorized type, the maximum of the permitted fine or term of imprisonment should be fixed by law. Only in this way can the integrity of the legislature's scheme of gradation of offenses and of the underlying principle that penalties should correspond in some fashion to the degree of blameworthiness of defendants' conduct be maintained. Only in this way can room be allowed for the beneficent operation of theories of reformation, while shutting the door to their tendencies toward cruelty.[64]

5. Should the legislature prescribe the *minimum* punishment, or the minimum severity of the treatment to be meted out, for particular types of crimes? The problem here is to make sure that society does not depreciate the gravity of its own judgments of condemnation through the imposition by sentencing judges of disproportionately trivial penalties. Yet, the virtues of individualization have their claims, too. Perhaps a suspended prison sentence, with probation, may be the best form of treatment even for a convicted murderer,

as it certainly may be for a convicted manslaughterer. A society which entrusts its juries with power to bring in a verdict of acquittal in cases of undoubted guilt ought to be able to trust its judges to exercise the lesser discretion of leniency in sentencing.

6. In cases in which convicted persons are to be sentenced to a term of imprisonment, how should power be divided between the sentencing judge (or jury) and prison and parole authorities in determining the actual duration of the incarceration? This question can best be left to be considered when the problems of the criminal law are examined from the point of view of those agencies.

IV. The Perspective of Police and Prosecuting Attorneys

To shift from the perspective of the legislature to that of police and prosecuting attorneys is to shift from the point of view of formulation of general directions to that of their application. These law enforcement officers, moreover, have power only to determine how their own functions shall be carried out. Unlike the antecedent determinations of the legislature and the subsequent determinations of courts, their decisions carry no authority as general directions to others for the future. They have a lesser role to play, accordingly, in the conscious shaping of the aims of the criminal law.

Nevertheless, what enforcement officials do is obviously of crucial importance in determining how the criminal law actually works. Their problems and the policies they pursue in trying to solve them need to be studied for the purpose not only of learning how better to control their activities—familiar enough questions—but for the purpose also of a better understanding, which legislatures sadly need, of what responsibilities ought to be given them and of the consequences of unwise imposition of responsibility.

This is not the place to pursue these questions in detail. A few suggestions only will be ventured.

1. The breadth of discretion we entrust to the police and prosecuting attorneys in dealing with individuals is far greater than that entrusted to any other kinds of officials and less subject to effective control. This discretion presents obvious difficulties in securing the lawful and equal administration of law. It presents also less obvious, or less noticed, difficulties of transferring from the legislature to enforcement officials the *de facto* power of determining what the criminal law in action shall be.

28

2. To the extent that the activities of enforcement officials are confined to securing compliance with what have been described as the basic obligations of responsible citizenship, their discretion will tend to be reduced to the minimum which the necessities of the administration of law admit. If social morale is good, there will be community demand for enforcement of these obligations and community support of it, and it will be feasible to provide an enforcement staff reasonably adequate to its task. Under these circumstances, reliance upon enforcement only on private complaint or newspaper insistence will be minimized. The exercise of discretion by police and prosecutors will consist largely of making specifically professional, and inescapable, judgments concerning the sufficiency of the evidence to warrant further investigation or formal accusation, what charges to make, what pleas to accept, what penalties to ask for, and the like.

3. The stupidity and injustice of the thoughtless multiplication of minor crimes receives its most impressive demonstration in police stations and prosecutors' offices. Invariably, staffs are inadequate for enforcement of all the criminal statutes which the legislature in its unwisdom chooses to enact. Accordingly, many of the statutes go largely unenforced. To this extent, their enactment is rendered futile. But it proves also to be worse than futile. For statutes usually do not become a complete dead letter. What happens is that they are enforced sporadically, either as a matter of deliberate policy to proceed only on private complaint, or as a matter of the accident of what comes to official attention or is forced upon it. Sporadic enforcement is an instrument of tyranny when enforcement officers are dishonest. It has an inescapable residuum of injustice in the hands even of the best-intentioned officers. A selection for prosecution among equally guilty violators entails not only inequality, but the exercise, necessarily, of an unguided and, hence, unprincipled discretion.

4. While the evils just described are common in the enforcement of most minor crimes, they are at their most acute in the sphere of regulation of conduct which is not intrinsically wrongful, and there a special phenomenon is likely to develop. Even though he ought not to seek the power in advance,[65] a conscientious prosecutor, faced with the fact of more violators than he can prosecute, is likely to single out for prosecution those whom he regards as morally blameworthy, in default of any better basis of selection.[66] Thus, he will

29

negate the legislative judgment that all violators should be prosecuted, regardless of moral blame. But at the same time, he will create a *de facto* crime, the main element of which is withdrawn from proof or disproof by due process of law.

5. In the area of traditional crimes, enforcement officials have an opportunity to put the dominant aim of the criminal law to inculcate understanding of the obligations of responsible citizenship, and to secure compliance with them, into a meaningful relationship with its subsidiary aim of rehabilitating people who have proved themselves to be irresponsible. In the area of regulatory crimes, this is possible only if "wilfulness," as earlier defined,[67] is an ingredient of criminality. The whole concept of curative-rehabilitative treatment has otherwise no relevance in this area.

V. The Perspective of Courts in the Ascertainment of Guilt

Courts look both backward and forward in the application of law. They look backward to the relevant general directions of the Constitution and the statutes, as interpreted and applied in prior judicial decisions. They look backward to the historical facts of the litigation. But when the facts raise issues with respect to which the existing general directions are indeterminate, they are bound to look forward to the ends which the law seeks to serve and to resolve the issues as best they can in a way which will serve them. This, of course, is the strength of the judicial process—that it permits principles to be worked pure and the details of implementing rules and standards to be developed in the light of intensive examination of the interaction of the general with the particular. But it is a strength existing sometimes in the potentiality rather than in the realization. Notably has this been true in this country in the development of the substantive law of crimes.

The inherited criminal law was rich with principles and with potentialities for their reasoned and intelligible development. But the multiplication of statutory crimes and the inadequacy of judicial techniques of interpreting statutes, coupled with unimaginative and unintelligent use even of familiar common-law techniques, have shaken much of the law loose from these moorings.

It is possible to see the beginnings of this development in some unfortunate decisions in the area of customary crimes touching sensitive matters of sex and family law.

A well-known example is that of statutory rape and kindred offenses against immature girls. Here, the courts came widely to hold that when the legislature had specified a fixed age of consent, the man's belief in the girl's age, and even his utmost good faith and reasonableness in holding the belief, were irrelevant.[68] They pictured the legislature, in other words, as saying to mankind: "If you choose to have intercourse with a willing female who may be over or under the age of consent, you will be playing a game with the law as well as with her. If she is of age, you win the law's game. If she is under age, you lose it and will be condemned as a felon, regardless of what she may have told you and regardless of the good reasons you may have had for believing her." When account is taken of the long tradition that ignorance of the fact excuses, it is evident that this interpretation was not a necessary one, if, indeed, it was even plausible. But it seems to have had important influence in encouraging the modern trend toward strict liability.

Similarly, in prosecutions for bigamy, and particularly when the bigamy statute was coupled with a presumption of the death of a missing spouse after a fixed period of unexplained absence, the courts tended to hold that a man or woman who remarried within the statutory period did so at the peril of criminal conviction if the spouse were actually alive.[69] In effect, such courts said: "Good faith and reasonable inquiry have nothing to do with this. We read the legislature's presumption as not merely avoiding the necessity of specific proof of good faith when the presumption is applicable, but as barring such proof when it is inapplicable. We attribute to the legislature a purpose to discourage the remarriage of abandoned spouses as socially impolitic, by requiring those who attempt it to take a gambler's chance of becoming a criminal." Once again, obviously, the interpretation was not a necessary one. And once again, currency was given to the notion that people can commit crimes without really doing anything wrong at all.

Closely and vitally related to the failure of American courts to develop adequate principles of criminal liability and an adequate theory of the aims of the criminal law as guides in the interpretation of statutes has been their failure to come to grips with the underlying constitutional issues involved. This failure is the more surprising because of the obvious concern of the Constitution to safeguard the

31

use of the method of the criminal law—especially, but not exclusively, on the procedural side—and the concern of the courts themselves, particularly in recent times, to give vitality to the procedural guarantees. What sense does it make to insist upon procedural safeguards in criminal prosecutions if anything whatever can be made a crime in the first place? What sense does it make to prohibit ex post facto laws (to take the one explicit guarantee of the Federal Constitution on the substantive side) if a man can, in any event, be convicted of an infamous crime for inadvertent violation of a prior law of the existence of which he had no reason to know and which he had no reason to believe he was violating, even if he had known of its existence?

Despite the unmistakable indications that the Constitution means something definite and something serious when it speaks of "crime," the Supreme Court of the United States has hardly got to first base in working out what that something is. From beginning to end, there is scarcely a single opinion by any member of the Court which confronts the question in a fashion which deserves intellectual respect.[70] The Court began with a few dicta suggesting that a crime is anything which the legislature chooses to say it is.[71] These were followed by a pair of narcotics cases, patently concerned with the evils of drugs rather than with the evil of disloyalty to a millennium of legal tradition.[72] Then came, only a few years ago, one of the most drastic of the Court's decisions, treating the whole matter as a *fait accompli*.[73] Not until the last term, in *Lambert v. California*,[74] did the Court discover that the due process clauses had anything to say about branding innocent people as criminals. But neither the majority nor the dissenting opinion in that case is persuasive of any need to qualify the second sentence in this paragraph.

The *Lambert* case involved a Los Angeles ordinance making it a criminal offense for any "convicted person," as defined, to be and remain in the city for more than five days without registering. The Court held that the application of this ordinance to one who had no actual or "probable" knowledge of it violated the due process clause of the fourteenth amendment. Yet, four members of the Court dissented. They were led by so sensitive a judge as Mr. Justice Frankfurter, who, pointing to the large body of legislation which he believed to be put in question by the majority's reasoning, expressed his confidence "that the present decision will turn out to be an isolated deviation from the strong current of precedents—a derelict on the waters of the law."

The opinion of the Court by Mr. Justice Douglas pinned its holding upon the fact that the conduct condemned by the ordinance was "wholly passive" and "unlike the commission of acts, or the failure to act under circumstances that should alert the doer to the consequences of his deed." Yet, it made no effort to analyze the nature of crimes of omission, as distinguished from those of commission.[75] It spoke vaguely of "the requirement of notice" as "engrained in our concept of Due Process." But it cited only inapposite cases,[76] left the unexplained suggestion that notice making for "probable" personal knowledge would be enough, and wholly ignored the fact that the theretofore unqualified doctrine of Anglo-American law has been that notice by due promulgation and publication of a statute is all that is required.[77] On the issue of criminal intent, the opinion said that "we do not go with Blackstone in saying that 'a vicious will' is necessary to constitute a crime." More atrocious even than the rhetoric of this statement is its moral insensitivity and the intellectual inadequacy of the reasoning offered to support it. Why the views of Blackstone should be thus cavalierly overridden in interpreting a Constitution written by men who accepted his pronouncements as something approaching gospel was left unexplained. What the essential distinction is between those states of innocence which permit conviction of crime and those which do not was left to guesswork.

The dissenting opinion did not have the virtue even of the majority's muddy recognition that being a "criminal" must mean something. It contented itself with flat assertion that human beings may be convicted of crime under the Constitution of the United States even though they "may have had no awareness of what the law required or that what they did was wrongdoing." To this, one can say only, "Why? why? why?" The opinion gives only one answer, "So it has been decided. So it has been decided. So it has been decided." The replication has to be, "But this is wrong, wrong, wrong. And it will continue to be wrong so long as words have meaning and human beings have the capacity to recognize and the courage to resent bitter and unwarranted insult."[78]

The importance of constitutional doctrine is not to be measured by the number of statutes formally invalidated pursuant to it or formally sustained against direct attack. Thinking in constitutional terms provides the points of reference which are necessary in building up a body of thought which is adequate to the task of statutory interpretation.[79] Correspondingly, the absence of such basic thinking is likely to result in a hiatus of thought when interpretive problems present themselves. Thus, the small handful of pre-*Lambert* decisions upholding the constitutionality of strict criminal liability helped to breed a multitude of other decisions blandly assuming, with no effort at ratiocination, that it was a matter of indifference whether ambiguous statutory language were to be read as importing a requirement of "criminal" intent or dispensing with it, and permitting slight evidence to tilt the scales in favor of dispensation. Correspondingly, what will be chiefly important to watch about the *Lambert* case will be the strength of the push it gives to interpretations insisting upon the necessity of a genuinely criminal intent. One may guess that the push would have been stronger if the majority opinion had been more muscularly written.

What are likely to be crucial in the development of any body of statutory law are the presumptions with which courts approach debatable issues of interpretation. For it is these presumptions which control decision when a legislature has failed to address itself to an issue and to express itself unmistakably about it. If the interpretive presumptions of the courts are founded on principles and policies rationally related to the ultimate purposes of the social order, then statutory law will tend to develop the coherence and intelligibility, and the susceptibility to being reasoned about, which a body of unwritten law tends always to have. Otherwise, it will tend to become a wasteland of arbitrary distinctions and meaningless detail.

Legislatures in our tradition have depended heavily upon the assistance of courts in giving statutory law this kind of in-built rationality. The articulation and use of interpretive presumptions by the courts is an essential means of providing this assistance. It involves no impairment of legislative prerogative, but, on the contrary, facilitates the legislature's work rather than hinders it. It serves to focus issues, to sharpen responsibilities, and to discourage buck-passing. It gives assurance that a legislature's departure from generally prevailing principles and policies will be a considered one. This, in turn, requires the courts to confront the resulting constitutional questions, if any, with recognition of the deliberateness of the legislature's determination and of the need for taking full account of the reasons for the determination before overturning it.

The need of some improvement in the shoddy and little-minded thinking of American legislatures about the problems of the criminal law is great. But adequate improvement cannot come from that source alone. Only if the courts acknowledge their obligation to collaborate with the legislature in discerning and expressing the unifying principles and aims of the criminal law is it likely that a coherent and worthy body of penal law will ever be developed in this country. For the most part, American courts have, thus far, failed not only in the fulfillment, but even in the recognition of this obligation.

VI. The Perspective of Courts in Making Decisions About Treatment

When an offender has been found guilty, the court's responsibility for the generalized statement of substantive legal doctrine is at an end. What ordinarily remains is only an individualized determination with respect to this particular defendant. This focus upon the defendant as an individual provides opportunities to be exploited. But it also points up tendencies to be resisted. For the defendant is a character in a much larger drama, and questions about his needs must not be allowed to push out of view questions about the effect of his treatment on other persons and on the well-being of society generally.

A. The Judgment of Conviction

If criminality is to be equated with antisocial conduct warranting the moral condemnation of society, then plainly the first and foremost function of the trial judge in every case, when a finding of guilt has been made, is to express to the defendant with all possible solemnity a judgment of condemnation of his conduct in society's behalf.

The trial judge, of course, can do this under existing law, as many do, when the defendant's offense is one which the community recognizes as blameworthy. But here we meet another of the hidden costs of the sacrifice of principle. For a conscientious judge who is called upon constantly to convict and to sentence defendants who have been guilty of bad luck more than anything else is forced to differentiate. Since he cannot, in honesty, tell such a defendant that his conduct is morally blameworthy, he is forced to draw a line among criminal defendants. This is not like drawing a line between genuinely criminal offenses of varying degrees of gravity. For this differentiation puts in question the very integrity and meaning of the concept of crime. The result may be that even the judge himself stops believing in the equation between criminality and blameworthiness.

A distinguished federal district judge said recently in private conversation that in entering judgments of conviction and passing sentence, he was careful always to refrain from expressing any view about the defendant's character or the morality of his conduct. One can respect the spirit of personal humility that lies behind this restraint. One can discern the main outlines of the supporting rationalization which the positivistic strain in American legal thought provides. One can understand why it is particularly easy for a federal judge, dealing with a considerably larger proportion of regulatory crimes than most state judges, to take such a view. Yet, it has still to be said that the practice described epitomizes the moral and intellectual debility of American criminal law. An able and sensitive judge does not consider that there is any difference between a criminal conviction and a civil judgment which it is worth while to try to communicate to the defendant. If this is so, what attention can ordinary people be expected to pay to the threat of a criminal as distinguished from a civil sanction?

The result, considered simply from the point of view of efficient social engineering, is a grievous waste. For all except the most hardened criminals, a judgment of community condemnation, solemnly and impersonally expressed, can be made a shaking and unforgettable experience. If legislatures had kept clean the concept of crime and sentencing judges were then enabled to tell a convicted criminal, in good conscience, that his conduct had been wrongful and deserved the condemnation of his fellow men, the very pronouncement of such a judgment would go far to serve the purposes of the criminal law by vindicating its threats and so to lessen the need for resort to other commonly less effective and invariably more expensive and oppressive forms of treatment.

B. *The Sentence: Herein Also of the Perspective of Prison and Parole Authorities*

A judgment of conviction having been entered, the trial judge must next face the harsh realities of imposition of sentence.

If what has been said is correct, the judge, in doing this, should be guided by two main, and interrelated, objectives. First, is the overriding necessity of a sentence which, taken together with the judgment of conviction itself, adequately expresses the community's view of the gravity of the defendant's misconduct. Second, is the necessity of a sentence which will be as favorable as possible, consistently with the first objective, to the defendant's rehabilitation as a responsible and functioning member of his community. The first objective stresses the interests of the community; but it does not ignore the interests of the defendant as an individual, since his rehabilitation requires his recognition of community interests and of the obligations of community life. The second stresses the interests of the defendant as an individual; but it does not ignore those of the community, since the community is interested in the defendant's realization of his potentialities as a human being and in the contributions he can make to community life.[80]

The community's condemnation of the defendant's conduct can be expressed in four main ways: *first*, by the legislature's prior grading and characterization, in general terms, of the offense of which he has been found guilty; *second*, by the trial judge's formal expression of condemnation of the particular conduct, taking into account all the special circumstances of it; *third*, by a determination that the defendant shall be vulnerable to unpleasant consequences *in the future* if his behavior thereafter fails to conform to prescribed conditions; and, *fourth*, by a determination that the defendant shall *presently* and forthwith undergo unpleasant consequences, such as fine or imprisonment. Under modern statutes, the judge's exercise of discretion in sentencing will consist largely of choices about the use to be made of the third and fourth forms of condemnation.[81] This paper will not attempt a detailed analysis of the judge's problems in making these choices, but a few broad suggestions in line with the general thesis of the paper may be appropriately made.

1. It is first to be observed that the best possibilities of an imaginative and effective reconciliation of the community's interests and the individual's in fixing sentences will lie ordinarily in the use of the third of the forms of condemnation just described. To declare that the defendant is to be vulnerable to future punishment can be, in itself, an impressive expression of the community's moral disapproval. At the same time, the conditional suspension of the

punishment, whether it be a fine or term of imprisonment, can provide an environment favorable to rehabilitation, both by conveying to the defendant a sense of the community's confidence in his ability to live responsibly and by giving him a special incentive to do so. It would seem to follow that a suspended sentence with probation should be the preferred form of treatment, to be chosen always unless the circumstances plainly call for greater severity.

2. Of all the forms of treatment of criminals, prison sentences are the most costly to the community not only because of the out-of-pocket expenses of prison care, but because of the danger that the effect on the defendant's character will be debilitating rather than rehabilitating. It would seem to follow that if some form of present punishment is called for, a fine should always be the preferred form of the penalty, unless the circumstances plainly call for a prison sentence.

3. Once it is decided that a defendant should be sent to prison, a problem arises about the division of authority and responsibility between the sentencing court and the parole authorities in deciding the time of the prisoner's release—assuming, that is, that the view earlier advanced is accepted that prison sentences ought not to be for a fixed term, neither more nor less.[82] The first aspect of this problem relates to the minimum length of the term. It was earlier urged that the legislature ought not to specify a fixed minimum term in such a way as to deprive the sentencing judge of power to give a suspended sentence.[83] But this was for the reason that the judge ought to have an opportunity to appraise the blameworthiness of the crime in the light of the particular circumstances of it. Should the judge, having made this appraisal, be empowered to fix a minimum prison term in such a way as to deprive the parole authorities of discretion to order an earlier release? Obviously, the judge is better qualified than the parole authorities to interpret the community's views of the blameworthiness of the defendant's conduct. Prima facie, therefore, it would seem that he ought to have the power to fix a minimum term, although the power should be used with caution, since its exercise will deprive the prisoner of an opportunity by his behavior in prison to justify an earlier parole.[84]

4. Should the sentencing judge also have power to fix a maximum term shorter than the statutory maximum so as to deprive the parole authorities of discretion to keep the prisoner in confinement for

the full statutory term? Undoubtedly there will be cases in which extenuating circumstances make the conduct of a guilty defendant less blameworthy than that of the general run of those who commit the same type of crime. This suggests that the judge, as the community's representative, should have the power to recognize these special circumstances in some fashion, either in his judgment of conviction or in his sentence.[85] Yet, it will be observed that whereas the minimum term has the sole function of seeing that the community's condemnation of the defendant's conduct is adequately expressed, different, or at least additional, considerations enter into the fixing of the maximum term. The statutory maximum has as its prime function the fixing of a limit upon the period during which the prisoner may be subjected to administrative control.[86] Judicial power to lower this maximum may be less essential than judicial power to see to the adequate expression of community disapproval.

5. In relation to both of the two points last made, a further and vitally important aspect of the problem of sentencing needs to be taken into account—namely, the necessity of avoiding anarchical inequality in the sentences handed down by different sentencing judges. The achievement of the purposes of the criminal law can never be satisfactorily approximated until this intractable problem is in some fashion reduced to minor, instead of major, proportions. The very ideal of justice is offended by seriously unequal penalties for substantially similar crimes, and the most immediate of its practical purposes are obstructed. Grievous inequalities in sentences are ruinous to prison discipline. And they destroy the prisoner's sense of having been justly dealt with, which is the first prerequisite of his personal reformation. Experience seems to show that large numbers of sentencing judges with power to fix both individualized minimum terms and individualized maximum terms will inevitably produce an indefensible heterogeneity of result. How can a reasonable degree of order be brought into this chaos?

6. Legal experience gives a relatively precise answer to the question just put. Consistency of result in similar cases can be secured either by the laying down of quite precise rules of decision (which here seems impossible), or by subjecting heterogeneous discretionary decisions to review and revision by a single tribunal, or in both ways. Appellate courts seem ill-adapted to the function of reviewing and revising the sentences of trial judges, besides being too preoccupied with other functions. The creation of a new authority, with the

single responsibility of equalizing sentences initially imposed, to the end of assuring that they reflect uniform concepts of degrees of blameworthiness, is a tempting possibility. Short of this expedient, the only institutional machinery presently available in most American legal systems is the parole board.

7. In an ideal system, perhaps, prison and parole authorities would receive prisoners from trial courts with sentences for predetermined, individualized maximum and, when appropriate, minimum terms. The correctional authorities would then have the sole responsibility of custody and treatment of each prisoner, with an eye single to determining, within those limits, first, what kind of custodial treatment would best promote the individual prisoner's growth in responsibility; and, second, when, after the minimum sentence, if any, had been served, growth had progressed to a point which made it proper to permit the prisoner to resume, on parole, the effort at responsible living. But if such a regime is to work effectively, prisoners must have some sense of reasonable equality, and hence justice, in the terms under which they are asked to work out their salvation. In the existing institutional structure, and in any alternative structure which seems feasible, parole boards seem to be the agency best qualified to take responsibility for bringing about this sense of equality. Occasional minimum sentences, which have the special justification already indicated, would not seriously interfere with the discharge of this responsibility. But regular, judicially-tailored maximum sentences would.[87]

VII. Conclusion

The views expressed in this paper are somewhat, but not widely, at variance with the statement of purposes and principles of construction contained in the present tentative draft of the American Law Institute's Model Penal Code. That statement would approximate these views more closely if it were revised to read as follows (new matter being in italics):

Section 1.02. PURPOSES: PRINCIPLES OF CONSTRUCTION.

(1) The general purposes of the provisions governing the definition of offenses are:

(a) *To foster the development of personal capacity for responsible decision to the end that every individual may realize his potentialities as a participating and contributing member of his community:*

(b) To declare the obligation of every competent person to comply with (1) those standards of behavior which a responsible individual should know are imposed by the conditions of community life if the benefits of community living are to be realized, and (2) those further obligations of conduct, specially declared by the legislature, which the individual either in fact knows or has good reason to know he is supposed to comply with, and to prevent violations of these basic obligations of good citizenship by providing for public condemnation of the violations and appropriate treatment of the violators;[88]

(c) To safeguard conduct that is *not blameworthy*[89] from condemnation as criminal;

(d) To give fair warning of the nature of the conduct declared to constitute an offense; *and*

(e) To differentiate on reasonable grounds between serious crimes and minor offenses.

(2) The general purposes of the provisions governing the conviction, sentencing, and treatment of offenders are:

(a) *To further the purposes of the provisions governing the definition of offenses;*[90]

(b) To promote the correction and rehabilitation of offenders;

(c) *To subject to a special public control those persons whose conduct indicates that they are disposed to commit crimes;*[91]

(d) To safeguard offenders against excessive, disproportionate, or arbitrary punishment;

(e) To give fair warning of the nature of the sentences that may be imposed on conviction of an offense;

(f) To differentiate among offenders with a view to a just individualization in their treatment;

(g) To define, co-ordinate, and harmonize the powers, duties, and functions of the courts and administrative officers and agencies responsible for dealing with offenders;

(h) To advance the use of generally accepted methods and knowledge in the sentencing and treatment of offenders; and

(i) To integrate responsibility for the administration of the correctional system in a State Department of Correction (or other single department or agency).

(3) The provisions of the Code shall be construed according to the fair import of their terms but when the language is susceptible of differing constructions it shall be interpreted to further the general

purposes stated in this section and the special purposes of the particular provision involved. The discretionary powers conferred by the Code shall be exercised in accordance with the criteria stated in the Code and, in so far as they are not decisive, to further the general purposes stated in this Section.

2. You're (Probably) a Federal Criminal

*Alex Kozinski and Misha Tseytlin**

When he was president of the Board of New York City Police Commissioners, Theodore Roosevelt decided to fully enforce New York's prohibition against selling alcohol on Sundays. He directed officers to make no exceptions and to arrest saloon keepers who had long counted on their political connections to protect them. Answering the ensuing public outcry, Roosevelt explained, "You have got to be law-abiding citizens, or free government will disappear and anarchy will follow."[1] Forty-five years later, Attorney General Robert Jackson took a different view of enforcing the law and explained, "Law enforcement is not automatic. . . . No prosecutor can even investigate all of the cases in which he receives complaints." For Jackson, this was not merely a problem of resources—there were so many laws that "a prosecutor stands a fair chance of finding at least a technical violation of some act on the part of almost anyone."[2]

Roosevelt and Jackson represent two starkly different visions of the criminal law and its enforcement. For Roosevelt, the law proscribes serious antisocial activities that government officials must suppress and punish in all instances. For Jackson, it is a broad-brush combination of prohibitions that officials should not try to fully enforce, lest they put everyone in jail. Under Roosevelt's view, the ideal law-enforcement agent nabs every lawbreaker; under Jackson's, he acts without personal or invidious considerations in choosing whom to target from among the criminalized citizenry.

Henry Hart's understanding of the criminal law dovetails with Roosevelt's approach. As Hart explained in the essay that is the subject of this symposium, the proper reach of criminal law "is not simply antisocial conduct which public officers are given a responsibility to suppress. It is not simply any conduct to which a legislature

---

*Alex Kozinski is a judge on the U.S. Court of Appeals for the Ninth Circuit. Misha Tseytlin earned his J.D. at Georgetown University Law Center and served as a law clerk to Judge Kozinski in 2007.

chooses to attach a 'criminal' penalty. It is conduct which, if duly shown to have taken place, will incur a formal and solemn pronouncement of the moral condemnation of the community."[3] Since criminal law reaches only actions that the community rightly condemns as seriously immoral, only those who deserve to be behind bars will violate its prohibitions. Hart and Roosevelt's understanding is intuitively appealing because it is woven into the logic of criminal law. Most of us assume that we've nothing to fear from the police because we're not like those nefarious criminals who have broken the social compact.

Unbeknownst to most people, Robert Jackson paints a more accurate picture of America's criminal law system. Violations are so common that any attempt to go after all criminals would sweep up untold millions of people. While Americans vote for politicians who pass laws that make most people criminals, they also support harshly punishing and socially ostracizing those convicted of crimes. In sum, most people think of criminals as bad people, who deserve punishment, while not realizing that they are criminals themselves.

While ubiquitous criminality has not undermined the criminal law's moral force, it has changed the identity of those who make the law, in the practical sense. Since most people have committed at least one crime carrying serious consequences, police and prosecutors choose who'll actually suffer for their crimes. Under the best circumstances, most targets will be unlucky schmoes who happen to catch the authorities' attention or people the prosecutors or the public think are particularly "bad." At worst, a ubiquitous criminal law becomes a loaded gun in the hands of any malevolent prosecutor or aspiring tyrant.

Are You a Federal Criminal?

It is impossible to know how many Americans are federal criminals. There are thousands of federal crimes and hundreds of thousands of federal regulations that can be criminally enforced.[4] Some criminals are murderers, rapists, gangsters, and other profoundly immoral people. These fit easily into Hart's understanding that criminals are people who have committed acts deserving the community's serious moral condemnation and punishment. However, these antisocial individuals are a minuscule fraction of America's criminal class. In fact, most Americans are criminals and don't know it, or suspect they are but believe they'll never get prosecuted. As you read this section, ask yourself whether you're a federal criminal. And if you decide you're not, consider whether the criminals described are more worthy of your community's solemn moral condemnation than you are—on your worst day. Also, keep in mind that these are only federal crimes, so they are just the tip of the iceberg since most criminal prohibitions in America are made at the state level.

Without further ado, have you ever . . .

Done Your Job Poorly?

There are thousands of laws and regulations that make people criminals for unwittingly breaking complex environmental, shipping, and worker-safety rules. In one typical case, a director of a public works project became a federal felon because he incorrectly thought the town he was supervising had a permit for disposing leftover road paint.[5] In another case, the defendant mailed some chemicals without abiding by regulations requiring the shipping papers to note the contents. As Justice Potter Stewart pointed out, "A person who had never heard of the regulation might make a single shipment of an article covered by it in the course of a lifetime. It would be wholly natural for him to assume that he could deliver the article to the common carrier and depend upon the carrier to see that it was properly labeled and that the shipping papers were in order. Yet today's decision [upholding the conviction] holds that a person who does just that is guilty of a criminal offense punishable by a year in prison."[6] Could you imagine yourself shipping something potentially dangerous while accidentally failing to follow one of the technical regulations about how to label, package, and ship the item?

Merely negligently supervising employees who do their jobs poorly can also make you an outlaw. In one such case, an employee accidentally ruptured a heating oil pipe while trying to clean up some fallen rocks during a railroad-building project. The jury convicted the employee's boss for negligent supervision under the Clean Water Act (CWA). The supervisor got six months in prison, six months in a halfway house, six months of supervised release, and had to pay a $5,000 fine. It didn't matter that he had no reason to learn about the CWA's labyrinth of regulations, since he was merely

45

a railroad-construction supervisor.[7] Have you ever supervised employees who violated some environmental or public-safety regulation? Are people who have conducted such poor supervision far worse than you?

Done Your Job Dishonestly?

The federal mail and wire fraud statutes prohibit depriving someone of the "intangible right to honest services." This provision makes criminals out of some professionals who violate their duties of loyalty to employers or their fiduciary duties to clients.[8] In one early case, an attorney sent two letters in connection with his representation of a client who was trying to gain a city contract. The problem was the attorney knew his firm was representing another client competing for that same contract. A jury convicted the attorney of mail fraud, without finding he misused the information for personal gain or even that his failure to disclose the conflict of interest harmed anyone.[9]

Courts have had little success limiting the "intangible right to honest services" doctrine. Most require that the government prove that the defendant's conduct could have influenced the behavior of his employer or client or that the defendant could reasonably have foreseen that his dishonesty would pose a financial risk. Yet, professionals still become criminals for breaching fiduciary duties if they foolishly believe their breach will not influence conduct or cause any harm.[10] It is unsurprising that courts have been unable to successfully confine this doctrine, since any number of actions could reasonably be seen as depriving an employer or agent of the "intangible right to honest services." As Chief Judge Dennis Jacobs has explained, it is plausible that the following people are federal criminals: "an employee who violates an employee code of conduct; a lawyer who provides sky-box tickets to a client's general counsel; a trustee who makes a self-dealing investment that pays off. . . ."[11] Have you ever violated your employee code of conduct? Maybe you should reach into the very bottom of your desk drawer and take a look.

Tried Illegal Drugs?

There's a good chance you have, since nearly half of American adults try illegal drugs during their lives.[12] Luckily for you, you're extremely unlikely to face any federal charges, because the federal

46

government convicts fewer than 400 people per year for drug possession. But keep in mind that those who lose this prosecution lottery
don't always get off so easy. Among simple drug possessors with
little or no criminal history, those receiving jail time get an average
of 8.6 months in prison.[13] Wouldn't that have ruined your junior
year of college?

Cheated on Your Taxes?

When the Internal Revenue Service began requiring taxpayers to
list the social security numbers of dependents, 7 million children
suddenly vanished.[14] It's not surprising that tax evasion is one of
the most popular federal felonies. Beyond the thousands who use
abusive tax schemes to avoid paying taxes, tens of millions of Americans take improper deductions, don't report some money they won
in Las Vegas, or decide to ignore some tips they made at work.
Many of these people know they're breaking the law and may even
be vaguely aware that they're committing a federal felony, punishable by up to five years in prison.[15] Of course, they'll likely never
get caught, and if they do get nabbed, they almost certainly won't
be prosecuted. Still, are you sure you've never cut any corners in
filling out your tax returns?

Lied to a Government Bureaucrat?

Your mom taught you not to lie, but she probably didn't tell you
that making a false statement to any federal official dealing with
any matter in his jurisdiction will make you a federal criminal.[16] Not
only that, lying to a private person who repeats this lie to a federal
agent is also a crime, even if you had no idea the person was going
to pass on the lie.[17] Be honest, have you always told the whole truth
on every federal form you've ever completed?

This prohibition against making false statements also prohibits
inaccurately claiming you've done nothing wrong. In one case, federal agents had ironclad proof that a union rep had taken an illegal
cash gift. They showed up at his home anyway and asked him if
he had taken this gift. When he denied any wrongdoing, it was easy
as pie to convict him for making false statements to federal agents,
even though his statements did nothing to impede the investigation.
Justice Ruth Bader Ginsburg explained the problem: "Because the
questioning occurs in a noncustodial setting, the suspect is not
informed of the right to remain silent. Unlike proceedings in which

a false statement can be prosecuted as perjury, there may be no oath, no pause to concentrate the speaker's mind on the importance of his or her answers."[18] If a federal agent came to your house and confronted you about your recent visit to the Mayflower Hotel in Washington, D.C., would you fess up immediately?

Put Money in a Bank, Bought Expensive Things, or Worked with Others?

Four businessmen decided to import some lobster tails. Unfortunately for them, among other transgressions, they transported the tails in plastic bags, rather than cardboard boxes, and some of the tails were less than 5.5 inches long. The jury found they violated Honduran fishing law, which was elevated to a federal crime under the Lacey Act. The appellate court upheld the conviction, even though the Honduran government explained that its fishing regulations were invalid. But that wasn't the end of it. Because these hardened criminals worked together and placed their money in a bank, the jury found them guilty of conspiracy and money laundering.[19] This issue illustrates how prosecutors can take dubious crimes and multiply the number of convictions and length of sentences defendants will face.

One useful way to turn a single offense into multiple offenses, while increasing a defendant's sentence, is to charge him with money laundering. After proving a defendant has committed a lucrative crime, the prosecutor merely has to show that he tried to conceal the profits through any financial transaction. For example, because the fishermen hid in a bank the money they made from selling their lobsters, they were guilty of multiple counts of money laundering. Of course, since the regulations they broke were invalid in Honduras, there was likely absolutely nothing wrong with their financial transactions. Nor is that all. If one of them had used $10,000 of the money he earned from selling lobsters to buy a car, with no intent to hide the source of the funds, he would be guilty of yet another count of money laundering.[20]

Another easy way to turn someone from a one-time criminal into a multiple felon is by charging that person with conspiracy. To add conspiracy to an already proven crime, the prosecutor merely needs to show that at least two people committed the crime together. Our fishermen were guilty of conspiracy because several of them were involved. A conspiracy conviction can severely increase a defendant's punishment, especially since the sentences for substantive and conspiracy offenses can run consecutively.[21]

* * *

How'd you do? If you're like most people, you probably committed at least one of these crimes. You should count your blessings that no one was looking when you became a federal criminal. Admittedly, breaking fiduciary duties, badly supervising employees, doing drugs, and lying to the feds aren't what you'd teach your kids. But it is striking that a system designed to allow the community to separate out those who commit serious anti-social acts makes most of that same community a bunch of crooks.

The Moral Force of Criminal Law

Yet, ubiquitous criminalization has done little to diminish the public's belief in the moral force of law. Most Americans continue to believe that those convicted of crimes have done something seriously wrong and should be treated far differently from the rest of us supposedly law-abiding folks.

Far from believing the law has lost its moral force, most people continue to support laws treating criminals, or at least felons, as distinctly different. Most states don't allow felons the right to serve as jurors and deny them the right to vote, sometimes permanently. In many states, a felony conviction serves as grounds for divorce and can play an important role in terminating parental rights. Federal law prevents felons from owning guns, and most states put additional restrictions on felon firearm possession. Some states require all felons to register with law-enforcement agencies.[22]

Many of us treat criminals as pariahs who have transgressed serious moral commitments. For example, many employers require job applicants to disclose whether they've been convicted of a crime and often don't read beyond a "yes" answer. This is especially true for white-collar criminals, who may lose their professional licenses and find themselves unable to get permits to work in other fields. Even if they don't work in a licensed field, their reputations are often so destroyed that they can't find even meager work in their chosen profession. Indeed, even being charged with a crime will often lead to being fired.[23]

It seems paradoxical that, even though most of us have committed crimes, we continue to support laws and social conventions that treat those convicted of these same acts as pariahs. The solution to this puzzle is that we have internalized Hart's understanding that "a criminal conviction carries with it an ineradicable connotation of moral condemnation and personal guilt."[24] If our government has deprived someone of his liberty, he *must* be a truly bad person. But do we ever ask ourselves why we haven't been convicted for our own crimes?

Enforcement of a Ubiquitous Criminal Law

Hart understood that criminals should be a small minority of antisocial actors who deserve to suffer serious consequences. Theodore Roosevelt is the ideal police officer for such a criminal law regime—the man who dispassionately goes after every criminal. Consider how you'd expect an officer to respond when hearing a credible murder or rape allegation. Under a system of law that only criminalized these sorts of serious offenses, a rogue officer would retain some authority to allow criminals to escape justice. However, this officer's ability to do harm would be limited to helping nefarious characters; he'd have no lawful authority to go after the law-abiding populace. These people would be shielded by their innocence, along with the constitutional and statutory protections that prevent the authorities from hassling them without good cause.

The situation is far different when most people have committed some crime carrying serious consequences. Under such a system, the authorities necessarily have vast discretion to choose who will remain free, well-respected members of society and who will be tossed in jail and lose their rights, their family, and their job. As Hart aptly explained, since there is no pretense that most criminal laws are seriously enforced, "The breadth of discretion we entrust to the police and prosecuting attorneys in dealing with individuals is far greater than that entrusted to any other kinds of officials and less subject to effective control." Indeed, this transfers "from the legislature to enforcement officials the *de facto* power of determining what the criminal law in action shall be."[25]

Recall that under Hart's view of criminal law, the dutiful officer's role was to nab every criminal and the rogue officer had no lawful authority over the law-abiding majority. Enforcement is far more problematic under a system of broad criminalization, especially one that accepts the moral force of law and, thus, imposes harsh penalties. Even the dutiful prosecutor will drift from randomly punishing whoever commits the most conspicuous crimes to trying to nab only the "worst" criminals to responding to the public's demand for enforcement of some laws or for prosecution of some individuals. And that is just the good news. The malevolent prosecutor, empowered by ubiquitous criminal penalties and harsh sentences, will have broad authority to punish almost anyone he chooses. This power will be especially dangerous if seized upon by an aspiring tyrant.

Dutiful Enforcement

A sprawl of criminality puts even the most dedicated officers and prosecutors in an untenable dilemma. Do they go after every criminal they can find, or do they prioritize crimes and targets? If they do prioritize, do they follow their own moral sense of who deserves punishment, or do they try to enforce laws in a way they think will please the public?

Random Enforcement. Since police and prosecutors only have the time and resources to go after a small percentage of the criminalized populace, they could try to enforce the law randomly. That is, they could catch and prosecute as many criminals, of any type, as their time and resources permit. This is an adaptation of Roosevelt's notion that officials should blindly enforce the law because everyone's "got to be law-abiding citizens."

When government agents randomly enforce sprawling criminal prohibitions, guilt becomes only a very minor factor in determining whether someone will remain a free person. Instead, ability to hide one's crime and luck will play the dominant roles. If police and prosecutors are busy catching and prosecuting every conspicuous violator, they'll never have time to bother with those who are hiding their criminality. Similarly, if the number of people who commit crimes dwarfs the number held accountable, anyone who ends up in jail will be extraordinarily unfortunate. You'd probably have to walk under three ladders and kick five black cats to get prosecuted for cheating on your taxes or smoking some pot.

Needless to say, conspicuousness and luck shouldn't be the most important factors in deciding whether a person gets locked up, loses his rights, and becomes a social pariah. Indeed, a society of criminals

51

that randomly locks up the unlucky or indiscreet can hardly claim it operates under a just system that respects lawfulness.

Selective Enforcement. Of course, police and prosecutors don't randomly enforce all criminal laws. As Attorney General Robert Jackson explained, conscientious prosecutors usually select those cases "in which the offense is the most flagrant, the public harm the greatest, and the proof the most certain."[26] That is, they choose which violators and crimes they will pursue within the confines of their limited resources. In doing so, they have to decide between listening to their own moral sense and trying to intuit which crimes and criminals the public wants them to target. Under either approach, they'll target the worst of the worst—the murderers and rapists—but deciding who else to go after will be extremely problematic.

On the one hand, the subjective judgment of authorities could serve as the determining factor in deciding which members of a criminalized populace will be punished. Under such a system, whether a person has his life torn apart will not depend primarily on his guilt, since everyone is guilty of something. Rather, it will turn on whether government officials believe that the person's crimes are particularly serious or that he is an especially bad person. For example, some government agents decided that Al Capone was a bad guy, and since they couldn't prove he committed murder or extortion, they threw him in prison for tax evasions. If that hadn't worked, perhaps they could have considered whether he negligently supervised the way some of his garbage businesses disposed of their trash. In short, allowing officers and prosecutors to use their judgment to select targets out of a criminalized population transforms the rule of law into the rule of men.

On the other hand, a government agent may realize that he can't simply rely on his own judgment, and so he may choose to use public opinion as his guide. Since prosecutors, police, and their supervisors are accountable to the people, this approach is sensible. Yet publicly responsive enforcement will simply end up targeting crimes the populace gets suddenly excited about enforcing. Consider the increase in white-collar prosecutions after the Enron scandal or the promises to crack down on new categories of criminals during state attorney general election campaigns. Even more troubling, the public often wants law enforcement to target particular individuals, because they are either famous or "bad" people. Consider this the next time you read about a celebrity or politician being investigated for tax fraud or lying to government agents or about a prosecutor's office pouring endless resources into a high-profile case. Ironically, a brash prosecutor can become so famous for catering to the public's desires that he may find himself the authorities' next target.[27]

Law enforcement officials trying to cater to the public's preferences will run into many of the same problems as those trying to enforce their own subjective judgments. Again, the most important factor in deciding whether someone ends up in jail will not be that he committed an objectively defined criminal offense; after all, we all do that. Rather, it will be whether the public finds him or his crime particularly distasteful at a given moment.

The pitfalls of selective enforcement exist under any system where government officials have discretion. However, these problems are far more serious when most people violate sweeping criminal prohibitions. Giving even the most well-intentioned officials power to select who they believe are the most morally culpable or publicly displeasing destroys the link between the impartial rule of law and the reality of criminal law-enforcement. It makes each person's claim to liberty and rights turn on the opinions of other people, rather than on objectively defined rules of conduct.

Malevolent Enforcement

The most common justification for broad criminal laws is that government officials will use good faith and sound judgment in discharging their massive authority. Besides leaving government agents no good way to enforce criminal prohibitions while respecting the rule of law, this grant of authority ignores America's time-tested distrust of vesting vast power in government officials in the hope that they'll use this authority judiciously. Accordingly, it's important to consider the damage malevolent prosecutors and would-be tyrants could do when empowered by ubiquitous criminal law.

Bad Apples. You stole a federal prosecutor's girlfriend. He's ticked and decides to snoop around your life. Maybe you failed to report some income or took a deduction you weren't entitled to; broke a fiduciary duty or negligently supervised some workers; or tried some drugs with people who are willing to talk. Even if he can't find sufficient evidence to prove all the elements of any crime, he can come to your house in the middle of the night and ask you sharp questions. If you figure he's got it in for you and lie, he's got you on the hook for the lie—which is itself a federal crime. Since your family and friends are probably federal criminals as well, he can give them the same treatment. Then he can offer them a pass if you'll plead guilty. In addition, once he's nailed you for one crime, he might be able to add money laundering and conspiracy charges to increase your sentence. Facing this, you'll likely plead guilty. And after you get out of jail, you won't be able to vote, sit on a jury, find a decent job, or exercise your rights under the Second Amendment. Meanwhile, he'll steal back his girlfriend, who'll likely want nothing to do with a criminal such as yourself.

Hopefully, few police and prosecutors behave this way. Yet, it is important to understand that a system of law that makes most everyone a criminal, also makes all its citizens *lawful* targets for malicious officers and prosecutors. Under such a system, substantive and procedural safeguards no longer protect citizens from official harassment. For example, the Fourth Amendment shields citizens from being hassled, searched, and arrested unless the authorities have good reason to believe they've committed crimes. However, if lots of inadvertent and common activities are crimes, this apparent protection actually empowers malevolent government officials to arrest citizens on the street, to search them because of that arrest, and then to search their homes for more evidence. Similarly, the guarantee that the government must prove every element of a crime beyond a reasonable doubt provides little protection for a criminalized populace, except by shielding those who hide their crimes particularly well or make friends with police and prosecutors.

Bad Leaders. A Russian oil executive got the authorities angry by supporting opposition parties and wanting to sell oil to foreign countries. Soon after, he found himself convicted of fraud, embezzlement, and tax evasion, and he was sentenced to 9 years in prison. Just when he was about to become eligible for parole, the prosecutors charged him with money laundering and embezzlement, and they began targeting his former associates for tax evasion. Defending his government's hard-line stance against one such associate, Russian President Vladimir Putin channeled Theodore Roosevelt and explained, "Everyone must understand once and for all—the law must be followed always."[28]

54

Nothing like this scenario is likely in America's near future. Nevertheless, it is noteworthy that post-Soviet Russia's return to autocratic rule was not inevitable. Using the moral force of law to justify cracking down on regime opponents has been one of Vladimir Putin's most effective tools in crushing his country's nascent democracy. Of course, all oppressive regimes cloak themselves with the imprimatur of law. But a society that criminalizes most of its members through a legitimate democratic process gives an incredibly valuable gift to an aspiring autocrat. He doesn't have to answer the argument that he created laws to put down his opponents; he can merely channel Theodore Roosevelt and turn the moral force of criminal law into a chain around his people's necks. He can deploy all of the powers that the bad-apple prosecutor has—from targeted investigations to stacking charges to multiplying sentences—only writ large.

* * *

The overwhelming majority of police and prosecutors try to enforce the law dutifully. After catching the few obvious hard-core crooks, they vacillate between randomly enforcing laws and selectively enforcing them based on their own judgment and the public's demands. This approach undermines the rule of law and makes luck, conspicuousness, and the subjective opinions of government officials the most important factors in determining whether someone ends up in jail. And that's just what happens in the best case. When malicious prosecutors or would-be tyrants get hold of a ubiquitous criminal law, fortified by the public's belief in the moral force of that law, they can go after pretty much anyone they choose.

Conclusion

Hart implied that constitutional amendments limiting the scope of the criminal law were the cure.[29] After 50 years of new criminal laws, long sentences, and post-incarceration consequences, he'd likely hold to this same position today. Yet, political support remains small for passing constitutional amendments and repealing federal laws. Indeed, if people don't believe that the ubiquity of criminal law is a significant enough problem to urge their public officials to stop enacting new criminal laws, they're unlikely to demand constitutional amendments to curtail criminalization.

55

So the question is not about the institutional method for change, but whether people think there's a problem. Do you believe well-intentioned police officers and prosecutors should have the freedom to select from among a criminalized citizenry based on their own judgments or the fleeting desires of the public? Do you think malicious officers and would-be tyrants are likely to abuse the power ubiquitous criminality gives them? Are you willing to accept that, if we limit the number of crimes, some bad people will be able to evade prosecution? In deciding how to answer these questions, recall that you're (probably) a federal criminal.

3. How Correct Was Henry M. Hart?

James Q. Wilson

The central issue in Henry Hart's essay is what behavior should our government define as a crime. Some writers have alleged that a "crime" is anything that is called a crime, but that cannot be correct. Such a vacant argument fails to distinguish criminal penalties from civil ones and does not take into account popular feelings that place great weight on how crimes differ from other failings. To Hart, a crime is "conduct which . . . will incur a formal and solemn pronouncement of the moral condemnation of the community." The matter can be put even more bluntly, as Hart does when he quotes, approvingly, another author who wrote that punishment for "moral delinquency" expresses "the community's hatred, fear, or contempt for the convict."

Writing in 1958, Hart does not discuss anthropological findings, many of which had not yet been published, about what most if not all cultures call crimes. In 1976, Graeme Newman published a survey he had completed of crime in six nations: India, Indonesia, Iran, Italy, Yugoslavia, and the United States. He did not ask about murder, a topic about which everyone would agree is a crime, but he did ask about several other offenses. In those very different countries, 99 percent of the respondents thought robbery was a crime and more than 90 percent thought that stealing public funds, factory pollution, and incest were crimes. Nearly 90 percent regarded taking drugs as a crime, but less than three-fourths thought that homosexuality was a crime and only about half regarded abortion, public protests, and not helping a person in danger as crimes.[1]

There also seems to be a remarkable degree of agreement among people about how crimes should be punished. In 1980, two scholars asked the inhabitants of eight countries (Denmark, Finland, Great Britain, Kuwait, the Netherlands, Norway, Sweden, and the United States) how violent, drug, economic, property, and sexual crimes should be punished. There were differences among these nations:

the four Scandinavian nations recommended shorter prison terms while the Americans, British, and Kuwaitis recommended longer ones. But the gaps were not large. The longest prison term for violent crimes was seven to eight years, the shortest was three to four years. In all nations, property and economic offenders were thought to deserve one to three years in prison, while sexual offenders should receive less than one year.[2]

Violent, property, and economic offenses were always regarded as crimes, but there was a lot of variation regarding abortion, homosexuality, and sexual offenses. Were the study done today, there might be even greater differences in opinion. For example, drug dealing is a capital offense in several Asian and Middle Eastern nations but only a minor offense (and one that is often not enforced) in Switzerland and the Netherlands.

These distinctions do not, in my judgment, alter Hart's argument. Even if people differ a bit on what ought to be called a crime and even think some things ought not to be crimes at all, for the great majority of what we regard as felonies there is little doubt that humans condemn them as moral failings and not just as correctable behaviors. His argument is plain on this matter: He has little use for psychiatrists who think criminals are sick people who ought to be treated and not punished. As Hart wrote, a "curative-rehabilitative theory of criminal justice tends always to depreciate, if not to deny, the significance" of guilt, leading the system to treat people based on what an offender is believed to be rather than on what he or she has done.

Suppose medicine devised a method, perhaps a pill, that would unfailingly cure rapists. Given recent advances in the biological sciences, this idea is not inconceivable. Would we then treat rapists with the pill rather than with prison? And if we did, how would we explain our treatment to their victims? And even if (implausibly) the victims would agree to this policy, what would such a strategy do to the frequency of rape? As Hart notes, we must work to ensure that the commands of the criminal law are effective as ways of influencing behavior.

At the time he wrote, most people probably believed that crime could be, up to a point, deterred. In the two decades that followed his essay, this argument was tested in ways that led many scholars to criticize the evidence that deterrence existed as too weak to warrant much confidence.[3] Since the mid-1990s, however, better studies have suggested that there is a substantial deterrent effect that results from enforcing criminal laws. That effect does not explain, however, all or even most differences among people and places in their crime rates. It may account for perhaps one-quarter of these differences, which is not a trivial amount.[4]

Deterrence is not the sole consequence of the criminal law. As Hart recognized, we hope not only to prevent some crimes, we also desire to take known offenders off the street and to create opportunities for such rehabilitative programs as may work to affect the behavior of offenders when they are back on the streets. The criminal law has a single principle (moral condemnation) but many purposes. Those purposes should not obscure the fact that the criminal law "defines the minimum conditions of man's responsibility to his fellows and holds him to that responsibility."

Obeying these minimum conditions might be weakened by human nature or a person's ignorance of the consequences of his own behavior. When Hart wrote, the general view was that all people are reasonably amenable to the sanctions of the law. But today, we know that there are important genetic differences between persistent offenders on the one hand and most people on the other. Various scholars have found evidence from studies of both twins and adopted children that some people are at much greater risk for habitual offending than others.[5] There is, of course, no "crime gene," and we have only a weak sense of what combination of genetic factors facilitates crime, but there is little doubt that some people find it harder to internalize social rules than do others.

Harder, but not impossible. Except for a few true psychopaths, everyone can learn rules. For some people, it may require quick and frequent rather than delayed and occasional rewards and penalties. Unfortunately, the criminal justice system, because of the need for it to be fair and impartial, usually cannot impose quick penalties. Because of the heavy workload on prosecutors and judges, it rarely imposes them very often. The great majority of felons in this country are on probation or parole. Despite this, the large increase in the prison population since the early 1980s has helped reduce the crime rate; some estimates put the prison-only effect on crime reduction at about 25 percent and other studies suggest it may be even higher.[6] The estimate of a 25 percent prison-based reduction is only an estimate; the true number could be lower or higher—even much higher.

After all, the typical offender commits 12 to 16 crimes a year while on the street. In theory, 100,000 more people in prison in the United States could mean a reduction of 1.2 to 1.6 million crimes. But even this estimate is a weak guess, since we do not know how many offenses the marginal prisoner commits (it might be many fewer than 12 or 16) and whether these are serious offenses or only minor drug charges.

The Hart argument that a crime is what the public morally condemns requires us to think about the changes that may have occurred in that condemnation. He wrote in 1958, just five years after the Otto Preminger film, *The Moon Is Blue*, appeared. After the motion picture moral code was first announced in 1934, it was the first movie in which the words "virgin," "seduce," and "mistress" were uttered. As with every other film then, it did not have anything in it that could be called pornographic. In 1958, I was a young man; when I think about those days, I recall that pornographic books and pictures were scarcely available anywhere except from a few friends who "knew somebody." Today, pornography is sold openly at many bookstores and is easily available on cable television. Public opinion has changed, whether people will admit it in surveys or not; the market reveals what they prefer.

But these changes are not simple ones. The public still is determined to prevent pornography from reaching children and supports local ordinances that restrict the ability of people to place stores selling pornography near schools or churches or, in some places, even too close to one another.

As we have seen, the criminal sanctions attached to the possession or sale of many addictive drugs vary greatly among nations. Clearly moral condemnation among these communities differs. In this country, the public thinks that the government's anti-drug efforts have failed, but (in 1998) only 14 percent thought that drug sales should be legalized.[7] More than a decade later, the public's views were much the same even though attitudes toward the medical use of marijuana had changed. In 2001, the Pew Research Center found that the great majority of Americans still believed that the United States is losing the war on drugs. But despite that, a majority favored stopping the importation of dangerous drugs and arresting drug dealers. When asked whether we should treat possessing small amounts of marijuana as a crime, men tend to say no while women, especially black ones, say yes.[8]

Since 1996, 12 states have legalized the use of marijuana for medical purposes. What "legalization" means in these states varies. In some, such as California, a doctor need only "recommend," not prescribe, the drug, and so its use may have increased owing to loose restrictions on so-called head shops. In some states, the possession of small amounts of marijuana has been decriminalized, meaning that the penalty is limited to a fine as opposed to a jail term. The few studies that are available suggest that, in states with such marijuana laws, there has been no significant increase in the use of the drug.[9]

Libertarian readers of this chapter probably feel that the sale of addictive drugs should be legalized, and so they may dispute my interpretation of Hart or Hart himself. But in doing so, they must provide a basis for the criminal law that does not rest on the principle of moral condemnation but on something else. My reading of the arguments supporting drug legalization is that most of them rest on utility, not morality. Ending the so-called war on drugs, it is alleged, would save money, keep people out of prison, lower the cost of drugs, reduce crime rates, or lessen political corruption.

Whether all of these things would happen is not clear. Obviously the prison population would be smaller and drug prices would be less, but it is not clear whether crime rates would be reduced or money spent on welfare would be less. Lower drug costs, combined with the reduced threat of being ripped off by an illicit drug dealer, would in all likelihood increase drug consumption as people discovered that it was much cheaper, both socially and economically, to consume substances that powerfully heighten one's sense of euphoria. With increased consumption, the users, many but not all of whom would be in a constant state of euphoria, would be unable to hold a job, stay in school, or maintain a marriage. The extent to which this would happen would vary with the drug, being least of all for marijuana and most of all for heroin and cocaine. Without a job or an education, this large group of addicts would either have to be supported by welfare payments or would resort to crime. If the former, it would cost the government more; if the latter, crime rates would rise.

For every utilitarian argument for drug legalization, there is a similar argument against it. To learn which set of arguments is correct, we would have to legalize drugs and inspect the practical results. We would learn which argument was right, but only at the risk of learning, too late, that the anti-legalization argument was correct.

Hart's argument suggests that we base the criminal law not on utilitarian concerns but only on moral ones. Readers may disagree with that view, but if so, they must reject the essence of their position and then construct, as an alternative to their view, an argument that would serve to justify the criminal law. If the case for legalizing drugs is that it would make society better off, then is it the case that it would be better off if we legalized public nudity? Or, to pursue the utilitarian thesis, could theft best be reduced by suing rather than incarcerating thieves? Or could rape best be reduced by suing rapists? Treating rapists as the objects of a civil action seems ludicrous, but if people think selling drugs is almost as blameworthy, then Hart's case for a criminal sanction seems to apply to both.

When the legislature determines the punishment that should be visited upon someone who commits a criminal offense, Hart argues that the legislature cannot state a single, definite, and unvarying penalty because the sanction must be tailored to fit the circumstances of the crime and the conduct of the accused. But it can and should set a maximum penalty and probably should set a minimum one as well. Anticipating the findings of research done in the 1970s and 1980s, Hart acknowledges that judges should not be allowed to set very different sentences for similar crimes and similar offenders. This would lead, he remarks, to "anarchical inequality." Hart said that one way to do so is by judicial review of sentences (which would place too great a burden on the appellate courts) or by the legislature laying down strict and narrow rules (which he thought impossible). He suggested the "creation of a new authority" that would be responsible for "equalizing sentences" so that they "reflect uniform concepts of degrees of blameworthiness." This argument foresaw work done by later scholars about unjustifiable differences among judges in sentencing and the congressional decision to create a Sentencing Commission that would do exactly what Hart had proposed several decades earlier.

The commission has produced a table that states, in months of imprisonment, what an offense and an offender deserve. Each offense is scaled in degrees of severity, and each offender is categorized on the basis of his or her past record and degree of involvement. At the intersection of each row (the offense) and each column (the offender), prison time is set forth in a range of months.

As we know, many judges dislike this constraint on their authority. My sympathies, however, are with Hart and against the judges except in those cases where the commission can be shown to have made a serious mistake. Tom Tyler and his colleagues have shown that convicted criminals have a better opinion of the law if they believe they have been treated fairly than they do if they have received a lenient sentence.[10] In another study of small claims courts in Maine, the scholars found that the chances of a party paying what he owed was greater when that person thought he had a fair hearing.[11] The task of the courts is, first and foremost, to do justice (which means treat like cases alike) and only secondarily to tailor penalties to personal theories of who deserves what.

Although it is easy to sympathize with judicial complaints, the evidence gathered in the 1970s and 1980s showed that when identical cases were shown to judges, they differed dramatically in the penalties they imposed. A National Academy of Sciences report summarized the evidence this way: "Despite the number and diversity of factors investigated as determinants of sentences, two thirds or more of the variance in sentence outcomes remains unexplained."[12] Unexplained, that is, except for what the judge ate for breakfast.

Sympathetic as I am to Hart's analysis, there are some matters about which we disagree. He worried about the extent to which prison would make its inmates worse off: its effect on the offenders' character would be "debilitating rather than rehabilitating." We now know from studies of offenders that, on balance, it leaves them unchanged. More precisely, some are deterred from committing future crimes and others learn to work harder at crime, with the net effect close to zero. For most prisons, what affects their inmates is the character they bring to the institution and how they return to the community. Today, perhaps the major unlearned lesson of modern criminology is how best to manage the return process in ways that minimize repeat offending.

To me, it is remarkable how well Hart's analysis has stood up a half century after it was published. When people, including me, study the criminal justice system, many of our favorite findings do not last for a year before they are refuted by new research. Hart did better.

4. Federal Criminal Law: Punishing Benign Intentions—A Betrayal of Professor Hart's Admonition to Prosecute Only the Blameworthy

Harvey A. Silverglate

In his seminal essay "The Aims of the Criminal Law," Professor Henry Hart proposed a moral foundation for the criminal justice system that modern-day practitioners of *federal* law know has been honored largely in the breach. The 50th anniversary of the publication of Hart's essay is an appropriate occasion to cause us to think, and perhaps do something about, the extent that federal criminal justice has veered from its moral underpinnings.

Hart argued in his essay that some degree of "blameworthiness" is necessary in order for our society to condemn an individual as a criminal. In some cases, Hart explained, blameworthiness is self-evident, because the behavior in question is "intrinsically antisocial," as in murder or rape. For our current purposes, it is enough to say that there is no justification for committing these acts, known as *malum in se*—acts that are bad in themselves. Offenders against these laws transgress not only the criminal code, but also society's underlying moral framework that provides the basis for that code. They are, in some rough sense, violations of certain of the Ten Commandments.

These are not the only types of crimes, however. Some individuals are condemned as criminals for engaging in behaviors that are not intuitively evil, but which have nonetheless been prohibited by the legislature to "secure some ultimate social advantage."[1] These *mala prohibita*—or bad because they have formally been deemed to be so—behaviors were designated by the legislature irrespective of whether the legislature "thinks the immediate conduct involved is either rightful or wrongful in itself."[2] Some of these laws, a cynic

65

might say, target behaviors that legislators simply don't *like*; modern-day libertarians concerned with the use of the criminal law to legislate morality or a certain lifestyle might, for example, fit *mala prohibita* recreational drug laws into this category.

In order for an offender against these statutes to be considered blameworthy, Hart reasoned, he must have been given fair notice that the conduct in question is prohibited, and he must have willfully ignored this warning. "[K]nowing or reckless disregard of legal obligation affords an independent basis of blameworthiness justifying the actor's condemnation as a criminal, even when his conduct was not intrinsically antisocial," he explained.[3] (Criminal defendants may sometimes claim accident, coercion, or other exigency as reason or excuse for breaking the law, and, when the facts support these defenses, such circumstances lessen the degree of the defendant's moral culpability because the defendant did not intend to break a legitimate and valid societal rule.)

Hart made a point of stressing the difficulties that attend delineating *mala prohibita* conduct. As the law shifts from the *malum in se* to the *malum prohibitum* framework, he explained that "it necessarily shifts its ground from a demand that every responsible member of the community understand and respect the community's moral values to a demand that everyone know and understand what is written in the statute books."[4] If those statute books become too confusing and impractical, wrote Hart, they also become useless and unjust. "To condemn a layman as blameworthy for a default of technical judgment in a matter which causes trouble even for professional judges is, in many cases, so manifestly beyond reason that courts have developed various makeshift devices to avoid condemnation in particular situations."[5]

Thus, Hart meant to imbue the criminal law with a necessary level of moral authority. After all, to punish individuals for committing acts that they had no reasonable way of knowing constituted crimes would be the moral equivalent of punishing an infant or a person with severely diminished mental capacity—something that the western legal tradition has long avoided to preserve the moral underpinnings of the criminal law.

Historical context is crucial in order to understand Hart's concern over the abusive or unfair use of *mala prohibita* crimes. Hart wrote during a transformative time in American lawmaking. The 1950s and 1960s were defined by a steady increase in the number of both state and federal laws.

On the state level, legislatures undertook major organized efforts to codify and standardize their laws. Previously, many states had relied heavily on the ancient common law as the basis for their criminal jurisprudence. Certain *malum in se* acts, such as homicide, were so commonly understood to be universally abhorrent that it was theretofore unnecessary to enact detailed statutes codifying the elements of that offense. These efforts to codify state criminal codes in the 1950s and 1960s were intended to modernize and organize— not to reject—ancient common law concepts, firmly establishing their place in the statute books. And the crafters of the new state criminal statutes were attuned to the need to keep the law linked to the moral notions of blameworthiness that underpinned the common law of crimes.

As the codification of state criminal law went forward, the federal criminal code was developing in a quite different direction in both scope and structure. The era of the New Deal had witnessed a veritable explosion of government rules, ranging from congressionally enacted statutes to myriad regulations promulgated by the administrative agencies to which rule-making authority had been delegated by legislation. These regulatory laws, and expansions of traditional fraud statutes, created crimes well beyond what the common law covered. For example, federal securities laws and insider trading regulations brought to the fore new notions of criminal fraud.

However, the federal criminal code's unhinging from the English common law did not begin with the Franklin Roosevelt administration. Rather, it was a consequence of early Supreme Court jurisprudence. Only three decades after the Revolutionary War, a Pennsylvania federal court dismissed a bribery case because Congress had not enacted a bribery statute. The court ruled that federalism and the limited jurisdiction of federal courts precluded the existence of federal common law crimes. The Supreme Court agreed, and, in the 1812 case *United States v. Hudson & Goodwin*, went on to announce that federal crimes were entirely creatures of congressional statute rather than of English common law.[6] Accordingly, Congress in writing statutes and the federal courts in interpreting them do not have the full benefit of the common law's wisdom and experience. Instead, as the Supreme Court said, ''because federal crimes are creatures of statute . . . , when assessing the reach of a federal criminal statute, we must pay close heed to language, legislative history, and purpose in order strictly to determine the scope of the conduct the enactment forbids."[7] Hundreds of years of common law experience, and the precision and wisdom that accompanied it, appear to have lost their precedential weight in federal jurisprudence in one fell swoop.

The consequences would eventually prove highly destructive to both liberty and the moral underpinnings of federal criminal law. Although Hart does not make the point directly in his essay, which is aimed largely at state and not federal criminal law, clues suggest that he had grappled with the problems posed by any detachment, whether in state or federal jurisdictions, from the common law's emphasis on the requirements of clarity and "fair notice." For example, to avoid the problem of the conviction of a person who simply did not understand the requirements of a statute he is accused of violating, Hart suggested various devices, such as "permitting a good faith belief in the legality of one's conduct to be pleaded and proven as a defense, or of providing a civil rather than a criminal sanction for nonwilful violations."[8] Further, Hart recommended that two words be changed in a provision to make it clear that the law should "safeguard conduct that is *not blameworthy* from condemnation as criminal."[9] And he left undisturbed the sentence of the American Law Institute's draft Model Penal Code that would have required criminal statutes "to give fair warning of the nature of the conduct declared to constitute an offense."[10]

Hart then ended his essay by proposing that the Model Penal Code's section on "general purposes of the provisions governing the definition of offenses" include the following purpose:

> "To declare the obligation of every competent person to comply with (1) those standards of behavior which a responsible individual should know are imposed by the conditions of community life if the benefits of community living are to be realized, and (2) those further obligations of conduct, specially declared by the legislature, which the individual either in fact knows or has good reason to know he is supposed to comply with."[11]

Though Hart was not writing with regard to federal criminal legislation, the lessons he provided could easily be adapted to the federal criminal code.[12]

I believe Hart's article can be seen as a sort of "backdoor approach" to reconnecting federal law and common law principles of blame-worthiness. I call it "backdoor" because, for one thing, Hart was writing specifically in connection with then-pending efforts to codify and update *state* criminal codes. And, further, Hart surely realized that it was too late to change the "creature of statute" approach to the drafting and interpreting of federal statutes. The deracinating work of the *Hudson & Goodwin* decision had already been done. Hart simply reminded the legal community of the *justifications* for punishment generally. Presumably, all criminal justice systems should follow these general and universal precepts.

Given the time and place Hart was writing in, it is highly likely that he was influenced by a similar attempted backdoor approach to fixing the federal criminal law that had taken place a few years earlier. Supreme Court Justice Robert H. Jackson—a former U.S. attorney general and the chief American war crimes prosecutor at Nuremberg—had penned the majority opinion in the much studied but somehow greatly underappreciated case of *Morissette v. United States*.[13] Though he could not reverse *Hudson & Goodwin*, Jackson wrote an opinion in the *Morissette* case that seems, at least to me, to have been a piecemeal attempt to limit the moral and ethical damage done when federal criminal law was delinked from the English common law notion of the joinder of act and intent in order to charge and prove a crime. Jackson sought, it seems, to restore the basic common law notions of fair notice and criminal intent to federal statutory criminal law. The similarities between Jackson's backdoor approach and Hart's subtle use of the Model Penal Code to tether the criminal law—including implicitly *federal* criminal law—to ancient common law principles are striking.

While at first glance *Morissette* may have looked unworthy of Supreme Court review, Jackson noted how truly important it was: "This would have remained a profoundly insignificant case to all except its immediate parties had it not been so tried and submitted to the jury as to raise questions both fundamental and far-reaching in federal criminal law," he wrote.

After being honorably discharged from the United States Army, Joseph Edward Morissette started a family in small-town Michigan. In order to support his wife and young son, he worked as a fruit stand operator during the summer months and as a trucker and scrap iron collector during the winter. His seemingly normal life came crashing down, however, when he was charged with stealing from the U.S. government.

Morissette's supposed crime was that he collected spent bomb casings that piled up on "a large tract of uninhabited and untilled land in a wooded and sparsely populated area of Michigan" owned by the federal government, which used it as "a practice bombing range over which the Air Force dropped simulated bombs at ground targets." The area "was known as good deer country and was extensively hunted." When Morissette failed to bag a deer to pay for his trip, he collected some of the casings, crushed them with his tractor, and sold them as scrap metal. The casings yielded him a net profit of $84.

The casings had been "dumped in heaps, some of which had been accumulating for four years or upwards, were exposed to the weather and rusting away." No signs were posted about the casings, and Morissette had no reason to believe they were anything but detritus. Nonetheless, Morissette was indicted in federal court on the charge that he "did unlawfully, willfully and knowingly steal and convert" property of the United States of the value of $84 in violation of a statute that provided that "whoever embezzles, steals, purloins, or knowingly converts" government property is punishable by fine and imprisonment. Morissette was convicted and sentenced to two months in prison or a fine of $200.

The trial judge forbade Morissette's lawyer to argue to the jury that his client acted with an "innocent intention," because the judge concluded that Morissette's guilt under the statute was obvious: the bomb casings were on government property, and Morissette took them without permission. It was irrelevant that Morissette might have reasonably believed the casings were abandoned property, essentially trash. Thus, he was convicted because the trial judge instructed the jury that as long as (a) the casings were on government property, (b) Morissette admitted he took the casings, and (c) he did not have express permission to take them, Morissette had no defense to assert. The question of whether Morissette *believed he was stealing* did not matter, as that was foreclosed in the government's favor.

The judge's approach to the statute departed from centuries of English common law tradition. As Hart rightly explained, the traditional understanding of the criminal law was that, with rare and narrow exceptions, those who act with innocent intent—presumably like Morissette—do not rise to the level of blameworthiness that would trigger the community's solemn disapproval. Instead, to convict one of a crime, the law generally requires proof that a defendant (a) knew what he was doing, (b) intended the consequences of his actions, and (c) understood that his actions were wrong. Of course, these three requirements are central to the criminal law's moral component, under which our society punishes only those who intentionally rather than inadvertently violate the law.[14]

In Morissette's case, Congress was silent about the intent required to be guilty of taking apparently abandoned federal property. Without a sufficiently clear intent requirement written into the statute, anyone charged with this crime apparently could be convicted, even if he had been utterly unaware his actions technically violated the statute. This omission was fatal for someone in Morissette's position because there were no signs posted on the bombing range warning that the rusted, heaped up piles of shell casings were not discarded and instead remained the property of the federal government.

When the United States Court of Appeals for the Sixth Circuit heard Morissette's appeal in 1951, it upheld his conviction by a 2-1 vote. While acknowledging Morissette took the casings in broad daylight with "no effort at concealment," the majority held that "federal courts long ago stopped overturning convictions on the technical niceties of pleading." By this logic, it became a "technicality" that Morissette neither intended to steal nor had any clue that the casings were other than abandoned scrap. When it comes to statutory crimes defined by Congress, the two-judge majority argued, intent or knowledge is irrelevant unless Congress specifically provides otherwise.

In its unanimous opinion, the Supreme Court threw out the appellate court's decision, and with it, Morissette's conviction.[15] Justice Jackson discussed the historical role of *intent* in criminal cases, as well as "the ancient requirement of a culpable state of mind" that must accompany a culpable act. For one to be convicted of a *malum prohibitum* crime, there must be "an evil-meaning mind with an evil-doing hand," the traditional common law notion of the combination of the *actus reus* and the *mens rea*.

Drawing on what appear to be centuries-old *common law* requirements, Justice Jackson concluded that intent must be read into federal criminal statutes unless Congress has explicitly dispensed with this requirement in drafting a particular statute. The courts could not presume from Congress's silence that it did away with criminal intent, as this "would conflict with the overriding presumption of innocence with which the law endows the accused and which extends to every element of the crime."

Justice Jackson noted that, had the jurors been allowed to consider Morissette's state of mind, "[t]hey might have concluded that the heaps of spent casings left in the hinterland to rust away presented an appearance of unwanted and abandoned junk," and from that, they might "have refused to brand Morissette as a thief." That the Congress was silent about the intent requirement did not authorize the trial judge to ignore it. Thus, Jackson rejected the prosecutor's suggestion, accepted by the trial judge, that criminal intent can be "presumed" from the mere act of taking the casings. If true criminal intent existed in this case, Jackson explained, the jury must determine it "not only from the act of taking, but from that together with the defendant's testimony and all of the surrounding circumstances."

* * *

Neither Hart nor Jackson could have predicted the degree to which their concerns over the trend in the direction of enforcing *mala prohibita* federal laws without adequate regard for the ancient requirement of intent would prove true beginning around the late 1980s. This has been accomplished not primarily by an intention of statute drafters to create absolute liability offenses (although some such offenses have indeed been created, largely as misdemeanors in the corporate arena) and not by any judicial declaration formally doing away with the ancient requirement that conviction attend conduct only where there is a joinder of a prohibited act and a mental intent to commit the act and to thereby break the law (the union of *mens rea* and *actus reus*). In other words, Justice Jackson's opinion in *Morissette* has not been formally overturned. Rather, seemingly ordinary citizens have become convicted criminals because of the advent of vague and therefore incredibly pliable federal crimes.

The principles in Hart's monumentally important essay—and the American Law Institute's attempts to carefully render a Model Penal Code—have been evaded not by a frontal attack on the notion of punishing only conduct committed in *knowing* violation of the criminal law, but, rather, by the practice of eviscerating this fundamental moral requirement of the law in the enforcement and interpretation of federal criminal statutes. Federal prosecutors find it easier to pursue their quarries when they are enforcing statutes with no apparent definitions of what constitutes the prohibited conduct—a luxury not available to prosecutors enforcing most state laws.

This legal development has been abetted by certain ancillary practices calculated to deprive a federal criminal defendant, as a practical matter, of the ability to defend on grounds of factual innocence. It is no wonder that it is widely viewed as nearly impossible for a defendant to beat a federal indictment and that the Department of Justice (DOJ) resolves the vast majority of its cases by defendants' pleas of guilty. Overall, between guilty pleas and guilty verdicts, the DOJ reportedly wins some 90 percent of its criminal cases.[16]

This development has largely escaped notice—and hence analysis—by legal scholars and theoreticians. It therefore falls to the system's practitioners, rather than to its scholarly students, to describe the phenomenon. A recent case from my own law practice perfectly demonstrates the modern problem infecting the moral underpinnings of federal criminal jurisprudence.

* * *

Bradford C. Councilman was the vice president of Interloc, Inc., a Massachusetts-based company that provided an online rare and out-of-print book listing service. Interloc supplied a number of its book dealer customers with an e-mail address and acted as an Internet service provider (ISP) for those customers. A rare book dealer using this e-mail service would obtain an e-mail address ending in "@interloc.com." Interloc was eventually merged into a corporation that dealt in used and rare books.

Councilman was charged with wiretapping in the federal district court in Massachusetts because he made extra copies of e-mail messages passing between used and rare book dealers on the Interloc system and Amazon.com, the giant Internet bookstore. The government charged that Councilman made the extra copies to learn the prices dealers were proposing and to give his company an unfair commercial advantage. Councilman maintained that he was not the one who actually did the copying, that he never read the messages, and that the copies were made solely for backup storage purposes.

Both the prosecution and defense agreed that the communications had been copied by somebody at Interloc while the messages were in temporary storage on Interloc's computer system on their way from sender to receiver, *not* while streaming through wires. Interloc's computer system, in other words, was a way station where the message stopped briefly during its journey. This fact raised an important question. Because the communications were in electronic *storage* rather than in electronic *transit*, as defined in the statute, could Councilman's actions truly be construed as wiretapping?

Councilman's chief trial counsel, my then–law partner Andrew Good, moved to dismiss the indictment for failure to charge an activity that amounted to a crime.[17] He was arguing, in effect, that while Councilman emphatically denied involvement in this course of conduct, the activity, even if he had done precisely what was alleged, would not have been a federal crime. The government, in contrast, took the position that a violation of the Wiretap Act had occurred even though the communications were not traveling in a "wire" when intercepted. It was, most observers of and even participants in the case agreed, the fabled "How many angels can dance on the head of a pin?" question. But it was a crucial technicality, for the answer determined whether the making of the extra copies, even for a perfectly benign purpose, violated a serious federal criminal statute.

Yet, there was another consideration that should have been taken into account: Was the correct interpretation of the statute—whatever interpretation happened to be correct—obvious enough so that the statute's scope and meaning were sufficiently clear such that Councilman could be said to have *knowingly and intentionally* violated the law?

It is crucial to understand that Councilman, working for an ISP, was not in the same position as an outside party seeking to tap into the line and intercept the e-mails involved. Such interception by a stranger would easily be deemed wiretapping; it would clearly violate the statute but would also constitute "intrinsically antisocial" behavior, in the words of Hart's essay. In contrast, Councilman, as an ISP, had lawful access to the e-mails while in electronic storage. Could a wiretapping statute be clearly applied to Councilman under such circumstances? There would have been, Councilman argued, a perfectly reasonable purpose for making an extra copy of a transmitted message—to provide backup in the event of a system failure. If such an action were to be declared a crime, it should be done by clear statute, not by twisting an existing law to perform a function for which it was not obviously meant or worded.

The difficulty of these questions threw the federal judicial system in Boston into paroxysms of confusion and disagreement. Judge Michael A. Ponsor, an intelligent and conscientious trial judge, initially ruled in July 2002 that Councilman's alleged conduct, at the very least, violated the *spirit* of the statute. He denied the motion to dismiss the indictment filed by Good and scheduled a trial.

But then, as Judge Ponsor was preparing to conduct the trial, he learned that the United States Court of Appeals for the Ninth Circuit decided a case, *Konop v. Hawaiian Airlines,* involving an interpretation of the same provision of the Wiretap Act.[18] The circuit ruled in favor of the same position being advanced by Councilman's lawyers. The *Konop* case involved a civil dispute between an employee and the company for which he worked. The employee claimed that the employer unlawfully gained access to the employee's secure website and disclosed its contents. Admitting that the statutory scheme was "a confusing and uncertain area of the law" because technology had gotten so far ahead of Congress, the Court of Appeals concluded that it did not constitute "wiretapping" for a party to access online communications after they no longer were *in transit* but instead had landed *in storage.*

Interestingly, the DOJ offered its amicus curiae view in *Konop* in which it encouraged the court to interpret the wiretapping statute exactly as defense counsel had in the Councilman case. Legal observers, with perhaps a touch of cynicism, speculated quite reasonably that in *Konop* the government narrowly read the statute in order to protect its agents and agencies from being sued for post-9/11 intrusions into stored messages. In other words, the government appeared to narrowly interpret the statute on the West Coast in order to protect its own agents, while on the East Coast it recommended a broad reading in order to convict a private citizen.

The Councilman team was curious to see how the Boston prosecutors would react to the startling fact that in *Konop* the DOJ had taken a diametrically opposite position on this crucial question to the statutory interpretation being advanced by the DOJ in Boston. Remarkably, the prosecutors in Boston argued that *Konop* should not control the Councilman case.

Our legal system is surely undermined when the DOJ is allowed to take one position in one jurisdiction when it fears being accused of invasion of a citizen's privacy, but an opposite position in another when it does the accusing. Judge Ponsor, attuned to the "fair notice" implications of allowing the government to put forth opposite interpretations of the same statute, dismissed the indictment against Councilman in February 2003.[19] He concluded that, of the two interpretations put forth, the Ninth Circuit's seemed more correct, and, hence, there was no illegal "interception" of e-mail in Councilman's case. As the Ninth Circuit put the matter, as simply and logically as was possible given the statutory morass, if the statute uses the term "'intercept' with respect to electronic communications," it obviously means that the message "must be acquired during transmission, not while it is in electronic storage." "This conclusion," said the Ninth Circuit, "is consistent with the ordinary meaning of 'intercept,' which is 'to stop, seize, or interrupt in progress or course before arrival,'" citing *Webster's Ninth New Collegiate Dictionary.* (How refreshing it was to have a court, when trying to figure out what the plain meaning of a statute would be to an ordinary citizen, resort to the same explanatory device to which the citizen would resort—namely, a dictionary of the English language!)

The DOJ appealed Judge Ponsor's dismissal. By a vote of 2-1, a panel of judges on the United States Court of Appeals for the First Circuit agreed with Judge Ponsor's legal analysis and *Webster's* definition. The dissenting judge, after a long and complex analysis of both the law and the technology involved, concluded, remarkably, that the statute did apply to Councilman's conduct largely because "I find it inconceivable that Congress could have intended such a result" that would exclude such conduct from the statute's ambit. Congressional intent, in other words, should trump what lawmakers actually write in a statute—an odd notion if citizens are supposed to be able in good faith to determine their legal obligations, as Hart and Jackson had demanded. Under this tortured logic, the citizen is supposed to see into the minds of legislators, rather than to follow the written word of the law.[20]

Because of intense public scrutiny, the First Circuit reconsidered the case *en banc* (that is, by the full membership of the court). On

August 11, 2005, the court, by a vote of 5-2, reversed the decision of the three-judge panel. The court's *en banc* opinion pivoted on a question central in the criminal law: "whether Councilman had fair warning that the Act would be construed to cover his alleged conduct in a criminal case, and whether the rule of lenity or other principles require us to construct the Act in his favor." The five-judge majority of the court claimed to "find no basis to apply any of the fair warning doctrines." Nor did they see fit to apply the "rule of lenity," which would hold, essentially, that if there were reasonable and articulable doubt over the interpretation of a criminal statute, the defendant had to be given the benefit of that doubt—a rule based in part on the presumption of innocence and in part on the clear notice concept inherent in due process of law.

The court's analysis was remarkable for the degree to which it dismissed all of the doubts previously expressed about the meaning and reach of the Wiretap Act. In response to Councilman's argument that the "plain text" of the statute did not cover his actions, the majority said, "As often happens under close scrutiny, the plain text is not so plain." But this lack of clarity, rather than working *for* Councilman, somehow worked *against* him. The majority purported to resolve "this continuing ambiguity" in the statute's language by looking to the legislative history of the enactment, a notoriously difficult task under the best of circumstances. Congress intended to give "broad" protection to electronic communications, they concluded, and so the panel's prior *Councilman* decision was deemed flawed.

The majority of First Circuit judges were obviously a bit self-conscious about reinstating an indictment that was so controversial and that had perplexed so many fine judicial minds on both coasts. The court could not entirely deny that there was *some* degree of an ambiguity problem here. But the rule of lenity, the majority intoned, applies only in cases of *"grievous ambiguity* in a penal statute" (emphasis supplied). In this case, there was only *"garden-variety, textual ambiguity"* (emphasis supplied). "The Wiretap Act is not unconstitutionally vague in its application here," concluded the majority. "From its text, a person of average intelligence would, at the very least, be on notice" that Councilman's activity was covered.

It was this last part of the majority's decision reinstating the indictment against Councilman that drew the ire of Circuit Judge Juan

Torruella, who issued a stinging dissent. While purporting (perhaps sarcastically) to give appropriate deference to the "erudite and articulate majority opinion," Judge Torruella termed the majority's rewriting of the statute "an unfortunate act of judicial legislation that no amount of syllogization can camouflage." This defect can be cured, he pointed out, only by Congress's rewriting the statute. "It is not by coincidence that every court that has passed upon the issue before us has reached a conclusion opposite to that of the *en banc* majority."

Even if the *en banc* majority's interpretation of the statute were correct, wrote dissenting Judge Torruella, the rule of lenity surely must be applied in a case such as this. "Councilman is being held to a level of knowledge which would not be expected of any of the judges who have dealt with this problem," concluded the dissenter, to say nothing of "men and women of common intelligence." "If the issue presented be 'garden-variety,'" as the majority decision claimed, "this is a garden in need of a weed killer."

Nine years after his alleged criminal act, Bradford Councilman was finally put to trial before a jury of his peers to determine the factual question of whether he was the person who copied the stored e-mails and, thereby, committed what the court of appeals said would be a federal felony. The jury returned a verdict of "not guilty" on February 6, 2007. Jurors have their own way, sometimes, of clearing weeds, whether garden variety or grievous.

Interestingly, at Councilman's trial, a government witness conceded that the copies of e-mails made by whoever copied them were periodically purged because the accumulation of duplicate copies intermittently overloaded the system. This made it unlikely that the copies were being made for some nefarious reason, such as to gain a commercial advantage by stealing customer data contained in the e-mails, since they were not being saved. Instead, this fact made it more likely that the copies were being routinely made by someone at the company to supply a temporary "backup" in the event of accidental deletion of the original message before it arrived at its destination. A Federal Bureau of Investigation agent testified at the trial that, when a cooperating witness tried to explain this to a prosecutor during a trial preparation session, the prosecutor balked and asked the witness and his lawyer to confer, whereupon the witness retracted the innocuous explanation for the backup procedure. Of course, had the court of appeals properly interpreted the statute, none of this maneuvering would have been possible. The case would not, and should not, have gone to trial.

* * *

The problem of prosecutions based on impossibly vague federal criminal statutes has become endemic to the system. Consider the sad fate of the late accounting giant Arthur Andersen, LLP.

The Department of Justice's scapegoating of Arthur Andersen, long-time Enron Corporation auditor, is a horror story that, despite Andersen's eventual Pyrrhic victory, almost certainly will be repeated again and again in other corporate and professional sectors of civil society. Indeed, it was later nearly repeated in connection with other national accountings firms. For example, both KPMG and Ernst & Young learned how futile it is to resist rather than "cooperate," regardless of claims that truth rightly should exert over expedience.[21] Each of these firms, having the Arthur Andersen experience in its rear-view mirror, chose to save itself by sacrificing individuals to criminal prosecution and by admitting error and even fraud where they may well not have existed.

While cries went up in the public sphere from those decimated by the Enron bankruptcy, there was serious debate within financial circles over whether Enron's reporting practices were in fact fraudulent or, rather, merely aggressive. But the public and the news media had little interest in such seemingly esoteric and hair-splitting arguments. Yet these same arguments seemed central to the question of whether the DOJ was going to be able to convict Enron's top executives. There was, in particular, the issue of whether the creation of certain complex investment partnerships, not detailed in Enron's financial statements, enabled Enron to hide substantial losses by "off-loading" those losses so that they would not appear on Enron's balance sheet and income statements and, hence, would not reduce reported earnings. The accounting devices used by Enron to dress up its earnings reports, while controversial, were arguably perfectly lawful, even if aggressive. The propriety and legality of such devices—deemed by Enron critics as artificial means of hiding the company's substantial earnings problems—will doubtless occupy experts and scholars for decades to come.[22]

But prosecutors could not confidently rely on ordinary jurors to deem criminal what experts could not agree on. Normally, the legality of such accounting devices might be tested by a *civil* proceeding brought against the company and its auditor by the Internal Revenue Service, the Securities and Exchange Commission, or even by a private investor challenging the accuracy of the company's financial statements. But political considerations seemed to dictate that the DOJ act swiftly in the criminal arena to avenge the loss of so many nest eggs.

A major obstacle toward a successful conviction of Enron's higher-ups was Arthur Andersen, the company's auditor and an internationally respected member of the "Big Five" group of accounting firms.[23] The controversial transactions that hid Enron's losses had been reviewed and approved by Andersen auditors. Enron or any individual corporate executive charged with fraud could invoke, as a highly effective defense, the fact that they relied on professional advice from one of the nation's premier accounting and auditing firms.

Recall from the beginning of the chapter both the descriptive and prescriptive elements of criminal law, explained by Hart, that required evidence of wrongfulness—that the wrongdoers knew or had reason to know that their actions were in violation of the law and that they intended to violate the law. Even in cases where the maxim "ignorance of the law is no excuse" might otherwise apply, statutes often contain provisions that only knowing, intentional violations of discernible legal duties are crimes. In such cases, the defense of good faith reliance upon expert advice, particularly in an area so complex that jurors almost certainly would not understand the nuances, can be particularly effective. (These defenses are also normatively desirable, since they protect accused defendants who have not committed the predicate elements of wrongfulness— knowledge and intent—that would trigger the community's moral disapprobation, at least for *mala prohibita* crimes.) Defendants would have to convince the jury not necessarily that they acted correctly, but merely that they relied in good faith on the experts and therefore intended to act properly and thought they were doing so. In order for this defense to succeed, the company (Enron) would have had to provide the auditors (Andersen) with all relevant information and documentation, the relationship between the auditing firm and the corporate client would have had to be honest and aboveboard, and the advice given would have had to be within a broad range of reasonableness such that the client would not have had good reason to believe the advice was erroneous or given in bad faith.

Two seemingly opposite paths emerged for the DOJ prosecution team: one, to ally with the Andersen firm and convince leading accountants to disown and testify *against*, not for, their clients; or, two, to sweepingly discredit the firm and disable it from testifying for the Enron defendants. Either way, as one experienced white collar criminal defense lawyer succinctly put it, "for the prosecution, the road to Enron went through Arthur Andersen."[24]

Recognizing this, the DOJ at first resorted to its traditional playbook and sought to make a deal with the auditing firm to defer prosecuting if the firm would agree to cooperate in the government's assault on Enron. Under such a deferred prosecution agreement, Andersen would have had to open up all of its records and make all of its employees available to the prosecutors, including an agreement to give court testimony if requested. Only after Andersen would prove its willingness to comply with the government's terms and to assist fully in the prosecution of the firm's former client would Andersen be allowed to go on its way. Such a deal would have saved the accounting firm from the destruction that was ultimately visited upon it, but it would not necessarily have reflected the truth of Andersen's position at the time it actually did the Enron audits, nor even later. Andersen would have had to join the crusade against Enron rather than choose to defend its, and its client's, accounting decisions and choices. One white collar criminal defense lawyer concluded that Anderson's refusal to buy the DOJ's offer of deferred prosecution amounted to an "inability of Andersen management to come together to save the firm."[25] This issue raises the disturbing question of whether an auditing firm has an obligation to tell the truth about an audit or, instead, do what is necessary to save itself.

Regardless of whether Andersen was motivated by principle or by insufficient skill in cutting a cynical deal to save itself by tailoring its testimony to the needs of the occasion, an agreement with the DOJ was not to be. And so the path for prosecutors became clear: Arthur Andersen had to be dealt with and destroyed. Destruction of a national or international audit firm is accomplished through the simple act of indictment, because that disables the firm from conducting credible and legally acceptable audits for clients.

Since the firm's auditing practices were not readily cast as criminal, the feds creatively indicted Andersen on a completely different but far simpler charge: obstruction of justice. They alleged that partners and employees intentionally and knowingly advised personnel to destroy relevant documents with the goal of obstructing the nascent government investigation. Years later, the obstruction of justice charges completely unraveled. Divorcing themselves from the bubbling public anger that fueled the Enron and Arthur Andersen prosecutions, all nine Supreme Court justices would join together to admonish the prosecutors for the indictment of the accounting giant on such a bogus charge. But it was too late for Arthur Andersen. With the help of a pliable obstruction statute and with the cooperation of a federal trial judge in Texas, the DOJ succeeded in disabling Andersen from playing any useful role in the defense of the Enron defendants.

No accounting firm can successfully operate once indicted, and Arthur Andersen rapidly, and predictably, disintegrated. Companies simply will not, and in nearly all jurisdictions may not, employ auditors living under the cloud of indictment to certify financial statements for certain purposes or with certain agencies. And so the indictment effectively destroyed the firm. To the extent there was anything left of the firm after indictment, the jury conviction in the federal district court in southern Texas administered the coup de grace. When the Supreme Court unanimously threw out the conviction in May 2005, this one-time auditing powerhouse had already gone from 28,000 employees in the United States to a staff of some 200. The skeleton crew's sole task was to clean up loose ends, mostly dealing with remaining litigation and other fallout facing the firm and its former partners.

The Supreme Court's decision to review the Andersen accounting firm's conviction for obstruction of justice took the legal and business worlds by surprise—and for good reason. By traditional criteria, it was hard to figure out why the Supreme Court would spend its time on the conviction of a defunct firm, reviewing the meaning and operation of an obstruction of justice evidence-tampering statute that, in any event, had effectively been superseded by a new statute enacted by a post-Enron Congress intent on appearing tough on "crime in the suites."

Deeply embedded in Supreme Court law and lore is the notion that the high court will not review a case unless the question presented is of direct and practical importance to the party seeking review. Further, the High Court normally will review only a case that presents an issue of more general application to other similar situations likely to arise in the future. In other words, the case has to have a practical impact on the party seeking review, but it also has to present a question of some importance to the development of legal doctrine. The requirement that a case has to directly impact the parties in some meaningful fashion is the way the court has always interpreted the Constitution's assigning the federal judiciary the power to decide "cases and controversies," rather than mere academic questions and issues. The likelihood that the Supreme Court would agree to review Andersen's conviction was seen as so remote that the solicitor general did not even bother to file an opposition to Andersen's petition seeking review.[26]

So it came as a shock to Supreme Court–watchers when the High Court announced on January 7, 2005, that it would review the obstruction of justice conviction won by the Department of Justice against Andersen. While the firm and its by-then scattered former partners doubtless had an emotional investment in getting the conviction reversed, as a practical matter, the case hardly registered on anybody's radar screen. After all, the mere indictment in March 2002 had shattered the firm and scattered its client base.

Nor was the Supreme Court faced with an issue of seemingly practical importance to the smooth future operation of the law. While there was a split among the circuit courts of appeals as to how to interpret the particular obstruction of justice statute, there was no compelling reason why the High Court should have felt the need to resolve the split, since the particular statute was unlikely ever to be used again. It had by then been superseded in the post-Enron era by the Sarbanes-Oxley legislation that sought to plug what were suddenly seen as "loopholes" in the federal regulatory scheme covering the reporting of financial results of publicly traded companies.[27]

A careful reading of Chief Justice William Rehnquist's opinion for the unanimous court—remarkably, there were neither dissents nor separate concurring opinions that joined the result but with different reasoning—indicates that the Court appeared suddenly concerned that the Department of Justice, in its zeal to rectify, or appear to rectify, the spate of high-profile corporate disasters, was cutting corners and risking the conviction of the innocent. While the Supreme Court did not, of course, mention any other cases—the purpose of appellate review, after all, is to decide a single case or controversy, not to deliver a civics lesson—it did note, seemingly caustically, that both the Congress and the Department of Justice shared the blame for the prosecution and consequent destruction of a presumptively innocent company.

The Supreme Court wrote that the Department of Justice erroneously interpreted the statute to allow the DOJ to prosecute the firm without proving that it intended to break the law. It also concluded that the DOJ had taken advantage of the "inelegant" manner in which the law had been written, leading prosecutors to destroy one of the then–Big Five national accounting firms, leaving, now, the Big Four.

The Supreme Court's criticism of the Department of Justice, of the trial judge who followed the department's lead in crafting instructions to the jury, and of the Congress that wrote such an obtuse statute, was even more stinging. "Indeed, it is striking how little culpability the instructions required," the justices wrote. (Professor Hart would be proud.) The Supreme Court was particularly taken aback by the judge's instruction to the jury that "even if [Andersen] honestly and sincerely believed that its conduct was lawful, you may find [Andersen] guilty." "The instructions," concluded the High Court, "also diluted the meaning of 'corruptly' so that it covered innocent conduct."[28]

A brief review of the scenario as it unfolded, when employees of Andersen for a period of time, upon advice of corporate superiors and in-house legal counsel, shredded and deleted documents relating to its audit of Enron, highlights the problem confronted by the Supreme Court. The statute made it a felony to "knowingly us[e] intimidation or physical force, threate[n], or corruptly persuad[e] another person . . . with intent to . . . cause" that person to "withhold" documents from, or "alter" documents for use in, an "official proceeding."[29] What was at issue, said the Supreme Court, were the meaning and elements of the phrase "corrupt persuas[ion]." This particular obstruction statute, it should be noted, did not make it a crime to actually shred documents, but simply to advise others to do so.

At this point, a word is necessary concerning the nature of corporate and other routine document retention-and-destruction policies. In the absence of a specified exception mandated by government or by corporate management, a company (or an individual, for that matter) is not required to preserve documents. Taxing authorities reserve the right to audit tax returns for a certain number of years after the filing date, and so taxpayers normally would preserve documents until then. And in the era of electronic storage of data, many more companies retain huge numbers of documents for a very long time, if not for the foreseeable future. However, such retention is voluntary, unless there is some government request or order—typically indicated by some kind of demand or subpoena—that particular documents be retained pending examination as part of an investigation. Most corporations, therefore, adopt formal policies regarding the length of time certain categories of documents should be retained before they are destroyed. Destruction of documents, unless they are subject to a subpoena or some such request for production or retention, is routine in corporate America. The Andersen case involved circumstances under which the company followed its routine document retention-and-destruction policy.

The Supreme Court laid out the scenario. When Enron changed its business during the 1990s to become an energy trading conglomerate, it adopted "aggressive accounting practices" and enjoyed "rapid growth." Andersen's David Duncan headed the "engagement team" for the Enron client. Enron began to falter in 2000 and 2001. On August 14, 2001, Enron's chief executive officer, Jeffrey Skilling, resigned. Shortly thereafter, Sherron Watkins, an Enron in-house accountant, warned Enron's new CEO, Kenneth Lay, that the company could "implode in a wave of accounting scandals." Later that month, the *Wall Street Journal* published an article suggesting accounting and business improprieties at Enron, and the Securities and Exchange Commission commenced an investigation.

By early September, noted the Supreme Court, the Andersen firm formed an Enron "crisis-response" team, on which an in-house lawyer, Nancy Temple, held a position. On October 8, Andersen hired outside legal counsel for any litigation that might arise out of its auditing of Enron. The next day, Temple discussed the Enron situation with fellow in-house lawyers, who agreed that "some SEC investigation" was "highly probable."

Michael Odom, an Andersen partner who was Duncan's supervisor, addressed a general training meeting of 89 Andersen employees, including some who worked on the Enron audit. He urged all those present to follow Andersen's document retention policy. That policy, replicated in some form in virtually every large or middling business enterprise in the country, was meant to regularize the accounting firm's practices concerning not only retaining certain documents for specified periods of time, but also destroying documents when the retention period ended. Documents were destroyed, of course, not only for space conservation purposes, but also to ensure the confidentiality of matters contained in those documents.

Andersen's retention policy provided, however, that "in cases of threatened litigation, . . . no related information will be destroyed," and that if the firm is "advised of litigation or subpoenas regarding a particular engagement, the related information should not be destroyed." The policy also contained "notification" procedures for whenever "professional practice litigation against [the Andersen firm] or any of its personnel has been commenced, has been threatened or is judged likely to occur, or when governmental or professional investigations that may involve [Andersen] or any of its personnel have been commenced or are judged likely."

Odom's admonition at the Andersen staff meeting concerning the firm's document retention policy focused on both aspects—its purpose to retain documents that might be called for in governmental or other investigations and to routinely destroy documents after a specified period of time as long as no investigation was known to be in progress. According to the Supreme Court, he told those assembled at the meeting that "if it's destroyed in the course of [the] normal policy and litigation is filed the next day, that's great. . . . We've followed our own policy, and whatever there was that might have been of interest to somebody is gone and irretrievable." Later, Odom's advice that Andersen employees follow the policy and destroy documents proved fatal, as this destruction proved to be the crucial issue in the case, the very basis of the indictment being brought.

Six days after Odom met with the Andersen staff to discuss the firm's document-retention policy, Enron released its third quarter financial results, including a $1.01 billion charge against earnings.[30] The following day, the Securities and Exchange Commission notified Enron by letter that it had opened an investigation back in August; it now requested information and documents. On October 19, 2001, Enron sent a copy of the SEC's letter to Andersen. The following day, Andersen in-house lawyer Temple, on a conference call of

Andersen's Enron crisis-response team, reiterated the earlier advice given by her colleague Odom; she instructed everyone to "[m]ake sure to follow the [document] policy."

This advice by Temple, while it later played a substantial role in getting Andersen convicted of obstruction of justice, was "the kind of thing lawyers do all the time," observed Stephen Bokat, vice president and general counsel of the U.S. Chamber of Commerce, which filed a friend-of-the-court brief on behalf of Andersen in the Supreme Court. "There but for the grace of God go I," he added in an interview by Tony Mauro in the *National Law Journal*.[31]

On October 23, Duncan met with members of Andersen's Enron team and directed compliance with the document policy. All of these steps, by various Andersen personnel, seeking to ensure compliance with the firm's document retention policy, the Supreme Court noted, were followed by substantial destruction of paper and electronic documents. This, of course, was entirely predictable, since the policy, like all such policies that are ubiquitous across all organizations that generate documents, directed not only *retention*, but also *destruction* of documents after a certain period of time, in the absence of a likely, threatened, or actual proceeding to which they might be relevant.

It was not until October 30 that the SEC opened its formal investigation and sent *Enron* a letter requesting accounting documents. Document destruction at *Andersen* continued, noted the Supreme Court, "despite reservations by some of [Andersen's] managers." It was not until November 8 that the SEC served Andersen itself with subpoenas for records. The next day, Duncan had his secretary send an e-mail that stated: "Per Dave [Duncan]—No more shredding. . . . We have been officially served for our documents."

Andersen was indicted in March 2002. The charge was that the firm "did knowingly, intentionally and corruptly persuade . . . [its] employees" to withhold and alter documents for use in "official proceedings."

The two sides argued vigorously at the trial over how the trial judge should instruct the jury on the meaning of the word "corruptly."[32] In the end, the jury was told by the judge that, "even if [Andersen] honestly and sincerely believed that its conduct was lawful, you may find [Andersen] guilty." As the Supreme Court noted, this instruction, which was approved by the court of appeals, "diluted the meaning of 'corruptly' so that it covered innocent conduct." The trial judge agreed with the Department of Justice's position and instructed the jury that it could convict "if it found [Andersen] intended to 'subvert, undermine, or impede' governmental factfinding by suggesting to its employees that they enforce the document retention policy." The jury convicted, and Andersen was fined $500,000, but the fine was the least of its problems by that time. No national accounting and auditing firm can function once indicted, much less convicted.

The Supreme Court noted that these instructions called for the conviction of Andersen merely because of the destruction of documents pursuant to the firm's document-retention policy. "No longer was any type of 'dishonest[y]'necessary to a finding of guilt," wrote the High Court, "and it was enough for [Andersen] to have simply 'impede[d]' the Government's factfinding ability."

The Supreme Court had problems with the jury instructions. The law was intended, said the court, to punish the act of "knowingly . . . corruptly persuad[ing] another to impede an official investigation." At the crux of the dispute was the notion—argued by Andersen, opposed by the Department of Justice, and accepted by the Supreme Court—that there could have been perfectly lawful reasons for Andersen, or any other party in a similar situation, to invoke its document-retention policy before receiving a formal notice from the government that an investigation was underway. Not every act that makes the government's work harder can be considered a criminal obstruction of justice. The High Court noted that persuading a person to "withhold" testimony or documents from a government proceeding "is not inherently malign." It gave some readily comprehended examples, such as "a mother who suggests to her son that he invoke his right against compelled self-incrimination . . . or a wife who persuades her husband not to disclose marital confidences." Indeed, it is not corrupt for a lawyer to persuade or advise a client to "withhold" documents from the government in the course of an investigation where, for example, those documents might be covered by a legal privilege. If there is a legal basis for the client's refusing to turn over documents to the government, the lawyer who gives such advice is surely "obstructing" the investigation and even intending to do so, but is not doing so with corrupt intent.

What the Supreme Court was trying to explain to the government is that citizens in a free society, and those who advise and direct them, have no inherent obligation to make the government's job easy. There are certain statutes and regulations governing when cooperation must be forthcoming and defining the nature of that cooperation. In the absence of a law clearly stating the citizen's obligation, the citizen is free to go about his or her business. It did not matter that the Andersen firm's document-retention (and destruction) policy made the government's job harder. Making the government's job harder simply was "not inherently malign," except when in violation of a specific law.

The Andersen firm, or at least some of its employees, did not want to have available more documents than it was required to retain, and so it followed a long-standing retention policy and destroyed documents right up until the point when its statutory duty of document retention kicked in—when it was formally notified of the SEC's need for and interest in those documents.

The underlying problem in the Andersen prosecution is, in fact, present in a very large (and growing) number of federal prosecutions, but it arose in this case in a form sufficiently stark that it caught the attention of the High Court. Yet the ubiquity of the danger did not escape the Supreme Court's attention. The *Wall Street Journal*'s Supreme Court reporter, Jess Bravin, reported that at oral argument Justice Anthony Kennedy told the government's oral advocate, Deputy Solicitor General Michael Dreeben, that the Department of Justice's definition of crime in this case amounted to a "sweeping position that will cause problems for every corporation or small business in the country."[33]

*   *   *

The prosecutions of the Andersen accounting firm and of Bradford Councilman are rich in the kind of drama and detail that surely would make the point of this essay, provided it can be shown that they are not sui generis but, rather, are indicative of a larger trend in federal criminal prosecutions. There is no statistical survey of which I am aware that can quantify the relative number of federal cases that fit into this category—prosecutions of members of civil society, on the basis of extraordinarily vague statutes, where the conduct at issue would not seem, intuitively or even on the basis of a modest study of the conduct and of the statute, to be felonious. However, I have undertaken to write a manuscript for an as-yet unpublished book, for which I have collected scores of such cases. Many of these cases are those in which my law partners and I have been engaged; the rest were handled by other lawyers. When I have discussed my thesis with other lawyers, most of them have reported a spark of recognition—an "aha moment" of sorts—that what troubled them about a particular case was the lawyer's sense that the client was not a criminal and that the conduct, alleged and even admitted, was not felonious. As one lawyer with considerable experience in the defense of both state and federal cases told me, he almost always could understand why the conduct alleged in a state prosecution constituted a crime, but his federal cases were far more puzzling in this regard.

In any event, I am a practicing criminal defense and civil liberties litigator, neither a legal scholar nor a social scientist. I do not purport to know statistically the prevalence of this phenomenon, except to say that I began to notice the trend in the last half of the 1980s, after I'd already been practicing law for two decades; and I have seen an acceleration of the trend, in both my practice and in my readings, to the present. And I doubt that Circuit Judge Toruella's reference, in his *Councilman en banc* dissent, to "a garden in need of a weed killer" was based on his frustration growing out of a single case.

There are many cases, both high-profile and more obscure, in which this problem is the basis for patently unjust prosecutions and even convictions of defendants who were not given adequate notice either by the statutes and regulations or by intuition, that they were committing indictable conduct when they went about their seemingly ordinary daily business. Even a brief survey of several cases that have attracted some degree of news media attention suffices to make the point.

William Hurwitz, M.D., a prominent physician in the suburban Washington, D.C., area, was indicted in 2002 for violating the notoriously subjective federal narcotics statutes in his prescribing the painkiller OxyContin to his patients. Despite lengthy efforts by the medical community to get the federal Drug Enforcement Agency to issue guidelines seeking to clarify the line between use of narcotics in good-faith medical practice and criminal dispensing of these substances, no satisfactory response has yet appeared on the horizon. He was convicted.[34]

Several employees of a pharmaceutical manufacturing company, C. R. Bard, Inc., were indicted in 1993 and convicted in 1995 for selling a cardiac angioplasty catheter device while failing to report to the United States Food and Drug Administration certain research and field results that the government insisted the regulations required be reported, but which the defendants indicated were simply not reportable under a proper interpretation of the regulations at issue. The government and the trial judge insisted that the regulations be interpreted in accordance with the "dictionary definitions" of the terms, while the defendants claimed that they properly relied on the technical definitions consonant with the entire statutory scheme. This war of definitions was ultimately resolved by the First Circuit, in the defendants' favor.[35] One of the interesting aspects of this case was that the government took a position that the common dictionary definition of a term was controlling, in a situation where that definition militated toward conviction, in contrast to the DOJ's later amicus position taken in the Ninth Circuit *Konop* wiretapping case where it argued *against* the dictionary definition. Of course, in a regulatory case such as the Bard prosecution, a defendant should not be convicted for relying on the strict and specific language that lays out a pharmaceutical manufacturer's manufacturing and testing obligations.

The indictment of Michael Milken, wunderkind of the now-defunct securities firm of Drexel, Burnham & Lambert, was indicted during the so-called decade of greed that spanned the late 1980s and early 1990s. He ultimately pleaded guilty to six felony counts and agreed to pay a $600 million fine, and he was sentenced to 10 years in prison (later reduced to two years), based on his agreement that he engaged in a number of financial transactions that the government deemed felonious. I was engaged, along with several colleagues, as post-conviction counsel, to analyze the plea, and to my dismay—but by then not my surprise—it turned out that none of the transactions could reasonably be deemed criminal. My and my colleagues' analysis was later confirmed by Professor Daniel Fischel of the University of Chicago in a careful and erudite academic analysis.[36] Indeed, Alan Rosenthal, a Milken codefendant, went to trial on one of the counts to which Milken pleaded guilty, and the judge directed a verdict of acquittal. The judge said from the bench that he understood how odd it was that he was acquitting Rosenthal on a count to which Milken had pleaded guilty. "I may say I make this ruling in the full understanding of the anomaly that those persons who participated in it and have testified thought it was unlawful."[37]

These cases are broadly representative of the trend that concerns me, in which federal prosecutors target individuals in all sectors of civil society for having broken laws by committing acts that they did not, and could not reasonably, know were illegal. The problem with vague or inadequately defined terms in federal criminal statutes is perfectly illustrated by the *Councilman* case. Federal prosecutors might object that they need leeway in the wording of statutes to be able to combat ever more creative criminals. The "social end" sought through prohibiting these acts would be best achieved, in this view, by allowing prosecutors to be proactive in their prosecutions and not constantly requiring revisions of the laws. After all, if statutes were strictly worded, resourceful would-be criminals could structure their marginally legal activities to ever-so-slightly evade the technical proscriptions of the law.

But such arguments are disingenuous in that they assume from the outset that the subjects of criminal investigations are in fact guilty. Bradford Councilman had thought that the routine data storage his company engaged in was not illegal, and the government's case against him was based on a counterintuitive reading of the statute that even ran against the government's own interpretation of the statute in a different judicial circuit! He could not have known ahead of time, in such a situation, that what his company did would open him up to federal indictment. The logic of the federal prosecutor—that they require a malleable tool in the form of vaguely worded criminal statutes in order to go after creative wrong-doers—is plainly undermined by cases like Councilman's, in which vague definitions in *mala prohibita* laws serve to ensnare those who did not intend to break the law and who believed in good faith that their conduct was lawful.

Councilman simply would not fall within the confines of the moral framework for the criminal law that Hart so cogently presented. He was not given adequate notice that his behavior could be considered criminal, and in cases where the prohibited act is not intuitively and inherently criminal nor clearly defined, the moral justification for criminally punishing someone for engaging in such behavior falls apart. But federal law allows for this kind of counterintuitive and alarming result, in part because federal law has become unmoored from the principles of blameworthiness that Hart expounded—and in part because the deck is so heavily stacked against criminal defendants to begin with.

One of the ways the deck is stacked against criminal defendants is through the government's essentially coercive use of deferred prosecution agreements and other vehicles for extracting cooperation or other guarantees from defendants. Pursuant to such an arrangement, the DOJ agrees to postpone bringing an indictment if the company undertakes certain internal investigations and reforms; agrees to a DOJ-appointed monitor; and cooperates in the prosecution of individual officers, employees, and even clients. Arthur Andersen was first offered a deferred prosecution agreement. When it declined, the Department of Justice turned next to a criminal indictment. In the wake of that indictment, its peer accounting firm, KPMG, crumpled when faced with an investigation of its own. The DOJ secured unparalleled cooperation from KPMG against partners whom the department proceeded to indict. Coupled with the high rate of plea bargaining—especially in federal cases, where defendants face extensive sentences if convicted without a deal—these tactics make an unlevel playing field that structures the enforcement and prosecution of federal crimes heavily in favor of the government. The practical effect is that many of these indictments never go to trial. This, in turn, means that prosecutors are able to become increasingly creative and to stray farther from what the laws prohibit to include ever more conduct at the margins of illegality. Such expansive applications of vague criminal statutes, because they are the subject of plea bargains, rarely face challenge in federal appellate courts.

Moreover, federal prosecutors have the broad use of tools for obtaining and even crafting testimony from individuals threatened with indictment. Long federal sentences, especially of late in white collar cases, pressure and convince individuals to cooperate with prosecutors, causing some witnesses, in the memorable phrase crafted by Harvard Law professor Alan Dershowitz, "to learn not only to sing, but also to compose." Indeed, in response to a claim by defense lawyers that the deals federal prosecutors make with witnesses violate federal subornation of perjury and obstruction of justice statutes, the Court of Appeals for the Tenth Circuit, in an infamous opinion that still causes widespread cynicism among defense lawyers and others, held that deals proffered by prosecutors to witnesses, "in light of the longstanding practice of leniency for testimony," do not run afoul of the federal witness bribery statute that literally appears to cover *all* testimony obtained in exchange for some benefit or favor.[38]

And federal agents, unlike police and investigators in many state jurisdictions, are not required to tape-record interviews of suspects and witnesses, thus enabling federal prosecutors to threaten a witness with a false statement prosecution unless the witness repeats before a grand jury and at a trial the testimony that federal agents *claim*, on the basis of an agent's handwritten notes, the witness told them when interviewed.[39] That testimony, of course, is almost invariably incriminating toward the target of the FBI probe.

* * *

The Supreme Court's decision to review the Arthur Andersen case was unexpected and exceptional in the context of that kind of prosecution. It is too early to predict whether the grant of certoriari— and the even more unexpected unanimous reversal of the conviction—portends the High Court's sudden interest in the problem of vague federal criminal statutes and the increasing delinking of certain federal crimes from traditional common law notions of intentionality and evil intent. But if, in fact, the trend of the past quarter century in federal criminal jurisprudence, is now being reexamined and rethought, it would be gracious, and quite appropriate, for us to thank Professor Hart for his legally sound, morally urgent, and remarkably prescient essay.

5. Henry Hart's "The Aims of the Criminal Law": A Reconsideration

*Richard A. Posner**

Henry Hart was a Harvard law professor of great distinction and of considerable academic influence. Among his well-known works is the essay[1] published a half century ago that the contributors to this book have been asked to comment on.

The essay, though a "classic," is not, in my opinion, a success. But it is an interesting failure, affording a glimpse of stubborn weaknesses of legal scholarship and of legal thought more generally.

The plan of Hart's article is to examine the aims of the criminal law from the perspectives of the different participants, beginning with "the makers of a constitution," that is, the persons "who are seeking to establish sound foundations for a tolerable and durable social order."[2] The first question they must consider is "What distinguishes a criminal from a civil sanction?" The answer Hart gives is "the judgment of community condemnation which accompanies and justifies [the criminal sanction's] imposition."[3] To be legitimate, that judgment must concern "conduct which, if duly shown to have taken place, will incur a formal and solemn pronouncement of the moral condemnation of the community."[4] The condemnation itself, divorced from tangible consequences such as imprisonment, is an important part of the criminal punishment: "the condemnation plus the added consequences may well be considered, compendiously, as constituting the punishment."[5]

When Hart was writing, an influential school of thought in penology regarded criminals as sick people, rather than as bad people deserving of moral condemnation, and wanted notions of punishment to give way to notions of treatment.[6] Hart makes a number of cogent criticisms of that approach. But his basic criticism, which

* The author wishes to thank Tara Kadioglu for research assistance and Dan Kahan for exceedingly helpful comments on a previous draft of this paper.

we'll see is not cogent, is that it undermines the role of the criminal law as a device for educating people in their basic responsibilities as members of society by exhibiting "the community's solemn condemnation of the accused as a defaulter in his obligations to the community."[7] The ultimate purpose of imposing criminal sanctions is "training for responsible citizenship."[8]

One might think that if criminals are not sick people, or unfortunates handicapped by low IQ or a bad upbringing, but instead persons deserving "the community's solemn condemnation," they should be punished severely. But Hart, because he regards the condemnation itself as a form of punishment, instead recommends lenity—and to a remarkable degree. He says that "a suspended sentence with probation should be the preferred form of treatment, to be chosen always unless the circumstances plainly call for greater severity;"[9] that "a fine should always be the preferred form of the penalty, unless the circumstances plainly call for a prison sentence;"[10] that "perhaps a suspended prison sentence, with probation, may be the best form of treatment even for a convicted murderer, as it certainly may be for a convicted manslaughterer;"[11] and that since "the treatment of criminals. . .should encourage, rather than foreclose, the development of their sense of responsibility. . .this consideration will point inexorably in the direction of eliminating capital punishment and minimizing the occasions and the length of incarceration."[12]

Turning from the perspective of the constitution maker to that of the legislator, Hart asks, "What *are* the ingredients of moral blameworthiness which warrant a judgment of community condemnation?" and can criminal punishment ever be justified "if the individual's conduct affords no basis for a judgment of moral condemnation?"[13] At one point, he intimates that the legislature should criminalize only "purposeful or knowing, as distinguished from reckless or merely negligent, conduct."[14] But elsewhere he allows for punishment of "an individual [who] knowingly takes a risk of a kind which the community condemns as plainly unjustifiable" and, thus, is "criminally reckless,"[15] and even of an individual who is negligent provided that, given what he knows, his failure to appreciate and avoid the risk that he creates by his conduct "involves substantial culpability."[16] But Hart is emphatic that unless the defendant's conduct is morally opprobrious (*malum in se*)—if instead it is conduct that would be regarded as proper were it not forbidden by a statute (*malum prohibitum*)—it should be punishable criminally only if the defendant knew about the statute and knew the facts that made his conduct violative of it. His violation must be knowing both as to the law and as to the facts.

Hart thus anathematizes strict-liability criminal laws (indeed suggests, in the section of the article on the aims of the criminal law from the perspective of the courts, that strict criminal liability is unconstitutional),[17] as when "the porter who innocently carries the bag of a hotel guest not knowing that it contains a bottle of whisky is punished as a criminal for having transported intoxicating liquor."[18] This "case" is Hart's variant of a real case, in which a common carrier's driver was punished for violating a statute that forbade common carriers or their employees to transport liquor into certain localities. The court, in a thoughtful opinion, explained that the legislature had been at its wits' end to prevent the illegal transportation of liquor, had doubted there were many instances in which the carrier or its employee didn't realize that it or he was transporting liquor illegally, and had hoped by imposing strict criminal liability to induce common carriers and their employees to be more careful.[19]

By altering the facts of the case that he cited (a misleading maneuver not to Hart's credit), in order to make strict-liability crimes seem ridiculous, Hart evaded having to consider the reasons for strict criminal liability. Those reasons are the difficulty of proving knowledge, skepticism that the defendants in such cases really are ignorant of the critical facts, and the incentive to take extra care that strict liability creates. Consider that it is not a defense to statutory rape that the defendant reasonably believed that the minor with whom he had sex was of age. (Hart offers this as an instance of "the notion," abhorrent to him, "that people can commit crimes without really doing anything wrong at all"[20]—which begs the question.) The effect is to induce men to steer well clear of young-looking women, a form of care they would be less likely to use if ignorance were a defense. This steering-clear effect of strict criminal liability reduces the likelihood of inadvertent commission of reprobated acts.

Hart conceivably may be right, as others continue to argue,[21] that voluntary compliance with criminal law would decline if people stopped thinking of that law as legitimate and that they would stop if the focus of that law ceased to be on morally blameworthy conduct. Maybe so. But what is implausible—and a conjecture for which Hart offered no evidence (no one has)—is that the pockets of strict liability in criminal law reduce that law's legitimacy in anyone's eyes (except Henry Hart's). Even if there were such a reduction, moreover, it would have to be balanced against the probable effects of such liability considered in the preceding paragraph.

Criminalizing harmless acts, exercising prosecutorial or sentencing discretion on political or other invidious grounds, and punishing victimless crimes that a large part of the population engages in are practices more likely than strict liability for some dangerous or harmful conduct to undermine the perceived legitimacy of the criminal law. Hart ignores such practices.

I conjecture that he did not consider the pragmatic reasons for injecting strict liability into the criminal law—though they had been pointed out decades earlier by his later collaborator Herbert Wechsler[22]—because he was so convinced that the criminal law must be a moral teacher. That conviction stemmed from his belief that the principal function of criminal punishment is not deterrence or incapacitation but education in the responsibilities of membership in a human society. "If legislatures had kept clean the concept of crime [clean of any element of strict liability, that is] and sentencing judges were then enabled to tell a convicted criminal, in good conscience, that his conduct had been wrongful and deserved the condemnation of his fellow men, the very pronouncement of such a judgment would go far to serve the purpose of the criminal law by vindicating its threats and so to lessen need for resort to other commonly less effective and invariably more expensive and oppressive forms of treatment."[23] Hart separated the criticism of a person that is implicit in condemning him as a criminal from what would ordinarily be regarded as punishment, and he allowed the first (the criticism) to do most of the work of the second.

There is more to the article, but I have described its thrust and main content. That thrust—that content—depends entirely on the assumption that the main significance of the criminal law is moral education; that tangible punishment is secondary to declaring a person a criminal; and hence that anything that dilutes the moral force of that declaration is to be avoided, as it will create a climate in which crime will flourish. The approach is sufficiently counterintuitive to require evidence to make it convincing, but, as I said, Hart presents no evidence. Not only no evidence that the moral force of a criminal judgment is a good substitute, even in a murder case, for a stiff prison sentence, but also no evidence that attaching criminal penalties to conduct that the defendant had no reason to think criminal increases the frequency of other crimes by reducing the moral force of criminal punishment.

He treats his idea that the essence of punishment is the declaration of guilt as self-evident. It is not; it is not even sensible. The moral force of a punishment (what is sometimes referred to as the "expressive" effect of punishment)[24] cannot be divorced from the punishment's severity. Suppose both petty theft and murder were typically punished with suspended sentences. Wouldn't that dilute the moral significance of a conviction for murder?

There is an expressive, a condemnatory, aspect of criminal law, no doubt, but Hart has reversed the main direction of causation. It is not, or at least not principally, that by condemning conduct as criminal the government educates the public in what is good and bad conduct. It is rather that the fact that the public condemns certain conduct, such as murder and robbery, creates a powerful impetus to criminalize the conduct. The public is not a body of slow learners that has to be educated by government to believe that murder and robbery are bad things so that once people learn this they will avoid doing them. Were the public such a body, the principal question about the propriety of strict-liability crimes would be whether their having been made criminal would have an educative effect by underscoring the harm of (for example) statutory rape or of serving liquor to intoxicated customers.

In thus ignoring the public's prelegal evaluation of harmful acts, Hart overlooked the role of the public's thirst for vengeance in shaping criminal law. In the simplest utilitarian approach, the function of punishment is to deter crime by subjecting the criminal to a degree of disutility that exceeds the utility he would obtain from the crime. Were the defendant affluent, the requisite disutility could often be imposed by fining the defendant rather than by imprisoning or executing him—or indeed by imposing punitive damages in a tort suit rather than subjecting him to any criminal sanction. James Fitzjames Stephen, the 19th-century English barrister, judge, and polemicist whose influential theory of criminal punishment Hart would have done well to ponder, argued that the public wouldn't be satisfied to see a criminal (other than the perpetrator of the most minor of crimes) fined. The imposition of a fine would not quench the public's thirst for vengeance because it would not make the criminal suffer enough. And this would be bad because, Stephen argued, the purpose of the criminal law was to provide a civilized substitute for vengeance.

As Stephen famously (or notoriously) put it, "it is morally right to hate criminals."[25] In fact, "it is highly desirable that criminals should be hated."[26] Vengeance is powered by hatred, for if one didn't hate the person who had done one (or one's family, or nation, etc.) an injury, one would hardly bother to incur the cost and possibly the risk involved in attempting to inflict a return injury on the person.[27] And so without the hatred, there wouldn't be strong pressure to enforce the criminal law unless people understood the utilitarian benefits of such enforcement. Stephen, notably contemptuous of the intelligence of the average person, probably thought that the public couldn't understand those benefits and therefore that the vigorous enforcement of the criminal law depended on emotion—and the relevant emotion was that of wanting revenge.[28] Law, in short, is "an emphatic assertion of the principle that the feeling of hatred and the desire of vengeance. . .are important elements of human nature which ought. . .to be satisfied in a regular public and legal manner."[29] He might have agreed with the philosopher Andrew Oldenquist that retributive justice is nothing more than "sanitized revenge."[30]

Stephen's emphasis on vengeance was natural because in his day, and certainly historically, the criminal law was privatized to a degree we would find strange. Prosecutors, rather than being public employees, were private lawyers hired on an ad hoc basis to prosecute criminal defendants; merchants could hire lawyers to prosecute thieves, and public police were a relatively recent innovation. Criminal law enforcement was, in short, far less professional and bureaucratized than it has since become and closer, therefore, to its roots in vengeance and more reliant on the emotion of the victims of crime. Although today the criminal-justice system is dominated by professionals who chase and prosecute and punish criminals not out of hatred but because they are paid to do those things, those professionals depend heavily on private citizens for aid in enforcement, including crime victims, the victims' families, bystanders, jurors, and others who rarely have a pecuniary stake in the apprehension and prosecution of criminals. The widespread popular support for capital punishment is based to a great extent on hatred of murderers.

There is no inconsistency between a utilitarian theory of punishment and a recognition that emotion plays a role in criminal law enforcement. Emotion, specifically vengefulness, is an alternative motivator to career incentives for bringing criminals to justice. Stephen was a utilitarian. He argued that "before an act can be treated as a crime, . . . it ought to be of such nature that it is worth while to prevent it at the risk of inflicting great damage, direct and indirect, upon those who commit it."[31]

Now a utilitarian might argue that if people get pleasure from seeing the people they hate punished, then that is an independent moral basis for criminal law. That seems not to have been Stephen's view. He was fiercely critical of witchcraft trials even though the women tried and executed as witches had been greatly feared and hated, as well as of the trials of Catholics falsely accused of plotting regicide, though they too had been greatly feared and hated. It was not that Stephen thought hatred the moral basis of criminal law or that criminals "deserved" their punishment in some moral sense, but that he thought, like the utilitarian that he was, that the law would not be effective unless criminals were hated.

Hart's concept of the grounds of criminal punishment is as remote from Stephen's version of retributivism as it is from conventional utilitarianism; it is also unexamined and incomplete. In insisting that no conduct should be deemed criminal unless it is done willfully, that is, unless the defendant knows that what he is doing is culpable, Hart ties criminal responsibility to Immanuel Kant's notion of moral responsibility, which in turn derives from Christian theology and makes the morality of conduct depend on the thinking that motivates it rather than on its consequences or on the community's evaluation of it. Hence, his notion that the statutory rapist does nothing wrong if he doesn't know that the girl is under age.

Hart does not mention Kant or Christianity, and he probably thought it self-evident that moral responsibility is a state of mind. In fact, the concept of moral responsibility prevailing in our society today, as in Hart's time, is more complex. A reckless driver who manages to avoid having an accident is unlikely to be punished by anything more painful than a traffic ticket, while if his reckless driving causes an accident in which someone is killed he may be prosecuted for a felony. If the accident causes two or more deaths, prosecution is a certainty. The state of mind is the same in all three cases, but the punishment is likely to differ very markedly. The reckless driver who avoids an accident has "moral luck"; the one who causes a fatal accident does not. What this means is that the morality of one's actions is a matter of consequences rather than just of one's state of mind.[32] Why else are attempts invariably punished less heavily than the completed crime even when the attempt is not interrupted and it failed to cause harm because of a fortuitous event, such as a sudden lurch by the intended victim of an assassination? Had Hart understood the complexity of our moral views he would not have been so quick to pronounce as morally atrocious the notion of punishing certain conduct criminally even when it is done with a good will in the Kantian sense.

Let me conclude. Conceptually, as well as empirically, Hart's theory of criminal justice is a thin and unsatisfying gruel. And it is an exemplary thinness—the thinness of the legal scholarship of his era, which was long on assertion and short on data, rhetorically powerful but intellectually cramped.[33] It is surprising that this should have been so in the field of criminal law, when one thinks of the distinguished proto-economic analysis of crime and punishment by Jeremy Bentham in the 18th century,[34] and the even longer tradition of philosophical and literary reflection on grounds for punishment (think of *Paradise Lost*),[35] to say nothing of the abundant historical, psychological, and sociological scholarship on crime and punishment.

The scholarship of criminal justice has moved well beyond Hart's article. Bentham's insights have been taken up and expanded into a comprehensive economic theory of criminal justice.[36] Other scholarly literatures have kept pace, as has sophistication in the collection and analysis of data on crime and punishment. I single out the economic approach because it is the one most congenial to me. It is also the one that offers the clearest pragmatic alternative to Hart's moralistic approach, as the reader will have glimpsed in my discussion of the reasons why there are strict-liability crimes.

6. How Would Henry Hart Have Approached the Problem of Suicide Terrorism?

Alan M. Dershowitz

When I was a law student, Professor Henry Hart's mimeographed class handouts were the stuff of legend. He published little but influenced many. The rumor was that he was never certain enough about his ideas to commit them to the permanency of publication. He and Professor Albert Sacks famously prepared numerous mimeographed versions of their course material for their popular and influential course "The Legal Process," which were finally published posthumously. I was fortunate enough to have taken Professor Hart's seminar on the legal process for potential law professors when I was a young assistant professor at Harvard. We are all fortunate that Professor Hart finally decided to allow his mimeographed handout on the "The Aims of the Criminal Law" to be published in 1958, so that it could receive a wider audience around the world and could become a staple of criminal law course, as it did in mine for many years.

Henry Hart was one of my early mentors. When I first arrived at Harvard in 1964, Henry transmitted to me a beautifully bound six volume set of the transcripts of the notorious Sacco-Vanzetti trial that had been transmitted to him by Felix Frankfurter when Henry began teaching in 1933. It had been transmitted to Henry by the future justice with the following inscription:

> To Henry M. Hart, Jr., the future historian of American law,
> these volumes, full of history and an important chapter of
> liberty and procedure are affectionately presented.

In presenting me with this gift, Henry said he hoped I would continue the tradition of Felix Frankfurter of combining scholarship and the struggle for justice. I now hold the Felix Frankfurter Professorship of law and have tried to meet Henry's hopes for me.

Henry and I worked as colleagues for only five years, because he died in 1969. While he was alive, I always sought his judgment on sensitive issues. He was a wise, serious, and principled man who, though shy and diffident, was generous with his time and ideas, especially with young colleagues. Following his death, I often found myself wondering "what would Henry think" about complex issues of the day, especially those involving tragic choices of evil. What institutional structures are best suited to making such choices in a democracy? What sources should be consulted, and what criteria invoked, in choosing between evils?

I wonder now what Henry Hart would think about the most recent, and in my view the most profound, change the criminal law is undergoing today. In this essay of appreciation and tribute, I will explore that question.

In "The Aims of the Criminal Law," Hart wisely argued that a penal code that "reflected a single basic principle would be a very bad one."[1] I have generalized that point in my own writing:

> We should not strive for the uniformity of one absolutely correct morality, truth, or justice.[2] The active and never-ending processes of moralizing, truth searching, and justice seeking are far superior to the passive acceptance of one truth. The righting process, like the truthing process, is ongoing. Indeed, there are dangers implicit in accepting—and acting upon—any single philosophy of morality. Conflicting moralities serve as checks against the tyranny of singular truth. I would not want to live in a world in which Bentham's or even Mill's utilitarianism reigned supreme to the exclusion of all Kantian and neo-Kantian approaches; nor would I want to live in an entirely Kantian world in which categorical imperatives were always slavishly followed. Bentham serves as a check on Kant and visa versa, just as religion serves as a check on science, science on religion, socialism on capitalism, capitalism on socialism. Rights serve as a check on democracy, and democracy serves as a check on rights. Our constitutional system of checks and balances has an analogue in the marketplace of ideas. We have experienced the disasters produced by singular truths, whether religious, political, ideological, or economic.[3]

A penal code, like any other code of conduct or law, must be eclectic both in its underlying broad philosophy and in the narrower goals.

It must also be subject to learning from experience and to changing in order to adapt to new challenges.

Despite Hart's eschewal of singular principles, his proposed code—indeed his entire approach to law in general and criminal law in particular—is based on a model of human behavior and interaction. For Hart, the major (or at least *a* major) aim of the criminal law is to "foster the development of personal capacity for responsible decision to the end that every individual may realize his potentialities as a participating and contributing member of society."[4] It follows from this that deterrence, through the threat of future punitive condemnation,[5] is to be preferred over treatment of a potential harm doer "for what he is believed to be."[6]

But Hart denies that deterrence should be "the overriding and ultimate purpose of the criminal law, important though it is." For Hart, deterrence is too "negative."[7] For him, the aims of the criminal law should be more positive:

> What is crucial in this process is the enlargement of each individual's capacity for effectual and responsible decision. For it is only through personal, self-reliant participation, by trial and error, in the problems of existence, both personal and social, that the capacity to participate effectively can grow. Man learns wisdom in choosing by being confronted with choices and by being made aware that he must abide the consequences of his choice. In the training of a child in the small circle of the family, this principle is familiar enough. It has the same validity in the training of an adult in the larger circle of the community.
>
> Seen in this light, the criminal law has an obviously significant and, indeed, a fundamental role to play in the effort to create the good society. For it is the criminal law which defines the minimum conditions of man's responsibility to his fellows and holds him to that responsibility. The assertion of social responsibility has value in the treatment even of those who have become criminals. It has far greater value as a stimulus to the great bulk of mankind to abide by the law and to take pride in so abiding.[8]

Although in his proposed introduction to a criminal code, Hart includes as one of its purposes, "to subject to a special public control those persons whose conduct indicates they are *disposed* to commit crimes,"[9] he also rejects the preventive-therapeutic approach:

> This, then, is the critical weakness of the two alternative
> constitutional provisions that have been discussed—more
> serious by far than losing or damaging a useful, even if
> imperfect, instrument of deterrence. The provisions would
> undermine the foundation of a free society's effort to build
> up each individual's sense of responsibility as a guide and
> a stimulus to the constructive development of his capacity
> for effectual and fruitful decision.[10]

At bottom, Hart's approach to the criminal law, as one important
means of enlarging "each individual's capacity for effectual and
responsible decision," contemplates a rational human being acting
in a rational manner for purposes of making an "effectual and fruitful
decision."[11]

This model of human behavior was challenged directly on September 11, 2001, by suicide terrorists who murdered more than 3,000
people in a carefully planned attack that they (or at least some of
them) knew would require their suicides. The new model of crime,
therefore, is mass casualty attacks that cannot be deterred by fear
of punishment or treated by therapeutic means. These terrorists were
neither mentally ill, by any conventional definition of that term, nor
deterrable by any means available to a civilized society.[12]

The new face of crime, one not seen by Henry Hart, is Zahra
Maladan.

Maladan is an educated woman who edits a women's magazine
in Lebanon. She is also a mother who undoubtedly loves her son.
Like every other mother, she has ambitions for him, but Maladan's
are quite different from most mothers in the West. She wants her
son to become a suicide bomber. At the funeral for the assassinated
Hezbollah terrorist Imad Moughnaya—a mass murderer responsible
for killing 241 marines in 1983 and more than 100 women, children,
and men in Buenos Aires in 1992 and 1994—Maladan repeated the
following admonition she has given to her son: "I tell my son, if
you're not going to follow the steps of the Islamic resistance martyrs,
then I don't want you."

Zahra Maladan represents the dramatic paradigm shift we now
face in the way we must fight to protect our citizens against enemies
sworn to kill them by killing themselves. The traditional paradigm
included the reality that mothers who love their children want them
to live in peace, marry, and produce grandchildren. Women in general, and mothers in particular, were seen as a counterweight to

macho belligerence. The picture of the mother weeping as her son is led off to battle—even a just battle—has been a constant and powerful image. Now there is a new image of mothers urging their children to die and then celebrating the martyrdom of their suicidal sons and daughters by distributing sweets and singing wedding songs instead of funeral dirges.

More and more young women—some married with infant children—are strapping bombs to their sometimes pregnant bellies, because they have been taught to love death rather than life. Read what is being preached by some influential Islamic leaders:

"We are going to win, because they love life and we love death," said Hassan Nasrallah, the leader of Hezbollah. He has also said: "Each of us lives his days and nights hoping more than anything to be killed for the sake of Allah. . . . The most honorable death is death by killing, and the most honorable killing and the most glorious martyrdom is when a man is killed for the sake of Allah, by the enemies of Allah, the murderers of the prophets."

Shortly after 9/11, Osama bin Laden told a reporter: "We love death. The U.S. loves life. That is the big difference between us." Afghani al-Qaeda operative Maulana Inyadullah explains: "We are not afraid of death. The Americans love Pepsi-Cola; we love death." Shiek Feiz Mohammed, leader of the Global Islamic Youth Center in Sydney, Australia, preached on video: "We want to have children and offer them as soldiers defending Islam. Teach them this: There is nothing more beloved to me than wanting to die as a mujahid." Ayatollah Ali al-Khamenei of Iran said in a speech: "It is the zenith of honor for a man, a young person, boy or girl, to be prepared to sacrifice his life in order to serve the interests of his nation and his religion. . . . Martyrdom-seeking operations demonstrate the pinnacle of a nation's honor."

How should western democracies, whose citizens do love life, fight against an enemy whose leaders preach a preference for death? The basic premise of the criminal law (as well as the law of war) has long been that soldiers and civilians prefer living to dying and can thus be deterred from killings by the fear of being killed.

This premise is being challenged by Zahra Maladan. Neither she nor her son—if he listens to his mother—can be deterred from killing by the fear of being killed, because they welcome death. Nor can they be educated or otherwise influenced by rational means, to choose life over suicide terrorism. They must be prevented from succeeding in their ghoulish quest for martyrdom. Prevention, however, carries a high risk of mistake. The woman walking toward the group of soldiers or civilians might be an innocent civilian. A moment's hesitation may cost innocent lives. But a failure to hesitate may also cost an innocent life. In February 2008, the media reported the case of a young female bomber who was shot as she approached a group of shops in central Baghdad. The Iraqi soldier who drew his gun hesitated as the bomber, hands raised, insisted that she wasn't armed. The soldier and a shop owner finally opened fire as she dashed for the stores; she was knocked to the ground but still managed to detonate the bomb, killing three and wounding eight. Had the soldier and other bystanders not called out a warning to others—and had they not shot her before she could enter the shops— the death toll certainly would have been higher. Had he not hesitated, it might have been lower.

As more and more women and children are recruited by their mothers and their religious leaders to become suicide bombers, more and more women and children will be shot at—some mistakenly. That too is part of the grand plan of many terrorist groups. They want us to kill their civilians, whom they also consider martyrs, because when we accidentally kill a civilian they win in the court of public opinion. One western diplomat called this the "harsh arithmetic of pain," whereby civilian casualties *on both sides* "play in their favor." Democracies lose, both politically and emotionally, when they kill civilians, even inadvertently. As the late Golda Meir once put it: "We can perhaps someday forgive you for killing our children, but we cannot forgive you for making us kill your children."

We need new rules, new strategies, and new tactics to deal effectively and fairly with these dangerous new realities. The laws cannot simply wait until Zahra Maladan's son—and the sons and daughters of hundreds of other Zahra Maladans—decide to follow their mothers' demand. Our laws must try to stop them before they kill themselves and many others in the process.

I have often wondered how Henry Hart's approach to the aims of the criminal law would deal with this new phenomenon of the mass-casualty suicide terrorist and the need for new rules to prevent rather than deter or treat.

The problem of preventing crime is not, of course, entirely a new one. Hart himself recognized "the purpose of preventing" crime as among the legitimate aims of the criminal law. But he was using "preventing" in the broadest sense to include deterrence as well as treatment.[13] He was using it the way Holmes had used it in the common law.

Oliver Wendell Holmes, Jr., in a celebrated passage from *The Common Law*, argued that "prevention" is the "chief and only universal purpose of punishment" and that "probably most English-speaking lawyers would accept the preventive theory without hesitation."[14] William Blackstone, the 18th-century British jurist who had considerable influence on the development of American law, in his chapter titled "Of the Means of Preventing Offenses," observed that "if we consider all human punishments in a large and extended view, we shall find them all rather calculated to prevent future crimes, than to expiate the past."[15]

Other legal authorities have argued in equally categorical terms that prevention has no proper role in the Anglo-American system of criminal justice. Francis Wharton, in his influential 19th century *Treatise on Criminal Law*, dismissed "prevention" as a "proper theoretical justification" for criminal punishment:

> If the [prevention] theory be correct, and be logically pursued, then punishment should precede and not follow crime. The state must explore for guilty tendencies, and make a trial consist of the psychological investigation of such tendencies. This contradicts one of the fundamental maxims of English common law, by which not a tendency to crime, but simply crime itself, can be made the subject of a criminal issue.[16]

The debate over the proper role, if any, of "prevention" in criminal punishment has not been limited to Anglo-American legal writers. The Marquis di Beccaria—one of the founders of modern-day criminology—in his classic 18th-century writing, *Essay on Crimes and Punishments*, put forth an essentially preventive justification for the criminal sanction:

> It is better to prevent crimes than to punish them. This is the fundamental principle of good legislation. . . . [T]he intent of punishment is . . . not to undo a crime already committed. [It is] no other than to prevent the criminal from doing further

injury to society and to prevent others from committing the like offenses.[17]

Immanuel Kant, the 18th-century German philosopher, in his *Metaphysical Elements of Justice*, took issue with Beccaria. For Kant, it was intolerable to impose punishment for any future-looking purpose:

> Judicial punishment can never be used merely as a means to promote some other good for the criminal himself or for civil society, but instead it must in all cases be imposed on him only on the ground that he has committed a crime.[18]

Some of the disagreement over the proper role of "prevention" in a system of criminal justice has resulted from a failure to define precisely what was being considered.

"Prevention," quite obviously, meant something very different to Holmes, for example, than it did to Wharton. The furthest thing from Holmes' mind was any kind of "psychological investigation" for "guilty tendencies" or a system of justice under which "punishment should precede and not follow crime."[19] What Holmes meant by "preventive" was simply a forward-looking approach designed to reduce the frequency of harmful events in the future:

> There can be no case in which the law-maker makes certain conduct criminal without his thereby showing a wish and purpose to prevent that conduct.[20]

Blackstone also defined "preventive" in a general way:

> [A]ll punishments inflicted by temporal laws may be classed under three heads; such as tend to the amendment of the offender himself, or to deprive him of any power to do future mischief, or to deter others by his example: all of which conduce to one and the same end, of preventing future crimes.[21]

When prevention is defined as broadly as Holmes and Blackstone define it, then most authorities—though probably not Kant—would agree that curtailing future crimes is one permissible function of any legal system.

The issue, therefore, is not whether prevention should play any role in a system of criminal justice: virtually all commentators (with the exception of strict Kantians) would agree that it should. The issue is how much and what kind of a role should it play. There is a considerable difference between a system that confines youngsters who have never committed a criminal act but who are predicted to be future criminals and one that authorizes confinement only after a consummated harm has been committed—though both may have as their purpose the prevention of future crimes. Prevention, as an element of criminal justice, is best seen as a continuum: some systems authorize preventive intervention of varying sorts relatively early in the process from dangerousness to ultimate harm, while others authorize preventive intervention later.

For purpose of this historical analysis, it is enough to distinguish three distinct but overlapping approaches to the control of crime that have, with varying emphasis, always been employed in the Anglo-American system of justice.

The Injury or Harm Approach

The first, which has characterized most primitive and simple societies, may be called the "injury" or "harm" approach. Cain kills Abel, and God punishes the killer (though perhaps not harshly enough because it was his first offense—indeed the world's first murder, according to the Bible). A serious physical injury, such as a death or maiming, is thought to require a response in kind. "Harm is harm and should be paid for. On the other hand, where there is no harm done, no crime is committed; an attempt to commit a crime is no crime."[22] In primitive societies, it is neither the law nor its agents that responds directly to harmful acts; the law simply authorizes those closest to the victim to seek blood revenge. Thus, the father of the accidentally killed child was expected to seek revenge against the killer or his family.[23] An "advance [was] marked" when the law moved "towards the suppression of blood-feuds" and private vengeance. This advance took the form of setting a price on the limbs and life of various victims. This system of compensation was, at least in part, preventive since its avowed purpose was "the suppression of blood-feuds."[24] The "bot" did, however, leave many dangerous criminals at liberty since its payment ended the "case."

Another preventive device, employed from the earliest times against criminals who were deemed especially dangerous, was total exclusion from the community and its protection. Exclusion could take the relatively benign form of "banishment," or it could take the extreme form of "outlawry," which was characterized as the capital punishment of a rude age.[25] Indeed, capital punishment (widely viewed today as the vestige of a retributive theory, or as an arguable general deterrent) had an important preventive component during an age when long-term confinement of dangerous offenders was not feasible. As imprisonment came into greater use, and dangerous wrongdoers could be locked away, the preventive component of the "harm-injury approach" became more obvious. But since only those people who had already committed a harmful crime could be locked up, the preventive component of imprisonment was limited by the requirement, inherent in its definition, that no intervention can be authorized until an actual injury has been sustained. Dangerous people, even those who had committed dangerous acts—such as throwing an axe at someone but missing—were allowed, at least in theory, to remain free to try again, perhaps this time with better aim. Thus, the father of the victims would not be punished until and unless he actually carried out his threat (if it was unlawful to kill the accidental killer of one's child).

The Dangerous Act Approach

This limitation is not inherent in the second approach, which may be called the "dangerous" or "inchoate *act*" approach. It is similar to the "harm-injury approach" in that it conditions intervention on the commission of a *past* criminal *act*. The essential difference is that under this approach the criminal act need not actually have caused any *injury* or *harm*; it is enough if the act is deemed "dangerous." Thus, throwing an axe, carrying a concealed weapon, driving above the speed limit, creating a fire hazard, or issuing a credible threat may all be made criminal acts without regard to whether an injury actually followed the act in any particular case. The acts themselves, and the situations they create, are deemed dangerous enough to warrant preventive intervention.

The purpose of the criminal punishment is to reduce the frequency of these acts because it is assumed that the more of these acts are committed—or the more these situations are permitted to exist—the more likely it will be that injuries will occur.

Included in this approach are the so-called inchoate crimes, such as attempted murder, solicitation to murder, conspiracy to murder, or incitement to kill. Again, no actual injury need be proved; it is enough that the act in and of itself was culpable and that it evidenced

112

dangerousness. If the father tried to kill his enemy but failed, he could be punished for attempted murder. Thus the father of the accidentally killed child could be punished for threatening to kill the child's murderer. This approach is considerably more "preventive" than the "harm-injury" approach since it authorizes intervention, indeed serious punishment, at a considerably earlier point on the danger-harm continuum.

The Dangerous Person Approach

Finally, the approach that is most obviously preventive may be called the "dangerous person approach." It does not require the commission of any past criminal act as a condition to intervention. A person may be confined because it has been predicted that he may commit a dangerous or harmful act at some future time. Most such predictions will, in fact, be based on suspicion that the person committed certain past acts; but these acts generally need not be proved; nor need they have been prohibited by law. Some obvious examples of the "dangerous person approach" are the confinement of predicted saboteurs or spies during wartime, commitment of mentally ill persons thought to be dangerous, pretrial preventive detention of criminal defendants on the basis of likely future criminality, the confinement of material witnesses and the imprisonment of suspected terrorists. Under this approach, the father might be confined in order to prevent him from taking revenge, even if he had not threatened or tried to kill, so long as it was very likely that he would try.

A related phenomenon is the age-old right of self-defense. John Adams, in his closing argument on behalf of the British soldiers accused of perpetrating the Boston Massacre, invoked what he called "the first and strongest principle in our nature": to prevent our own deaths by killing those who are about to attack us. This too requires a prediction of sorts and an assessment of the dangerousness of the attacker and the imminence of his attack.

It is the "predictive" approach to "dangerous persons"—and the lack of a jurisprudence governing it—with which Henry Hart might have had the greatest difficulty.

One important reason why we lack a jurisprudence or philosophy of preventive intervention is that so many intellectual, judicial, and political leaders have denied the legitimacy—even the existence—

of such intervention throughout our history. If we don't believe in, or practice, a particular mechanism of social control, then there is no need to construct a jurisprudence or philosophy that rationalizes and regulates it. Indeed the very act of articulating such a jurisprudence is sometimes believed to lend legitimacy to an otherwise illegitimate mechanism.[26]

The new paradigm of the mass-casualty suicide terrorist has some similarities with, but many differences from, those "dangerous" offenders whose crimes were sought to be "prevented" at common law. First, the "wholesale" suicide terrorist is far more widespread and dangerous than the occasional "retail" perpetrator. It may be true that it is better for 10 guilty murderers to go free than for one innocent person to be wrongly convicted and executed. But it does not follow that it is better for 10 potential suicide terrorists to commit their acts of mass-casualty mayhem than for one innocent person to be wrongly detained for several months. The stakes are different, and the rules should be different.

Hart wisely understood that

> It is evident that the view which the constitution-maker takes of the function of criminal law will be important in shaping his attitude on inclusion in the document of many of the traditional guarantees of fair procedure in criminal trials. Most of these, such, for example, as indictment by a grand jury or even trial by a petit jury, are largely or wholly irrelevant to the offender's need for, or his susceptibility to, curative-rehabilitative treatment. Indeed, as already suggested, even the basic concept that criminality must rest upon criminal conduct, duly proved to have taken place, would come into question under a purely rehabilitative theory. Present laws for the confinement and care of mentally-ill persons do not insist upon this requirement, and, if criminality were to be equated with sickness of personality generally, its rationale would not be readily apparent. But if what is in issue is the community's solemn condemnation of the accused as a defaulter in his obligations to the community, then the default to be condemned ought plainly to consist of overt conduct, and not simply of a condition of mind; and the fact of default should be proved with scrupulous care. The safeguards which now surround the procedure of proof of criminality or the essentials of them, in other words, will appear to be appropriate.[27]

114

But what if the issue is not only the "community's solemn condemnation of the accused as a [past] defaulter in his obligations to the community,"[28] but also the community's equally solemn obligation to protect its citizens from future acts of terrorism by employing the criminal law in a proactive and protective way? What kinds of safeguard are appropriate to this mechanism of criminal law? What ratio of false positives to false negatives is acceptable in this enterprise?

The answer should depend, at least in part, on *how* the criminal law is used to prevent mass-casualty terrorism. Going back to the tripartite categories discussed earlier—(a) "the injury or harm approach," (b) "the dangerous act approach," and (c) "the dangerous person approach"—it is clear that the dangerous person approach creates the sharpest conflict with Hart's approach. This is especially true if the criminal law were to condemn an individual "for what he is or is believed to be, rather than for what he has done."[29] But, in practice, the dangerous person approach, especially in the context of terrorism, would detain suspected future terrorists primarily on the bases of what they have done—or are believed to have done.

But the decision whether, in fact, they had done the acts attributed to them would be made not on the basis of the rigorous procedural safeguards required for criminal convictions, but rather on the basis of prosecutorial suspicion.

Hart spoke to this issue as well, at least indirectly, when he condemned

> the arrogant assertion that it is proper to visit the moral condemnation of the community upon one of its members on the basis solely of the private judgment of his prosecutors. Such a circumvention of the safeguards with which the law surrounds other determinations of criminality seems not only irrational, but immoral as well.[30]

How then should the criminal law deal with the suspect who investigators, intelligence agents, or prosecutors honestly believe is readying himself for a suicide bombing mission? The two extreme approaches—waiting until this nondeterrable potential mass murderer kills thousands, or detaining him based on the slightest suspicions (based perhaps on ethnic or religious profiling) that he might someday engage in terrorism—are untenable and would almost certainly have been rejected by Henry Hart. An intermediate alternative, which would have been acceptable to Hart, can perhaps be found in the dangerous act approach.

Under this approach, the legislature designates certain acts, which have not yet produced actual harm, to be sufficiently dangerous to warrant their prohibition on pain of criminal punishment. There are several categories of such dangerous acts. The first, and simplest, is to list the acts themselves as separate crimes. Thus, carrying a concealed weapon, speeding above the road limit, and creating a fire hazard are all crimes. Everyone is on warning not to commit them. It is no defense to prove that you would never use the weapon to cause harm, that you are a careful driver even while speeding, or that you never actually had a fire. The crime is completed with the prohibited dangerous act.

The second approach is to legislate broad and general inchoate crimes, specifically related to substantive crimes that do cause harm. Attempted murder, conspiracy to murder, solicitation of murder, and assault with intent to murder are examples of this category.

The third approach is a variation of the second and includes such new crimes as facilitating, contributing to, inciting, and supporting harmful results such as terrorism. This last category (and to some degree the second as well) is plagued with problems of vagueness, overbreadth, line-drawing, and fair warning. Entirely innocent acts can sometimes facilitate, contribute to, incite, or support terrorism, for example, providing legitimate legal or medical services to a terrorist may meet the open-ended definitions of these terms. An imam, minister, priest, rabbi, or teacher may incite without intending to do so or without even realizing he is. The words of Jesus, Mohammad, and Marx have incited much violence along with many good acts.

Conspiracy (along with its ugly big brother, the Racketeer Influenced and Corrupt Organizations statute [RICO]) too can be vague and open-ended. Attempts, solicitations, and assaults with intent to kill or maim are somewhat more protective of autonomy. The most protective is a clearly drawn criminal statute specifying with precision the exact acts that are deemed so dangerous as to be prohibited. The crime of contributing money to an entity on a designated list of terrorist organizations is relatively clear, but raises other problems.

Let us return to Zahra Maladan. Should it be made a crime to encourage someone to become a suicide terrorist or to preach the virtues of becoming a suicide bomber? Could a narrow statute be crafted to cover only those who have crossed the line into conscious criminality? What words—*actus reus*—would have to be spoken? What intent—*mens rea*—would have to be proved? Would any such criminal statute be consistent with the First Amendment?

These are daunting questions, but they are well within the traditional scope of our criminal and constitutional law systems. As I wrote in my book *Preemption: A Knife That Cuts Both Ways*:

> In the end any jurisprudence will inevitably reflect the broad value choices of a society. In eclectic, heterogeneous democracies, no jurisprudence will ever reflect a single ideology or worldview. Nor should it. It should incorporate Benthemite utilitarian principles that weigh costs against benefits, but it should also reflect some Kantian imperatives and absolutes. The experiences of the diverse peoples and groups that comprise any polity must figure into any widely accepted jurisprudence. Process, politics and compromise will produce some inconsistency, as they have in every other area of governance. The jurisprudence that emerges will be a work in process, a dynamic process rather than a static product. If a camel is a horse produced by a committee, then the resulting jurisprudence may resemble a lumbering dromedary more than a sleek equine. But we live in a barren desert today when it comes to the rules governing preemption and prevention. A camel would be a useful start.[31]

If the readers perceive in these words the enduring influence of Henry Hart, they are right.

7. The Community's Role in Defining the Aims of the Criminal Law

James B. Jacobs

Professor Henry Hart's essay, "The Aims of the Criminal Law," covers so much ground that it might seem churlish to point out what he hasn't thoroughly canvassed. However, in seeking to flesh out Hart's analysis still more broadly by focusing on the "community's role" in the design and operation of the criminal law and the criminal justice system, I do not imply fault with his magisterial article.

Hart's strategy for illuminating the aims of the criminal law is to analyze the "institutional considerations" of constitution makers, legislators, courts, prosecutors, and corrections officials. The community is not an "institution," but, as Hart recognizes, community condemnation does play an essential role in defining what is distinctive about the criminal law. There is no other body of law that draws its purpose and meaning from community values as starkly as criminal law. Using Hart's references to the community as a starting point, I attempt to illuminate the various ways that the community shapes the criminal law. In the second part of the chapter, I offer some reflections on shaming sanctions and on the current proliferation of criminal background checks.

Hart's Understanding of the Role of Community

In "The Aims of the Criminal Law," Hart frequently mentions "the community." The following passages mostly conceive of the community as a reservoir of moral values that justify the existence and use of criminal law.

> (1) pp. 1–2:
> Suppose, for example, that the deterrence of offenses is taken to be the chief end [of the criminal law]. It will still be necessary to recognize that the rehabilitation of offenders, the disablement of offenders, the sharpening of the community's sense of right and wrong, and the

satisfaction of the community's sense of just retribution may all serve this end by contributing to an ultimate reduction in the number of crimes.

(2) p. 4:
What distinguishes a criminal from a civil sanction and all that distinguishes it, it is ventured, is the judgment of community condemnation which accompanies and justifies its imposition.

(3) p. 5:
The method of the criminal law, of course, involves something more than the threat (and, on due occasion, the expression) of community condemnation of antisocial conduct. . . . Indeed, the condemnation, plus the added consequences may well be considered, compendiously, as constituting the punishment.

(4) p. 6:
The core of the difference [between civil commitment and penal incarceration] is precisely that the patient has not incurred the moral condemnation of the community, whereas the convict has.

(5) p. 8:
Or should the legislature be enabled to say, "If you violate any of these laws and the violation is culpable, your conduct will receive the formal and solemn condemnation of the community as morally blameworthy, and you will be subjected to whatever punishment, or treatment, is appropriate to vindicate the law and to further its various purposes"?

(6) p. 12:
If what was said in part two [of "The Aims of the Criminal Law"] is correct, it is necessary to be able to say in good conscience in each instance in which a criminal sanction is imposed for a violation of law that the violation was blameworthy and hence deserving of the moral condemnation of the community.

(7) p. 14:
If the legislature does a sound job of reflecting community attitudes and needs, [the defendant's] actual knowledge of the wrongfulness of the prohibited conduct will usually exist.

120

(8) p. 19:

> To engage knowingly or recklessly in conduct which is wrongful in itself and which has, in fact, been condemned as a crime is either to fail to comprehend the community's accepted moral values or else squarely to challenge them.

(9) p. 25:

> In determining that described conduct shall constitute a crime, a legislature makes necessarily the first and the major decision about the appropriate sanction for a violation of its direction. For it decides then that community condemnation shall be visited upon adjudged violators. But there remain hosts of questions about the degree of condemnation and the nature of the authorized punishment.

(10) p. 26:

> Are comparatively severe punishments to be favored over comparatively lenient ones? . . . Punishments should be severe enough to impress not only upon the defendant's mind, but upon the public mind, the gravity of society's condemnation of irresponsible behavior.

According to Hart, U.S. criminal law begins with the community. (In most other countries, the creation and application of criminal law is much more a matter for the state and the criminal defendant.) The criminal law gives expression to the community's values and, in addition, shapes those values. Unless there is community condemnation of a particular species of conduct, there should not be a criminal law prohibiting that conduct. Unless there is community condemnation of a particular offender's criminal law violation, no criminal sanction should be applied.

Hart recognizes and approves the deterrent role of community condemnation. "[A constitution maker] will be likely to regard the desire of the ordinary man to avoid the moral condemnation of his community ... as a powerful factor influencing human behavior which can scarcely with safety be dispensed with" (p. 8). In other words, deterrence is served by the would-be law violator's anticipation of being condemned, embarrassed, and humiliated in the community. I will ask later whether this necessarily means that members of the community have an obligatory or permissible role to play in communicating condemnation to the convicted offender.[1]

The community is also involved in the construction and implementation of the criminal law in some ways that Hart does not deal with. For example, there is the institution of the grand jury (in about half of American states) and the petit jury (constitutionally required for all states). The Anglo-American criminal justice process, unlike most other countries', gives lay representatives of the community responsibility for making the ultimate determination of guilt or innocence. And the commitment to general jury verdicts (guilty or not guilty) means that the petit jurors have the de facto power to nullify the criminal law if it does not correspond with their view of right and wrong. Moreover, up until the 20th century, juries in many states also exercised sentencing authority. Jury sentencing is rare today except when it comes to capital sentencing, where we still require a community determination of whether the defendant should or should not be executed. This alone, I think, makes a strong case for including the community in the list of factors that make the criminal law unique.

The Community and the Creation of Criminal Law

For Hart, criminal law begins with "the community" because, in his view, community condemnation is what makes criminal law necessary and meaningful. He is highly critical of criminal offenses that prohibit conduct that the community does not regard as morally wrong, and he favors purging such offenses from the penal code. But this assumes that there is a community consensus on the morality of a vast range of conduct and that such a community consensus can be reliably determined.

According to Hart, it is the legislature's job to discern community values; where legislators find community condemnation, they should create criminal laws. Hart does not explain how he or a legislator could determine which conduct commands sufficient community condemnation to warrant a criminal law and which does not. He does not tell us what percentage of public opinion should be regarded as "sufficient" or how solid or intense this opinion needs to be. How can we tell when the legislature has gotten it right or wrong? What if, as is often the case, the legislators disagree among themselves?

It is not easy to identify the existence, much less the extent and intensity, of community condemnation in a large, diverse society like ours. The morality of many behaviors (e.g., drunkenness, abortion, resistance to military recruiting, music and video sharing, marijuana possession for personal use, sharp business practices, sports gambling, physically disciplining children, dog fighting, aggressive tax shelters, recording conversation without the other party's knowledge, lying under oath about sex, donating huge sums to a political candidate) is contested. Substantial populations believe all these behaviors to be wrongful and properly punished criminally; substantial minorities disagree. How strong must the community's consensus be to warrant a criminal law? Might not community opinion change or fluctuate based on a particularly egregious case, increase in the frequency of a particular type of injurious conduct, or prestigious and persuasive advocacy? And how is the conscientious legislator to know how to vote on a proposal to increase or decrease the maximum or minimum sentence for a particular offense?

How is the conscientious legislator to determine whether a community consensus that warrants use of criminal law exists? Would Hart favor direct voting as the preferred way of deciding on new criminal laws? Even if direct voting were thought desirable, would a criminal law be justified by a bare majority or should supermajority support be required? Would it matter if only 25 percent of eligible voters bothered to vote? Can legislators intuit their constituents' attitudes toward arguably immoral conduct? Should legislators only consider "informed opinion"? Do we want legislators to weigh the rationality of community opinion and so play a modulating role in "toning down" the passions of the community that might fixate on the most egregious examples of a species of conduct?

Would Hart think it permissible for a legislator to campaign for (and vote for) a new criminal law that is not yet, but might soon be, supported by majority or supermajority community condemnation? Politicians and interest groups frequently believe that passing a new criminal law will call attention to conduct whose injuriousness was previously insufficiently appreciated. The campaign for criminalization (highlighting a particular form of injurious conduct) may itself change public opinion. Moreover, once the conduct is criminalized (or made punishable by a more severe sentence) more community members might regard it as morally condemnable or *more* morally condemnable. In other words, just as community sentiments lead to criminal laws, so too do criminal laws shape community sentiments.

Is a criminal law ever warranted when majority opinion does not support it? Suppose, for example, the majority does not condemn a type of conduct that involves victimization of a minority (e.g., gay bashing, providing abortions); should that automatically exclude use of criminal law? If not, what criteria should legislators use in deciding whether to vote for a criminal law that conflicts with majority opinion?

Hart offers an essay in criminal law jurisprudence, not sociology of law. It is not part of his project to explain how new crimes are added to the books, how old ones are removed, and how (maximum and minimum) sentences are increased or (rarely) decreased. If we were inclined to expand his article in a more sociological direction, we could examine how and why certain interest groups and "moral entrepreneurs" seek to pass new criminal laws or to increase punishments for existing offenses.

Community Condemnation and the Application of Criminal Sanction

Hart sees community condemnation playing a crucial role in the *imposition* of criminal sanctions in individual cases. In pronouncing judgment and imposing sentence, the judge should, in Hart's view, communicate the community's moral condemnation. In fact, Hart chides a federal judge, whom he knows personally, for being unwilling to lecture convicted defendants on the wrongfulness of their conduct. For Hart, this formal expression of community condemnation is an essential, perhaps *the* essential, part of the judge's role. In a large percentage of cases, it constitutes the criminal justice system's principal response to criminal wrongdoing.

How can and should the judge determine the right amount of condemnation in each case? This is even more complicated than the legislator's task of deciding whether there should be a criminal law. While the community might have a view about a species of injurious conduct *in the abstract*, there will be no discernible community consensus about the degree of immorality and wrongfulness in a situation based on a thick package of facts involving the circumstances of a particular crime and a particular offender. The defendant's defense counsel will always argue extenuating and mitigating circumstances. Criminal cases almost always look more morally ambiguous when all the details are filled in.

Because most cases are the product of a plea bargain, the judge herself may have limited knowledge of the offense and offender. Defendants are often permitted to plead guilty to offenses less serious than the most serious one they committed (or arguably committed). Should the judge express condemnation in accord with the offense to which the defendant pled guilty or in accord with the conduct the defendant (apparently) engaged in?

How should the community's condemnation be communicated to the defendant? If Hart is correct about the importance of the judge's communication of community condemnation to the convicted defendant, it is striking how little judicial and academic attention has been paid to the subject of judicial lectures to convicted defendants. Is there a preferred tone, script, and body language? Are there certain words and expressions that judges should employ or should refrain from employing? How does the same or similar condemnation not lose force and authenticity when repeated over and over again in case after case? Is it only necessary that the community's condemnation be expressed or, for the criminal law to work properly, must it be taken to heart? Does it matter whether the defendant internalizes the judge's expression of the community's condemnation, is indifferent to it, or even rejects it?

Once the judge communicates the community's condemnation to the convicted defendant, is the community condemnation fully spent? Should it ever or never be mentioned again? Should probation officials have a duty to integrate community condemnation into their work with the defendant? Or do they have a duty not to integrate that condemnation into their work? In the event that the defendant is sent to prison, should correctional officials seek to reemphasize and reinforce societal condemnation? Or should they avoid the subject? (My own experience in studying prisons is that moral condemnation plays no role whatsoever in the contemporary "correctional" regime.) Is it appropriate to deny parole on account of the strength of community condemnation?

The Community's Role in Expressing Moral Condemnation in Individual Cases

If a conviction carried no negative community reaction whatsoever, wouldn't deterrence be undermined, especially if the sentence did not involve a jail or prison term? Suppose a citizen were to embrace the convicted defendant, loudly telling him that what he did (say, theft or fraud) doesn't matter, is acceptable, even praiseworthy? Wouldn't that subvert the criminal law? Doesn't that situation arise in the prosecution of organized crime groups and street gangs making such criminality very difficult to deter?

Should members of the community themselves communicate condemnation to the convicted defendant? Should they communicate conditional or unconditional forgiveness? Should they seek to avoid knowing whether neighbors, acquaintances, and business associates have been previously convicted of criminal offenses and, if they do find out, pretend that they do not know?

In recent years, so-called shaming sanctions have become increasingly popular. They seek to mobilize public opinion and public action against the law violator in order to shame that person and deter potential offenders.[2] Shaming has been frequently used in the effort to deter street prostitution. For example, in 2005, the Chicago Police Department launched a website posting the names and photos of men arrested for soliciting prostitutes.[3] In addition to posting arrestee information on its website, officials in Arlington, Texas, mail postcards to the arrestee's home in order to get the attention and presumably mobilize the condemnation of spouses and family members.[4] Fort Worth, Texas, runs "John TV" on its community cable television station and posts arrest information on its website.[5] Arizona Stop DUI posts DUI arrests for all cities within Arizona that wish to participate.[6] Orlando posts the names of individuals arrested for prescription drug fraud.[7] Maricopa County, Arizona, posts all arrests for three days,[8] and it maintains a "deadbeat parents" "Hall of Shame," naming parents who owe child support.[9] Similar programs seem to be sprouting all over the country.

Some academic commentators, most notably Australian criminologist Professor John Braithwaite, argue that to be effective in reforming criminals the criminal law needs the support and participation of the community. According to Braithwaite, "Crime is best controlled when members of the community are the primary controllers through active participation in shaming offenders, and, having shamed them, through concerted participation in ways of reintegrating the offender back into the community of law abiding citizens."[10] Braithwaite argues that unless there is community involvement in responding to convicted defendants, the "rule of law will amount to a meaningless set of formal sanctioning proceedings which will be perceived as arbitrary."[11] Therefore, he advocates "reintegrative shaming," sanctions that "shame while maintaining bonds of respect or love," but disapproves of "stigmatizing shaming" that alienates the convicted defendant and pushes him toward the embrace of a criminal subculture.[12] Likening reintegrative shaming to behavioral controls used by functional families and to the role of neighborhood gossip, Braithwaite favors gossip with which the convicted offender is never confronted (but which he knows is occurring) combined with openly expressed regret, acceptance, and support for the defendant in the future. "Secret indirect gossip is combined with open direct gestures of reintegration."

Braithwaite may wish and exhort the community to forgive and embrace the ex-offender, but shaming is hard to channel and control. U.S. politicians and law enforcement personnel are more likely to emphasize the deterrent, rather than restorative, impact of shaming. Certainly, the john websites are intended to embarrass, humiliate, and deter customers of prostitutes. If shaming sanctions are wrong or undesirable, does that mean that the community should be morally neutral with respect to convicted offenders? If so, wouldn't that conflict with Hart's view?

Should Criminal Convictions Be Public or Confidential?

Should public policy seek to disseminate to the public information about individuals' criminal histories or to keep this information as confidential as possible? One of the most distinctive U.S. constitutional choices with respect to criminal procedure is the commitment to courts that are open to the public. Not only is the defendant guaranteed a public trial, but the public and the media have an independent right to attend trials and to examine court records. This means that a law violator cannot count on anonymity and that a rational actor contemplating the costs and benefits of a future crime should factor in the costs of community condemnation and loss of reputation. Is this an unintended feature of the administration of criminal justice? Or is it intended as an essential component?

In recent years, powered by the information technology revolution, the trend has been toward making criminal records increasingly more accessible to the public. Approximately half the states make criminal record information available to any member of the public, usually for a small fee. Several states post on websites the names and background information of state prisoners. For example, the Kansas Bureau of Investigation launched Kansas's online criminal records database in 2004.[13] This database is available to the general public and allows a searcher to retrieve any individual's criminal history record simply by entering the name and birth date of the search subject.[14] These criminal histories include convictions for offenses classified under Kansas state law as felonies or as class A, class B, or certain types of class C misdemeanors.[15] The criminal histories also include records of arrests that occurred less than a year before, unless there has been a dismissal or acquittal.[16] There were 3,000 public searches of this database in the first month of the website's availability.[17]

In addition, a whole industry of information providers now stands ready, for a modest fee, to conduct a criminal background search of any person about whom a client has an interest. Many private information services companies prominently advertise on the Worldwide Web. An Internet search for "criminal records" yields dozens of companies offering, for a modest fee, to carry out criminal background checks for employment, housing, and other purposes. Some companies have constructed their own databases by purchasing criminal history records in bulk from courts and state record repositories. For example, National Background Data claimed as of spring 2003 to provide real-time access to more than 126 million records covering 38 states. Another vendor, ChoicePoint, claims to have in excess of 17 billion public records, including more than 90 million criminal records. ChoicePoint reported conducting approximately 3.3 million background investigations in 2002, the overwhelming majority of which included a criminal records search.

A recent report by the National Task Force on the Criminal Backgrounding of America points out that criminal background checks are proliferating in a variety of contexts, especially employment and residential rentals.[18] We may be moving inexorably to a society where everybody's criminal record is readily and cheaply (if not freely) available. Should this be regarded as inconsistent with the aims of the criminal law? I think not.

The openness and publicness of criminal courts is a vital part of our criminal justice system and, arguably, of American democracy. It allows "the community" (via media, scholars, interest groups) to monitor who is being arrested, prosecuted, sentenced, and for what offenses. In the absence of such information, the criminal justice system's legitimacy would be undermined by all sorts of surmises, accusations, rumors, and conspiracy theories. A criminal justice system with fragile legitimacy would weaken the overall legitimacy of the state.

It is another question entirely whether a system of public and easily accessible criminal records is consistent with Hart's view of the aims of the criminal law. On the one hand, he might see it as consistent in that it will contribute to a citizenry that is better informed about patterns of crime and crime control and about individual criminal cases. On the other hand, he might see it as inconsistent with the aims of the criminal law in that it facilitates, perhaps encourages, members of the community to express their personal condemnation to defendants and to otherwise shun and discriminate against convicted offenders. Such actions could undermine the goals of rehabilitation and reintegration that Hart also recognizes as important. It is unfortunate that we do not have him here to opine on this dilemma.

8. If the Criminal Law Don't Fit, Civilly Commit

*Richard B. Sanders, Jacob Zahniser, and Derek Bishop**

Our thesis is this: The criminal law has served us well. It honors our humanity by holding each individual accountable for his acts, not his thoughts, not for who he is. Importantly, the criminal law—through its process, rules, and protections—chains the beast of unrestrained government; it guards our liberty.

But our thesis is also this: The blessings bestowed on us by the criminal law are under attack. Not a frontal attack, but an attack on the flanks, much as Adolf Hitler's panzers flanked the Maginot Line—and just as effective. We are referring to "noncriminal," "civil," or other forms of executive imprisonment.

The subject of this chapter is the so-called sexually violent predator (SVP) laws. However, the same concerns arise whenever someone is imprisoned outside the confines of the criminal law, whether it is civil commitment or detention by the commander-in-chief in the worldwide battlefield of the so-called War on Terror.

Like Hitler's panzer crews, the attackers speak a different language. Those subject to their attack are not "convicted," "sentenced," or "punished." Instead, they are confined for "treatment." Nor are they "imprisoned." Instead, they are "detained," perhaps as the new "residents" of an exclusive gated community. Nevertheless, the actuality of this "detention" for "treatment" is as restrictive as any imprisonment. Unless we repair to the first principles of our criminal justice system, we fear that the War on Liberty that has been declared may overpower the public's first line of defense—our courts.

* Richard B. Sanders is a justice on the Washington Supreme Court. Jacob Zahniser earned his J.D. at St. John's University and served as a law clerk to Justice Sanders between 2007 and 2008. Derek Bishop earned his J.D. at the University of Washington and served as a law clerk to Justice Sanders between 2007 and 2008.

Henry Hart analyzed the criminal law using a set of principles: the criminal law is the mechanism by which the community condemns unacceptable conduct, and the criminal law is the procedure to punish the perpetrator.[1] In other words, the criminal law engenders social order by setting forth minimum obligations of conduct, which vary depending on the institutional actor: the constitution maker, the legislator, the judge, and even the criminal.

However, the criminal law not only engenders social order, it also protects us from a government that would destroy our liberties. When reading the Bill of Rights, we discover a majority of its words address criminal investigation, process, and punishment.[2] These rights are not aimed at catching, convicting, and punishing criminals. To the contrary, these rights protect us against the awesome power of the state, which may overwhelm not only the criminal but everyone else.

If the aims of the criminal law are to engender social order while protecting our liberty, how is it doing? Since the early 1990s, the aims of the criminal law have been co-opted in pursuit of a goal never imagined by Hart or the Framers: to make the community feel safe. We say "feel" safe because the criminal law does not actually make the community safe; for as long as there has been a criminal law there have been criminals. "[T]he practical fact must be faced that many crimes . . . are undeterrable."[3] Nevertheless, the notion that the state should enact a law to make the community feel safe seems to be the motive behind the recent rash of SVP civil commitment laws. This chapter analyzes these SVP laws within the framework of Hart's analysis of the criminal law, as well as our own.

The Socio-Political Environment of SVP Commitment

Washington's SVP statute was the first of its kind in the nation, and it has since been copied throughout the country. Currently, 16 states and the District of Columbia allow civil commitment of sexually violent predators.[4] Because Washington was the first in the nation to enact SVP legislation, and that legislation has been used frequently as the model for other states, it is appropriate to look to it to draw conclusions about SVP statutes in general.

On the evening of May 20, 1989, Earl Shriner met a young boy riding a bike.[5] Shriner suggested he and the boy ride their bikes together through the nearby woods. When Shriner and the boy were in the woods, Shriner anally and orally raped the boy, stabbed him in the back, strangled him, and cut off his penis. Shriner left the boy to die in the woods. A family discovered the boy and rushed him to a hospital. Somehow he survived.

Prior to this brutal attack Shriner had a lengthy and violent criminal past. He had been jailed for 10 years for abducting two 16-year-old girls. The state believed Shriner was still dangerous and sought to keep him jailed beyond his 10-year maximum sentence. But because Shriner could not be further imprisoned for his criminal convictions, the state sought to continue his confinement under the existing mental health civil commitment scheme. However, the court found he did not meet the criteria for civil commitment and released Shriner after he fully served his sentence.

Media reports quickly began to reflect the public belief that Shriner's release from prison demonstrated a failure in the criminal justice system. Newspaper headlines throughout the state reflected public sentiment and read "Outrage Over the Attack, Over the System"[6] and "Protection of Society: Justice System Fails."[7] One editorial, titled "Put Mutilators Away," suggested, "The legal system needs to be changed to make it possible to remove the criminally insane from society, quickly and permanently. In such obvious cases as this, the law should err, if it errs at all, on the side of protecting the innocent."[8] In no respect did the public seem concerned with treating Shriner's underlying "insanity." The only interest of the public and policymakers was, in the words of Governor Booth Gardner, "keep[ing] violent and dangerous people off the streets."[9] To put it simply, fear captured the public and their elected representatives. Fear is a powerful, if not irresistible force, which, unfortunately, our institutions have not always been strong enough to contain.[10]

The political situation surrounding the enactment of the SVP statute demonstrates that the motive for enactment was not driven by a need to rehabilitate, but by a desire to segregate the so-called predator from the general public.[11] But community protection is ordinarily a result of the criminal law, although the crime prevention purpose is qualified by the more important purpose of establishing social order and maintaining constitutional safeguards to liberty.[12]

The SVP Commitment Process

To fully understand how civil commitment imitates, but actually undermines, the aims of the criminal law, we first examine how

133

SVP proceedings actually work. Each jurisdiction with an SVP commitment process requires some history of harmful sexual misconduct. All jurisdictions require the subject of commitment to be at least charged, but not necessarily convicted, with a sex offense as a predicate to civil commitment.[13] Some jurisdictions suspend the pending criminal process when the petition for commitment is filed.[14] Relatedly, some jurisdictions require the subject of commitment be confined at the time the petition is filed.[15] Other jurisdictions, such as Washington, do not require the person be confined at the time the petition is filed provided the person has not committed a "recent overt act."[16]

All jurisdictions specify the types of offenses to qualify a person for SVP commitment. Additionally, the person must exhibit some mental condition that supposedly "makes" the individual likely to reoffend, although each jurisdiction uses differing terminology to describe the mental condition and the standard of commitment.

A majority of jurisdictions require the state to prove beyond a reasonable doubt the person satisfies the criteria for commitment.[17] The remaining jurisdictions require the state to prove by clear and convincing evidence the person satisfies the criteria for commitment.[18] A majority of jurisdictions provide that the finder of fact may be a jury, with either the state or the subject of commitment requesting jury determination.

All jurisdictions provide that the subject of commitment has a statutory right to counsel and, if indigent, have court-appointed counsel at the public's expense. Moreover, all jurisdictions provide the subject with a right to request an expert and have the public pay for the costs of that expert. All jurisdictions provide that the subject of commitment has a right to attend the proceeding and cross-examine the state's witnesses; however, the jurisdictions are split as to whether the subject of the proceeding has the right to remain silent. In Washington, for example, the subject of the petition has no statutory or constitutional right to remain silent.[19]

Once the subject is determined to be a sexually violent predator, some jurisdictions require the court to commit him or her to a special commitment center. Other jurisdictions permit the court to commit the subject to the least restrictive alternative appropriate. In either event, the person is committed to a department of health, not a department of corrections, even though the treatment programs are typically housed in prisons.

Lastly, most jurisdictions require the subject to be confined until he or she is no longer "dangerous." About half the jurisdictions provide for some annual review of the subject to determine continuing "dangerousness."[20] At this annual review, the burden of proof shifts to the supposed "predator" to show that he or she is no longer "dangerous."

As Hart observed, if conduct is equated with sickness and punishment with treatment, there would be no requirement for condemnable conduct to have actually taken place.[21] Yet, the supposed "predator" is obviously subjected to the "community's solemn condemnation" so, according to Hart, "the default to be condemned ought plainly to consist of overt conduct, and not simply of a condition of the mind; and the fact of default should be proved with scrupulous care."[22] As will be seen, it is not.

The Civil Commitment Jurisprudence

To understand SVP civil commitment, one must understand the evolution of civil commitment laws in general. Despite certain fundamental differences, the U.S. Supreme Court drew from its general civil commitment jurisprudence to analyze the constitutionality of SVP civil commitment.[23]

Beginning in the 1930s, "sexual psychopath" laws authorized civil commitment of persons charged with or convicted of sexual offenses and deemed to be dangerous. These laws consigned the so-called sexual psychopath to a mental institution for treatment. The U.S. Supreme Court upheld Minnesota's sexual psychopath law in *Minnesota ex rel. Pearson v. Probation Court*.[24]

With this constitutional imprimatur, other jurisdictions passed similar laws. By 1960, more than half of the states passed some kind of sexual psychopath law, ostensibly to provide treatment for so-called sexual psychopaths.[25] It is important to note, however, these precursor laws to SVP commitment provided a civil procedure to mandate treatment in lieu of punishment, not in addition to punishment.[26]

By the late 1970s, however, treatment programs for so-called sexual psychopaths were severely curtailed due in large part to a series of reports, which became the foundation for the "nothing works" philosophy.[27] The major tenet of this philosophy was no amount of treatment or rehabilitation curbs criminal recidivism, especially the recidivism of sex offenders. As this view became widely accepted, legislative focus shifted from indeterminate sentencing and involuntary treatment-based models to determinate sentencing wherein the convicted criminal serves his or her justly imposed sentence and is released regardless of treatment.

Some critics viewed determinate sentences as insufficient punishment for violent, recidivist sex offenders, yet legislative commitment to determinate sentences and prohibitions on retroactive punishment restricted how violent sex offenders could be appropriately punished.[28] One commentator calls this perceived problem the "incapacitation gap."[29]

Hart warned of the "incapacitation gap" when he observed that determinate sentences did not adequately account for the individual criminal defendant's circumstances.[30] Hart posited that a sentencing judge could consider the individual circumstances of the convicted defendant, such as undeterrability, when crafting an individual sentence and that a parole board could ensure equality of sentencing, thus, implicitly eliminating any need for post-conviction civil commitment.[31] Hart's astute observation has been lost in the rush to commit the so-called predators living among us.

As we shall see in the cases to follow, the U.S. Supreme Court attempts to balance society's wish to be protected from "predators" against the clear deprivation of liberty inherent in civil commitment. Without limits, however, the simple weighing of the social benefit of avoiding harm potentially caused by the recidivist criminal against the harm of depriving a single person's liberty will always favor the state. A single criminal recidivist, such as Earl Shriner, can cause significant psychic harm to a community, and physical harm to an individual, whereas depriving him of liberty is seen as a much smaller harm.[32]

Hart recognized a double danger to this approach:

> [It] tends always to depreciate, if not deny, the significance of [the criminal law] and to focus attention instead on the individual. . . . The danger to the individual is that he will be punished, or treated, for what he is or is believed to be, rather than for what he has done. . . . The danger to society is that the effectiveness of the general commands of the criminal law as instruments for influencing behavior so as to avoid the necessity for enforcement proceedings will be weakened.[33]

The balance the Supreme Court struck was to require the state to prove a mental illness that causes a person to be dangerous. However, relying on amorphous concepts, such as mental illness and dangerousness, is like pinning down fog; they may provide a comforting poultice for the constitutional injury, but they provide no real limitation on the government's ability to civilly detain its citizenry. For a state to detain a person based on such amorphous concepts threatens the liberty of us all.

O'Connor v. Donaldson was the first case to link mental illness and dangerousness as the predicate conditions to civil commitment.[34] In *O'Connor*, Kenneth Donaldson brought suit alleging his involuntary commitment violated his constitutional right to liberty. During his 15-year involuntarily commitment, he received no treatment for his mental illness (paranoid schizophrenia), and the state never claimed he was dangerous to society.[35] The Supreme Court held Donaldson's commitment unconstitutional; "[a] finding of 'mental illness' alone cannot justify a State's locking a person up against his will and keeping him indefinitely in simple custodial confinement . . . there is still no constitutional basis for confining such persons involuntarily if they are dangerous to no one and can live safely in freedom."[36] Importantly, the Supreme Court did not address how dangerousness could be proven. In the end, the decision in *O'Connor* left more questions unanswered than it resolved.

The next case to address one of the predicates to civil commitment, albeit in an indirect manner, was *United States v. Salerno*.[37] *Salerno* involved a substantive due process challenge to the Bail Reform Act of 1984, which permits preventative pretrial detention of a person charged with certain serious felonies based solely on a prediction of dangerousness.[38] The Supreme Court upheld the constitutionality of the act, reasoning

> [w]hile the Government's general interest in preventing crime is compelling, even this interest is heightened when the Government musters convincing proof that the arrestee, already indicted or held to answer for a serious crime, presents a demonstrable danger to the community. Under these narrow circumstances, society's interest in crime prevention is at its greatest.[39]

Explicit in the "narrow circumstances" of *Salerno* is the temporal limit to the commitment being challenged; the detainee's right to a speedy trial with all attendant constitutional protections ensures a determinate commitment length.[40] But the facts explicit in *Salerno* render it inappropriate to support SVP commitment; pretrial criminal detention predicated on dangerousness is significantly different than indefinite civil detention.[41]

The most important case to address civil commitment was *Foucha v. Louisiana*.[42] *Foucha* concerned the constitutionality of a Louisiana statute allowing indefinite involuntary commitment of persons found not guilty by reason of insanity when the person was dangerous but not mentally ill.[43] The issue before the court was whether an individual with "an antisocial personality," which is not a mental disease or illness, may be civilly committed.[44]

The Supreme Court held that the Louisiana statute violated due process because it permitted civil commitment without mental illness. The Supreme Court reasoned that although an insanity acquittee could be committed,[45] he is entitled to release when either he has recovered his sanity or is no longer dangerous.[46] Since Foucha was not mentally ill, the basis for holding him as an insanity acquittee disappeared; the state could no longer hold him. In other words, mental illness *and* dangerousness were necessary predicates to civil commitment.

Three important elements should be teased out of the *Foucha* decision. First, the Supreme Court was concerned with the possibility of indefinite detention, as opposed to the limited detention based solely on dangerousness in *Salerno*.[47] Second, where the detention was indefinite, dangerousness alone was insufficient to justify civil commitment.

> [A] convicted felon serving his sentence has a liberty interest, not extinguished by his confinement as a criminal, in not being transferred to a mental institution and hence classified as mentally ill without appropriate procedures to prove that he was mentally ill. "The loss of liberty produced by an involuntary commitment is more than a loss of freedom from confinement."[48]

In other words, a high likelihood of reoffense is insufficient to justify civil commitment; something more must separate the dangerous, but ordinary, criminal recidivist from the dangerous, and extraordinary, mentally ill person.[49]

Third, the Supreme Court failed to set out any parameters to define mental illness. It explicitly rejected the notion that mere recognition of a disorder by the psychiatric community is a mental illness sufficient to justify civil commitment.

> [T]he State asserts that because Foucha once committed a criminal act and now has an antisocial personality that sometimes leads to aggressive conduct, a disorder for which there is no effective treatment, he may be held indefinitely. This rationale would permit the State to hold indefinitely any other insanity acquittee not mentally ill who could be shown to have a personality disorder that may lead to criminal conduct. The same would be true of any convicted criminal, even though he has completed his prison term. It would also be only a step away from substituting confinements for dangerousness for our present system which, with only narrow exceptions and aside from permissible confinements for mental illness, incarcerates only those who are proved beyond reasonable doubt to have violated a criminal law.[50]

The court rejected "personality disorder" and "antisocial personality" as mental illnesses to justify civil commitment. Hart echoes this observation: "It is not simply antisocial conduct which public officers are given responsibility to suppress."[51] However, the Supreme Court and Hart stop short of setting out any parameter that *could* justify civil commitment. In a concurring opinion, Justice Sandra Day O'Connor opined the state could civilly commit a person upon a showing of dangerousness and "some medical justification."[52] Needless to say, following *Foucha*, it was clear that mental illness was a constitutional requirement for civil commitment, but it was unclear what constitutes a mental illness, except that Foucha's personality disorder was insufficient.[53]

To summarize, *O'Connor* rejected civil commitment based on mental illness without dangerousness. However, *O'Connor* did not address how dangerousness could be proven. *Foucha* rejected civil commitment based on dangerousness without mental illness, but the *Foucha* ruling left considerable ambiguity surrounding the exact nature of the mental illness requirement. The stage was now set for the U.S. Supreme Court's review of SVP civil commitment.

Leroy Hendricks was convicted in Kansas in 1984 for taking "indecent liberties" with two teenage boys; he was sentenced to 5 to 20 years in prison.[54] Shortly before Hendricks's scheduled release, the state invoked its newly enacted SVP statute, seeking to commit Hendricks as an SVP.[55] Hendricks moved to dismiss the petition on constitutional grounds.[56] The trial judge reserved ruling on Hendricks's motion and found probable cause to proceed to trial.[57]

At trial, Hendricks stated he could not control his urges to molest children.[58] The state presented expert testimony that Hendricks suffered from pedophilia, was likely to sexually reoffend against children if not confined, and pedophilia qualified as a "mental abnormality" under the Kansas SVP law.[59] A jury unanimously found Hendricks to be a sexually violent predator beyond a reasonable doubt.[60]

Hendricks appealed to the Kansas Supreme Court, arguing his commitment violated the Constitution's Due Process, Double Jeopardy, and Ex Post Facto Clauses.[61] The Kansas Supreme Court held the SVP statute did indeed violate the Due Process Clause of the Constitution because the "mental abnormality" required under the statute fell short of the requirement of "mental illness" as a predicate for civil commitment.[62] The U.S. Supreme Court granted certiorari and reversed, rejecting Hendricks's claims.

The Supreme Court first addressed Hendricks's claim that substantive due process requires that civil commitment be based on a "mental illness," as that term may be defined by the psychiatric community. The Supreme Court held the Kansas law's mental disorder requirement satisfied the requirements of substantive due process because "[t]he precommitment requirement of a 'mental abnormality' or 'personality disorder' is consistent with the requirements of . . . other statutes that we have upheld in that it narrows the class of persons eligible for confinement to those who are unable to control their dangerousness."[63] The Supreme Court stated that "the term 'mental illness' is devoid of any talismanic significance."[64] Rather, it observed, "we have traditionally left to legislators the task of defining terms of a medical nature that have legal significance."[65] In other words, according to the Supreme Court, a "mental illness" is whatever the state legislature says it is, although it must result in some "inability to control . . . dangerousness."[66]

Putting aside the semantic quibble that it is not a person's dangerousness that must be uncontrollable but a person's conduct, the Supreme Court's reasoning might be viewed to collapse the mental illness requirement into the dangerousness requirement. Recall in

140

Foucha that the civil commitment was reversed because an antisocial personality disorder, although leading to uncontrollable dangerousness, was not a "mental illness," talismanic or not.[67] Perhaps because Hendricks admitted his dangerousness *and* his mental illness, the Supreme Court felt comfortable to collapse the requirements of dangerousness and mental illness into one another.[68]

To answer Hendricks's double jeopardy and ex post facto arguments, the Supreme Court characterized the commitment as civil, not criminal: "As a threshold matter, commitment under the Act does not implicate either of the two primary objectives of criminal punishment: retribution or deterrence." In addition,

> the Kansas court's determination that the Act's 'overriding concern' was the continued 'segregation of sexually violent offenders' is consistent with our conclusion that the Act establishes civil proceedings . . . especially when that concern is coupled with the State's ancillary goal of providing treatment to those offenders, if such is possible.[69]

Yet, if the Supreme Court were to approach the civil and criminal distinction in a principled way, it might do well to look to the purposes underlying that distinction. Hart offers one such principled method when he posits that the difference between civil and criminal sanction is "the judgment of community condemnation which accompanies and justifies [the criminal sanction's] imposition."[70] According to Hart, criminal acts "incur a formal and solemn pronouncement of the moral condemnation of the community."[71] Accordingly, acts not morally condemned by the community may be subject to civil sanction.

Other experts view the distinction differently. For example, Professor John C. Coffee views the distinction from a utilitarian standpoint. For Coffee, the difference "lies in the distinction between 'pricing' and 'prohibiting.'"[72] Civil sanctions are intended to "price" the action, and they cause the actor to "internalize the social costs of an activity."[73] Because a civil sanction requires the actor only to pay the social costs, the punishment is not punitive and, "arguably the full constitutional safeguards applicable to criminal prosecutions need not apply."[74] Criminal sanctions on the other hand are imposed on actions with no social utility and, therefore, must be prohibited in all cases.[75]

The question presented by SVP laws may also be approached differently than either Hart or Coffee. The question may not be whether SVP laws are criminal or civil but whether there are adequate safeguards on the state's ability to restrict a person's liberty.

For example, Professor Randy Barnett proposes a satisfying method to determine the legitimacy of laws.[76] This view begins with the Framers' deep mistrust of majoritarianism, and understanding the representative system put in place by the Constitution allowed the electorate, not to pass laws, but instead work as a check on those who do.[77] Therefore, the government cannot consent to the abridgement of any individual rights. Since there is no consent to the abridgement of rights, the use of government power is legitimate only when it is "(1) *necessary* to protect the rights of others and (2) *proper* insofar as [such powers] do not violate the preexisting rights of the persons on whom they are imposed."[78] These rights, as properly understood by the Framers, go well beyond those enumerated in the Bill of Rights and encompass all "inherent rights" held by citizens, which are so pervasive as to be innumerable.[79] He urges a presumption of liberty, making any deprivation of rights by the state illegitimate unless the state meets its burden to show procedural and substantive safeguards ensuring that the rights of the individual are respected.[80]

With this approach, the classification of SVP commitment as civil or criminal is immaterial; instead, only the substantive and procedural protections attendant to the deprivation of liberty are important. Where an individual faces forced confinement of indeterminate length, he is completely deprived of liberty; therefore, to be a legitimate use of government power, the protections attendant to the deprivation must also be complete.

By focusing on the formalistic labels of "civil" versus "criminal," however, we lose sight of the practical realities of SVP commitment: communal condemnation and dehumanization, lack of meaningful clinical criteria, lack of clinical consensus on predictive ability, and the overall depreciation of the criminal law and social order.[81] It is to these realities we now turn.

The Practical Realities of Sexual Violent Predator Commitment

Communal Condemnation and Dehumanization

Undoubtedly, no one is more reviled than the sexually violent predator. The name itself dehumanizes, expressly referencing a wild animal. A "predator" is something to be shunned or eliminated.[82] Yet, even if the highest constitutional protections were in place, incarceration based on who an individual is, as opposed to what that individual has done, is an unacceptable affront to the conception of liberty upon which this country was founded.[83]

Labeling a person a "predator" and incarcerating that person based on the label alone "undermine[s] the foundation of a free society's effort to build up each individual's sense of responsibility as a guide and a stimulus to the constructive development of his capacity for effectual and fruitful decision."[84] Such incarceration assumes either the person is incapable of choosing to act responsibly or, having such capacity, the person will not act responsibly. Both assumptions dehumanize, viewing the person as a dangerous animal or an automaton, lacking the free will to make a choice.[85] "In the dark heart of the sex predator statute is the legislative denial of free will and individual responsibility."[86]

Yet, as Hart observed, "Man is a social animal, and the function of law is to enable him to realize his potentialities as a human being through the forms and modes of social organization."[87] All of us have free will, the potential for good and evil; it is up to each to decide.

Lack of Meaningful Clinical Criteria

Under *Hendricks*, a simple reference to the fourth edition of the American Psychiatric Association's *Diagnostic and Statistical Manual of Mental Disorders* (*DSM-IV*) satisfies the mental illness prong of the substantive due process test.[88] However, even the authors of *DSM-IV* recognize the error of relying on its normalization of mental conditions to justify civil commitment.

> When the *DSM-IV* categories, criteria, and textual descriptions are employed for forensic purposes, there are significant risks that diagnostic information will be misused or misunderstood. These dangers arise because of the imperfect fit between the questions of ultimate concern to the law and the information contained in a clinical diagnosis. *In most situations, the clinical diagnosis of a* DMS-IV *mental disorder is not sufficient to establish the existence for legal purposes of a "mental disorder," "mental disability," "mental disease," or "mental defect."* In determining whether an individual meets a specified legal standard (e.g., for competence, criminal

143

responsibility, or disability), additional information is usually required beyond that contained in the *DSM-IV*
diagnosis.[89]

Moreover, as the Supreme Court recognized subsequent to *Hendricks*, "the science of psychiatry . . . informs but does not control [the] ultimate legal determination."[90] Notwithstanding these stern admonitions, the invocation of a *DSM-IV* diagnosis continues to support civil commitment.[91] However, this undermines the protections of the criminal law because it fails to provide any meaningful substantive limitation and merely punishes people for "for what he is or is believed to be."[92] This is true for three reasons.

First, relying on the *DSM-IV* to provide the legal standard of commitment fails to provide a significant limitation on preventative detention.[93] Arguably every criminal manifests some antisocial personality, as demonstrated by his willingness to break society's rules to personally enrich himself. It seems likely the state could find an expert to diagnose these recidivists with a personality disorder causing them to commit crime.[94] As such, the state could avoid the protections of the criminal law by creating some civil mechanism to commit undeterred criminals measured for the dangerousness of criminal recidivism.[95] There simply does not appear to be any principled method of limiting preventative detention to those who are truly likely to commit a violent sexual act in the future.[96]

Second, the reliability and validity of a *DSM-IV* diagnosis as determinative of sexual violence is questionable.[97] Psychiatry is not a science lending itself to highly reliable outcomes in that different examiners, assessing the same individual, may not assign the same diagnosis.[98] Yet, even if psychiatry were able to reliably diagnose mental illness, the question of whether that mental defect is necessarily the cause of an individual's sexual offense is a separate one. Current research suggests sexually violent behavior results from a complex interaction of a variety of factors, mental illness not necessarily being one of them.[99]

Third, use of *DSM-IV* undermines protection afforded individuals subject to preventative detention because more must be proven. The state must also prove a causal relationship between the mental illness and the individual's dangerousness or likelihood of reoffending. Although not explicitly stated in *Hendricks*,[100] the Supreme Court later clarified the requisite causal link between mental illness and dangerousness in a subsequent case, *Kansas v. Crane*.[101] But using *DSM-IV* provides no insight into a person's dangerousness.

> The fact that an individual's presentation meets the criteria for a *DSM-IV* diagnosis does not carry any necessary implications regarding the individual's degree of control over the behaviors that may be associated with the disorder. Even when diminished control over one's behavior is a feature of the disorder, having the diagnosis in itself does not demonstrate that a particular individual is (or was) unable to control his or her behavior at a particular time.[102]

To the contrary, if a lack of volitional control is satisfied by simply having a history of sex offending, such reasoning is tautological: one is a sex predator because one has prior sex offenses.[103] In this way, the simple use of the *DSM-IV* removes one safeguard on the state's ability to restrict an individual's liberty.

The inconvenient truth about so-called sexually violent predators may be that sexually violent behavior is a choice rather than an uncontrollable compulsion. Intentional acts are properly punishable by the criminal law, a fact recognized when the very offenders who are deemed "predators" were previously imprisoned for the exact same behavior on the assumption their behavior was *not* due to mental illness.[104] In the final analysis, civilly committing people based on a *DSM-IV* diagnosis merely punishes people for "what [they are] believed to be, rather than for what [they have] done."[105]

Lack of Predictive Ability

Since the danger of sexual-criminal recidivism is the primary justification for depriving individuals of their liberty through civil commitment, the state's power to detain individuals must be focused on only the most dangerous. The Washington State Supreme Court construed its statutory standard for commitment as identifying persons whose "likelihood of re-offense is extremely high."[106] Other jurisdictions use similar semantics.[107]

The question becomes, What are the criteria for predicting dangerousness, and do these criteria accurately predict which individuals will reoffend? The science of predicting dangerous recidivism is too complex and outside the scope of this chapter, but a general understanding is important to allow the reader to understand that the method currently used fails to engender social order or to protect our liberty.

Generally, the state's forensic psychiatrist, or psychologist, gives an opinion on the likelihood that the individual will engage in future predatory acts of sexual violence. This opinion is based on one of three approaches: a purely clinical approach; a purely actuarial approach; and a combination of the two, sometimes referred to as an "adjusted actuarial approach."[108]

In a strict clinical approach, the clinician is the sole judge of dangerousness based on his or her clinical observations and expert knowledge. In a strict actuarial approach, predictions of dangerousness are based on statistical probabilities determined by a defined set of weighted predictors. In the adjusted actuarial approach, an actuarial assessment is made, which is then adjusted by the evaluator based on factors not included in the actuarial tool.

Each of these approaches based on existing science may be nothing more than propensity testimony without regard to a causal connection to the diagnosed condition.[109] Studies have shown that evaluators who rely strictly on their clinical assessment will over-predict the recidivism risk while a strict actuarial assessment, relying primarily on static factors, such as prior offenses, age, and substance abuse history, fails to account for the changing dynamic factors of the subject's emotional state and treatment progress.[110] In other words, a clinical approach relies too much on the individual evaluator, and a strict actuarial approach relies too little on individual considerations and the link, if any, to a mental defect. As one judge noted, "Not only are the statistics concerning the violent behavior of others irrelevant, but it seems to me wrong to confine any person on the basis not of that person's own conduct but on the basis of statistical evidence regarding the behavior of other people."[111]

In the adjusted actuarial approach, wherein the evaluator adjusts the actuarial assessment up or down based on the dynamic factors not included in the actuarial instrument, the criticisms inherent in the other approaches merge. As Professor John LaFond observes, "Why not convert our criminal sentencing system into a game of chance? Release from prison could be decided by a flip of a coin."[112] As will be shown, Professor LaFond's wry observation is not far off the mark.

This brings us to the judge's role as gatekeeper when deciding whether to admit expert testimony. In the context of civil commitment, expert testimony is usually necessary and given great weight, which requires the accuracy and reliability of that testimony to be of paramount importance. But the judiciary fails to fulfill its basic role as neutral arbiter of justice if it admits expert testimony based on largely unproven science.

Depending on the jurisdiction, the trial judge uses either the *Frye* or *Daubert* test to ensure scientific evidence is sufficiently reliable for consideration by a fact finder.[113] Under the *Frye* test, the trial judge determines whether the proffered expert testimony is generally accepted by the relevant scientific community.[114] Under the *Daubert* test, "the proposed testimony must be supported by appropriate validation—i.e., 'good grounds,' based on what is known."[115] In other words, the proffered expert testimony must be scientifically valid.

However, there is currently no scientific consensus that predicting dangerousness based on a mental or personality disorder is possible. In fact, all the current studies point the other way; "study after study has shown that this fond hope of the capability to accurately to predict violence in advance is simply not fulfilled."[116]

In a survey of the seven most commonly cited studies on the ability of mental health professionals to predict dangerousness, between 54 and 92 percent of individuals predicted to act violently *failed* to do so over a three- to five-year follow-up period.[117] This means *at best* the so-called science of prediction is wrong *half the time.*[118] As one commentator observes, "The validity of prediction testimony becomes so attenuated that it is ineffective to establish the requisite certainty of harm to make the state's interest in preventing that harm 'compelling' (thus resulting in a violation of the due process clause)."[119] In sum, "Despite 25 years of research, social scientists have barely scratched the surface of risk assessment as a predictive tool."[120]

Nevertheless, courts regularly rely on these unproven measures of predicting dangerousness to justify civil detention. The majority of appellate courts have either ruled a *Frye* or *Daubert* analysis as unnecessary[121] or dismissed concerns over scientific methodology as going to credibility subject to the discretion of the trial judge.[122] But a more reasoned approach would seem to be scientific evidence is not "helpful" to a jury when it is not based on solid science.[123]

Ultimately, courts appear reluctant to be the first to say that "the emperor wears no clothes," as that would undermine the well-established practice of basing judicial decisions on a prediction of dangerousness; to admit the emperor wears no clothes is to "eviscerate the entire law of involuntary commitment as well as render dubious the numerous other areas where psychiatry and the law intersect."[124] We suppose the same could be said of witch trials in Salem. When the prestigious American Psychiatric Association reports the science is lacking to predict dangerousness but predictions of dangerousness lacking scientific basis are still admitted in court as dispositive of a person's liberty, there must be more at work in the judicial mind than simply and impartially searching for the truth.[125]

The Depreciation of the Criminal Law and Social Order

If Hart is right that the criminal law provides the mechanism to allow society to vindicate its interest in prohibited conduct and engender social order, it would depreciate the role of the criminal law to shift away from punishment based on individual conduct. Hart observed that

> the criminal law has an obviously significant and, indeed, a fundamental role to play in the effort to create the good society. For it is the criminal law which defines the minimum conditions of man's responsibility for his fellows and holds him to that responsibility. The assertion of social responsibility has value in the treatment even of those who have become criminals. It has far greater value as a stimulus to the great bulk of mankind to abide by the law and to take pride in so abiding.[126]

Under this view, if an individual has committed a crime, he or she must be criminally punished not only as a matter of social right, but also as a matter of individual responsibility. The criminal law is the teacher, and punishment is the lesson. Where an individual is not criminally punished but civilly committed, the lesson is lost and the community's desire to condemn the conduct is left unfulfilled.

Concomitantly, detaining a person in the name of treatment is to render the punishment arbitrary, undermining the proscriptive force of the law because "the very ideal of justice is offended by seriously unequal penalties for substantially similar crimes."[127] The perception of arbitrariness is simple. Take two individuals who have committed the same crime: the first is punished pursuant to the criminal law and after he serves his criminal sentence, rejoins society; the second is punished pursuant to the criminal law, but in lieu of, or in addition to, his criminal sentence, he is also committed for treatment based on speculation of what he may do in the future. Such a system is easily perceived as arbitrary, especially when considering the lack of any causal link between criminal conduct and mental disorders.[128] As Hart observed, unequal punishment "destroy[s] the prisoner's sense of having been justly dealt with, which is the first prerequisite of his personal reformation."[129]

Relatedly, labeling a person a "predator" absolves the person from taking responsibility for the conduct, enabling the person to commit future criminal conduct and to further undermining the proscriptive force of the law.[130] Formal punishment, on the other hand, enables the offender the opportunity to comply with the basic strictures of society. To deny punishment in the name of treatment is to depreciate the criminal law as well as the criminal. In the end, it is society that suffers.

Conclusion

Restating the original query, if the aims of the criminal law are to engender social order while providing a bulwark against deprivation of liberty, how is it doing? Well, that bulwark is not impenetrable, and it appears a goal never imagined by Hart or the Framers has co-opted the criminal law. The goal of community safety may one day breach that bulwark unless the courts recognize that the deprivation of liberty for any reason should be the sole bailiwick of the criminal law, with all its attendant protections. As the jurisprudence currently stands, a state is permitted to civilly detain a person indefinitely based on a limitless standard of mental abnormality and a guess about future dangerousness.

President Abraham Lincoln once quipped, "How many legs does a dog have if you call the tail a leg? Four. Calling a tail a leg doesn't make it a leg."[131] Similarly, calling incarceration "civil" should not demolish the formidable bulwark guarding our liberty. As one scholar observed, "The Framers, for all their prescience, did not anticipate post-modernism. They apparently thought they knew what the 'criminal' process was."[132]

We should be wary when government targets individuals who are already the object of the public's abhorrence. We should be doubly wary when the government suspends the formidable protections afforded those people under the criminal law to use a civil process in order to prevent an unknowable future. So-called sexual predators are the canaries in the coal mine, the first to fall when the forces of tyranny breach the borders of liberty.

Soon, because only some mental abnormality is required, nearly anyone deemed potentially dangerous could be civilly committed. Such a process neither engenders social order nor protects people from the awesome power of the state. Such a process fails Hart's aims of the criminal law as well as our own.

9. Substantive Limitations on the Criminal Law: Random Thoughts of a Judicial Conservative

Stephen Markman

The following are several hopefully not-too-random thoughts that come to mind on rereading Professor Henry M. Hart's classic article.

Random Thought 1—The Need to Organize Thought

During my nine years on the Supreme Court of Michigan, I have reviewed an estimated 15,000 criminal appeals. While these cases have involved questions of considerably varying degrees of complexity, in each I have sought to an appropriate extent to reflect on the "aims of the criminal law" and their relevance to the case at hand. This is necessary not only, as Professor Hart recognizes, to "organize thought,"[1] but also to bring consistency to bear in decision-making. For if the rule of law is built on any single principle, it is the equal application of the law. While many of the "aims" that I view as most pertinent to the ordinary criminal appeal—and whose consideration best enable me to "organize my thoughts"—are focused on the criminal *justice system*, rather than on the criminal *law*, all appellate judges must attempt in some fashion to place criminal appeals in a broader context by considering these "aims."

Random Thought 2—Criminal Appeals in Perspective

What distinguishes the criminal appellate process and makes it especially susceptible to the consideration of larger "aims" or purposes—most often unstated because judicial opinions and orders typically are not vehicles for the articulation of first principles—are the following: (a) the sheer volume of criminal appeals, especially within the states, requiring the appellate judge as a practical matter to develop internal benchmarks for placing cases in some larger context; (b) the recurrence of certain broad categories of cases and controversies (for example, Was the judge or jury biased against the defendant? Was the defendant unfairly prejudiced by certain testimony? Should the accomplice be held responsible for the acts of the principal? Was the defendant's sentence proportionate?); (c) the prevalence of broad legal concepts, such as "due process," "harmless error," "reasonable" searches and seizures, and "sufficiency of the evidence," which necessarily call on the judge to a significant degree to look inwardly, rather than to outside sources of law; and (d) the strong sense that the criminal justice system constitutes a particularly unified system within which the judge must be especially cognizant of the impact of decisions today upon decisions tomorrow. Thus, sentences must be relatively commensurate, sentences must take into account the deterrent impact on potential future offenders, and even minor procedures must be rendered as consistent and as uniform as possible in light of their constitutional provenance.

Random Thought 3—The Aims of the Criminal Justice System

In "organizing my thoughts" concerning the "aims of the criminal justice system"—to be distinguished from the "aims of the substantive criminal law," principally focused on by Professor Hart—there are several premises that invariably assist me in placing the individual appeal in some initial perspective.

First, as a believer in limited government, I understand the responsibilities of government to be relatively few. However, more specifically as a believer in limited *constitutional* government, as a judge, I must abide by the precedents of the U.S. Supreme Court, I must give respect to the precedents of my own court, I must accord reasonable deference to the judgments of the representative branches, and I must be cognizant that the federal and state constitutions do not always reflect my own preferences concerning government. Indeed, what arises from this belief in limited government, and that most shapes my thinking concerning the "aims" of the criminal justice system, is its corollary—namely that where governmental responsibilities clearly *do* exist, they must be carried out well.

To me, the establishment of a criminal justice system (along with the maintenance of a strong national defense) constitutes the primary responsibility of government. This right is the first civil right of every citizen to be free from the criminal predator, and it was, I

would surmise, toward this end that governments were first established by our distant ancestors. The criminal justice system is the
principal tool for vindicating the right to personal security, and there
is no more fundamental individual right. This right is the sine qua
non of any decent society. Thus, among my various responsibilities
as an appellate judge, there is none more essential than serving as
a steward for this system.

While I do not fully agree with Professor Hart concerning the
inferences to be drawn from the constitutional detail to the criminal
justice system,[2] I do concur that this emphasis strongly communicates that a conviction for a crime is truly a "distinctive and serious"
matter.[3] What this suggests to me as a judge on the court of last
resort in my state—a court with essentially plenary discretion to
hear only those appeals it chooses—is that summary denials of
"leave to appeal" (or what is called certiorari in the Supreme Court)
should only rarely be issued in a criminal appeal on the grounds
that such appeal lacks "jurisprudential significance," a common
rationale for declining to hear an appeal of a factually bound civil
case even where the appellate judge may believe that the lower
courts have decided a case wrongly. Instead, given the importance
of the criminal justice function, result-changing errors in criminal
cases, in my judgment, will almost always be of considerable jurisprudential significance and warrant correction. Similarly, the notion
that state supreme courts do not typically sit as "error-correcting"
bodies, but rather as "law developing" bodies, seems inapt when
errors have been made in the criminal justice process.

For the consequences of failing to correct such errors are simply
not tolerable by society. It cannot be countenanced that an innocent
person be convicted, that a predator unnecessarily be returned to
the community that he has already harmed, or that a convicted
person be confined for a period beyond that provided for by law.
Such mistakes are necessarily tragic mistakes and must be avoided
wherever possible. Although "harmless errors" will almost certainly
arise during the course of any criminal trial, errors potentially affecting the final disposition of a case can rarely be harmless and must
be addressed by the appellate court. Just as both proponents and
opponents of capital punishment agree that the death penalty is
different from other types of punishment, so too are criminal appeals
different from other types of appeal where potential errors must
sometimes be tolerated.

153

Second, I believe that the Constitution does not merely limit, but empowers, the criminal justice system. As Professor Hart recognizes, we obtain our "broadest view" of the aims of the justice system if we view these from the perspective of the "makers of a constitution—of those who [were] seeking to establish sound foundations for a tolerable and durable social order."[4]

What the preamble describes as "this" Constitution established a system of self-government that authorized the people through their representatives to make and enforce laws to "establish Justice" and "insure domestic Tranquility." To emphasize exclusively those provisions that protect people's rights "against the government" is to engage in a fundamentally distorted reading of our basic law by according lower priority to provisions that protect people's rights in spheres in which government is properly empowered to act. So understood, it is evident that the provisions of the Bill of Rights relating to criminal procedure were not written only to limit law enforcement; they were written to protect the public from criminal offenders as well. In this dual function, these provisions provide a check against excesses of government, while simultaneously acknowledging the right of the government to exercise essential law enforcement powers for the common good.

Thus, the Fourth Amendment *allows* reasonable searches and seizures; the Fifth Amendment *permits* the use against a defendant of incriminating statements made voluntarily and without compulsion; the Eighth Amendment *authorizes* the imposition of even severe punishment if it is not cruel and unusual; and so on. In addition, the Bill of Rights secures rights and practices that promote the interests of society and defendants alike in criminal proceedings that are neither arbitrary nor unfair, but rather conducive to the search for truth. Among these are the right to trial by jury, the right to confront witnesses, the right to a speedy trial, and the right to the assistance of counsel.

Third, the search for truth defines the principal mission of the criminal justice system, and evidence is essential to that mission.[5] For if truth cannot be discovered and acted upon, the system can only fail in its basic mission. The search for truth is not merely one of many functions of the justice system, any more than the justice system is merely one of many functions of government; rather, these define the core mission of those institutions. The discovery of truth is essential to the successful operation of the justice system's mechanisms for controlling crime and mitigating its consequences. To bring the incapacitative and specific deterrent effects of the system into play against a criminal, law enforcement authorities must have the ability to identify him as the perpetrator of an offense and to obtain and use evidence establishing his guilt.

Compromises of the truth-seeking function are also inimical to the general deterrent and value-defining function of the system. If criminals perceive that the system is full of loopholes and arbitrary advantages in their favor, they are emboldened in their criminality. And if the public perceives that the objective of reliably apprehending, convicting, and punishing criminals is too readily subordinated to other interests, the system's essential moral message that criminality is abhorrent and must be condemned is clouded. Moreover, when the justice system suppresses evidence of guilt and thereby frees an offender, the victim of a serious crime may perceive this as an expression of indifference for his life and his security, and the juror may believe that he or she has been misled by having been presented only a part of the available evidence. The integrity of the system can only be diminished in the public mind.[6]

Random Thought 4—The Importance of Criminal States of Mind

I emphatically agree with Professor Hart that the continuing trend toward the criminalization of regulated conduct is deeply troubling and that criminal laws that dispense with a criminal state-of-mind requirement are pernicious. Such laws (a) are unfair to persons who may be charged with and convicted of crimes despite lacking any intention to violate social norms; (b) trivialize the criminal law by separating out from that law the concept of moral blameworthiness; (c) facilitate arbitrary government by affording prosecutors an unjustifiably broad arsenal of tools with which to leverage plea agreements; (d) undermine public respect for the criminal law by rendering irrelevant the deterrent, rehabilitative, and incapacitative functions of the criminal law and by effecting the punishment function in an unwaveringly disproportionate manner; (e) engender among some a sense that the justice system is unfair when courts attempt to compensate for the lack of *mens rea* in regulatory crimes by sentencing offenders to what appears to be more lenient sentences than those given other offenders; and (f) divert limited public resources from the prosecution of crimes that are most destructive to persons and property. Thus, in my judgment, a necessary ingredient of the substantive criminal law should be a criminal state of mind.

Random Thought 5—The Aims of the Criminal Law

The most obvious and fundamental of the "aims of the criminal law" is to establish a "law." This requires that an appellate judge address issues necessary in resolving legal disputes of every kind: What does the law say? What facts have been determined? What measure of deference is owed to courts and juries that have determined these facts? Is the law at variance with the federal or state constitutions? Thus, I believe the paramount function of the appellate judge in all cases, criminal and civil, is to preserve the integrity of the law. This is best achieved, I believe, when judges give faithful meaning to the law and when they exercise the "judicial power" only to say what the law "is," rather than what it "ought to be." The judge thereby recognizes that the "law" is equally binding upon the courts as upon individual citizens.

Random Thought 6—Historical Context of Past 50 Years

In fairness to Professor Hart, much, but by no means all, of my perspectives concerning his thesis is a function of developments in the criminal justice system during the latter half of the 20th century, that he could never have fully anticipated 50 years ago—the Warren Court's criminal procedural revolution, the nearly complete incorporation of the Bill of Rights, the expanded realm of federal criminal jurisdiction, the transformation of habeas corpus, the enormous increase in levels of violent crime in our urban areas, and federal and state sentencing guidelines. Nor could Professor Hart have fully foreseen the continued concentration of federal governmental power, especially that within the federal judiciary, in the ensuing half-century, resulting from such Supreme Court decisions as *Mapp v. Ohio, Miranda v. Arizona, Roe v. Wade, Baker v. Carr, Garcia v. San Antonio, Fay v. Noia, Katzenbach v. Morgan, South Dakota v. Dole, Heart of Atlanta Motel v. United States, Lemon v. Kurzman, Shapiro v. Thompson,* and *Dunn v. Blumstein.*[7] Nor, lastly, could he have discerned the particular contours of the current debate over the role of the judiciary—the increasingly divisive confirmation battles over

Supreme Court nominations, the growing partisanship and paralysis of the judicial appointment process, the soaring costs and contentiousness of state judicial elections, the transformation of the American bar, the language of "originalism" and "interpretivism," the constitutional "right of privacy," Edwin Meese versus William Brennan, the dissents of Antonin Scalia and Clarence Thomas, the emergence of the Federalist Society, and the Reagan–Bush judiciary.

It is against this backdrop that Professor Hart's thesis must be evaluated. Quite conceivably, Professor Hart himself might have been influenced in his views by these developments. For my own part, I am not inclined at this particular juncture in our history to endorse a judicial role in the defining of "crimes" that would further diminish the role of the states within our constitutional system and further enhance the role of the federal judiciary. The balance of our constitutional system, in my judgment, is already askew and ought not to be rendered further askew.

Random Thought 7—The Judicial Obligation to Be Faithful to the Law

My fundamental disagreement with Professor Hart stems from my understanding of what I have described as the first aim of the criminal law—the establishment of a "law"—and the consequences of this for a judiciary acting within constitutional boundaries. While Professor Hart acknowledges that "each agency of decision must take account always of its own place in the institutional system"[8]— by which, I assume him to be referring principally if not exclusively to our "constitutional system" and its architecture of separated powers—he is highly critical of the judiciary for its toleration of what he views as noncriminal "criminal laws," that is criminal laws lacking scienter requirements. Professor Hart chastises the judiciary for failing to develop principles for interpreting statutes[9] and, indeed, for failing not only in the fulfillment, but even in the recognition of this obligation.[10] Still worse, American courts have "failed" to "collaborate with the legislature in discerning and expressing the unifying principles and aims of the criminal law."[11] Moreover, it is a "vacant" concept that a "crime is anything which is called a crime," and it is a "betrayal of intellectual bankruptcy" that a "criminal penalty is simply the penalty provided for doing anything which has been given that name"[12] by the Congress or the legislature.

157

The judiciary has not yet succeeded in "thinking through" these problems,[13] which failure is reflective of the "moral and intellectual debility of American criminal law."[14]

These criticisms are predicated on a view of the judicial role with which I respectfully disagree. While the criminal justice *system* is the primary responsibility of the judiciary, the substantive criminal *law* is the responsibility of the legislature. It is the overriding obligation of the appellate judge to give meaning to the criminal law just as he gives meaning to other laws and deeds and contracts, by looking to its words, to its grammar and syntax, to its surrounding context and manifest purpose, and by applying well-understood rules of interpretation. Professor Hart would undoubtedly consider these to be "inadequa[te]," "unimaginative," and "unintelligent" judicial techniques for interpreting statutes.[15]

Sympathetic as I am to Professor Hart's substantive views concerning the undermining of the criminal law by the failure to incorporate traditional scienter (criminal intent) requirements, in our system of self-government, the people are sometimes empowered to do foolish or imprudent things without necessarily running afoul of the Constitution. The determinative question is whether there is something in the Constitution that precludes this particular exercise in unwise lawmaking, or whether a remedy must instead arise through popular and academic debate and discussion, from the lessons drawn from our experience with the prosecution of strict liability offenses, from popular discontents and dissatisfaction, from the reconsidered decisions of thoughtful legislators, from the exercise of judgment by actors within the criminal justice system in areas in which they retain legitimate discretion, and from a better-educated and informed citizenry. Not all policy solutions must come from berobed attorneys.

Random Thought 8—The Conception of the Judicial Role

Mine is a different conception of the judicial role than that of Professor Hart, a truly seminal scholar, who has succumbed, in my judgment, to the idea that good public policies are required by the Constitution and bad policies prohibited. It is of a kind with the eternal judicial temptation to "do good things" and to eschew "doing bad things," never mind that these judgments are properly left to the determination of other institutions of government.

Rather, I believe that ours is a Constitution under which representative processes are allowed to work their will, absent clear limitations within that charter. That there will sometimes be excesses or mistakes made within these processes that cannot be corrected by the judiciary is not troublesome to me, for there are at least as many mistakes that have been made over the years by the judiciary that are uncorrectable by other branches. When I take a long view of the American experiment in self-government, I believe that our Constitution—one built on federalism, the separation of powers, limited government, and the rule of law—has afforded this country an unprecedented level of freedom, prosperity, and stability.

Moreover, I believe that departures from constitutional values have had adverse consequences for these same ends as often as not. Particularly since Professor Hart's article was written, the growing role of the central government, and the diminishing sovereignty of both the states and the individual, have gone hand in hand with an increasingly assertive Supreme Court, which in alternative bursts has both accommodated this transformation through excessive "restraint"[16] and facilitated this by excessive "activism."[17] I do not accept the premise that the republic flourishes when the Supreme Court grows strong, but that it flourishes when the Supreme Court acts within its proper boundaries.

Professor Hart's criticism of the courts for not acting more aggressively to oversee the definition of criminal offenses is misplaced and better directed toward legislatures, in particular the Congress. Confident as I occasionally am in my own judgments, I do not view myself as the "adult supervisor" of the people or of their representatives. Nor is it an aspect of the "judicial power" to second-guess or to "improve" on the work-product of the lawmaker—or to strike down enactments of the legislature, the county commission, or the city council—merely because I view these as shortsighted or even counterproductive.[18] It is not within the judicial authority to undo the bargains and compromises and pork-barreling of the representative branches. I am not their scold, and I am not under typical circumstances their "collaborator." Rather, it is my principal duty, so long as the Constitution has not been disregarded, to fairly parse the work of the lawmaker, declare what is the law, let the chips fall evenhandedly where they may, and by this means resolve cases and controversies.

Professor Hart is correct that there is "room for growth" in the criminal law "as conditions and attitudes in society change."[19] However, it is up to the Congress and the legislature to make these assessments, not the judiciary.[20] The judiciary must be faithful, not to the "community's understanding of what is morally blameworthy," but to the law—a law that presumably reflects this very "understanding."[21]

Random Thought 9—The Absence of Constitutional Barriers

In assessing a criminal statute on appeal, the threshold question is whether a legislative body possesses the constitutional authority to enact that statute. However, given that this is so rarely in doubt, it is the unusual case in which the constitutional authority of a jurisdiction to enact a particular law is significantly addressed by the courts. Nonetheless, the Tenth Amendment serves as a useful, if an increasingly and regrettably anachronistic, starting point for this analysis. It specifies that a state may enact any criminal law that is "not prohibited to it" by the Constitution, and the federal government may only enact a law that is a function of some power "delegated to the United States by the Constitution."

Given the breadth of authority of the Congress to legislate as a result of Supreme Court interpretations of the Commerce Clause, the dispositive question in assessing the kind of criminal laws condemned by Professor Hart seems to be whether there is something in the Bill of Rights that prohibits the Congress or the states from enacting a criminal law dispensing with a criminal *mens rea*. Professor Hart essentially says that we know a "criminal law" when we see it, that from time immemorial such laws have required intentional or purposeful or willful conduct, and that laws purporting to criminalize conduct absent a sufficient *mens rea* are unconstitutional, probably under the Due Process Clause of either the Fifth or Fourteenth Amendment.

As I have indicated, were I a member of the Congress or a state legislature, I would be hard-pressed ever to cast a vote to impose a criminal punishment absent Professor Hart's prerequisites. Similarly, as a judge of a state court, it is difficult to imagine the promulgation of a common-law criminal offense lacking a *mens rea* requirement. Such crimes were unknown to the common law, and I am unaware of anything in our social evolution that would warrant the transformation of the criminal law in this direction. And, of course, unlike the positive law, there is no legislative body positioned to communicate that a deviation from the common law was intended.

Nonetheless, I suppose I bear out Professor Hart's worst suspicions that there are some who truly do believe that a crime is "anything which a legislature chooses to call a 'crime'"[22]—at least in the absence of clear constitutional barriers. The criminal law has always reflected the sense of the community by identifying the harms that warrant criminal sanction, by defining aggravating and mitigating circumstances, and by imposing appropriate punishments. Unlike Professor Hart, I do not see constitutional barriers to the substantive criminal laws that we both deplore. By contrast, a criminal law, for example, that imposed disparate sanctions on black and white persons would certainly run afoul of the Equal Protection Clause of the Fourteenth Amendment; a criminal law that sought today to penalize what was lawful yesterday would certainly run afoul of the Ex Post Facto Clause; and a criminal law punishing conduct of a noncitizen of a state for conduct that would be legal if done by a citizen might well run afoul of the Fourteenth Amendment's Privileges or Immunities Clause. But what constitutional provision requires that there be a particular state of mind or *mens rea* before a criminal law can be enacted? Perhaps there ought to be, but there is not, and I am not inclined to read such an obligation into the Constitution in the guise of "interpreting" it.

The Constitution provides that "due process" be afforded all persons in their dealings with government. "The fundamental requisite of due process of law is the opportunity to be heard."[23] It encompasses "traditional ideas of fair procedure."[24] By these standards, a criminal law dispensing with a state of mind would not implicate due process, so long as the traditional elements of the criminal justice process have been preserved, the right to a fair charging procedure, the right to counsel, the right to an unbiased judge and jury, the right to be heard and to present evidence and to secure the testimony of witnesses, the right to confront witnesses, and the right to a lawfully authorized punishment.

There is, of course, the concept of "substantive due process"—a doctrine in which due process is understood to contemplate a variety of substantive as well as procedural protections. In my judgment, this doctrine is essentially incompatible with each of the two words

at issue, "due" and "process," as well as with historic understandings of the judicial role. It is an essentially standardless doctrine by
which the judge imports into the supreme law of our land, through
what is essentially a Rorschach-type legal analysis, policy values
that he believes to be important, whether the expansion of slavery,
laissez faire free enterprise, sterilization, or abortion. Can I say, in
the face of this doctrine, that there is clearly *not* a constitutional
right to be convicted only of crimes for which there is a *mens rea*
requirement? No, not really, at least no more than another can say
that there clearly *is* such a right. All that I can confidently say is
that there is nothing in the actual language of the Constitution that
clearly speaks of such a right, there is no discussion of such a right
in the *Federalist Papers* or in any of our other founding documents,
there is no state or federal court that has ever affirmatively identified
such a right, and there is no Supreme Court decision that has ever
imposed such an obligation.[25] So, while I can say with some assurance
that neither James Madison nor Alexander Hamilton ever probably
intended that their Constitution would forbid strict-liability criminal
laws—had they the occasion to give thought to these—I cannot say
with any assurance that a majority of four or five federal or state
justices will never come together who believe that due process has
a substantive component and that such component compels that
strict-liability crimes be forbidden.

To the extent that the Constitution is "written on water" with
regard to substantive due process, who can say for certain what it
will mean tomorrow? There are no apparent standards. There is
nothing that meaningfully binds any individual judge from doing
personal "justice," at the expense of "justice under law." There is
no external law that circumscribes the judge. There is no rule that
affords any predictability as to what eventually will be deemed to
fall within the Constitution and what will not.

Still, in considering this question and trying to determine whether
Professor Hart asserts a sufficiently "fundamental right" to elevate to
constitutional status, and thereby to forbid ever again any legislative
body from enacting a strict-liability crime, no matter what the circumstances, no matter what the exigencies, no matter what the
nature of the potential harm and thereby to strike down what may
well be a larger number of statutes in one fell swoop than in any
other decision of the Supreme Court,[26] one should ponder that the

legislatures that have enacted such laws—in particular our national legislature and presumably the people whom they represent—obviously did not view this as a "fundamental right." Maybe they should, but by the steady enactment of these laws, it is clear that they do not.

While on the substantive issue I am on Professor Hart's side, there *is* at least some semblance of a debate, one that, of course, would be abruptly terminated by the establishment of a new substantive due process right. Defenders of strict liability basically contend that there are a growing number of activities in modern society that, if undertaken negligently or carelessly, carry potentially severe consequences for large numbers of persons and that it is a legitimate tool in seeking to avoid these harms that strict accountability be imposed when one is involved in conduct within these areas. Strict liability may cause persons to act with greater care within these spheres of activity or, perhaps better yet, cause them to avoid becoming involved with such activities in the first place. Thus, it may encourage responsible decisionmaking by nontraditional means. Moreover, "An action does not become innocuous merely because whoever performed it meant no harm."[27] If the "object of the criminal law is to prevent the occurrence of socially damaging actions, it would be absurd to turn a blind eye to those which were due to carelessness, negligence or even accident."[28] These are not such unreasonable positions, in my judgment, that the courts, such as the Supreme Court, should intervene, declare the victors, and restrict further debate to legal and academic journals.

For myself, I am not in the market for exotic, or even mildly "creative and innovative," theories by which the least representative and accountable branch of our government, the judiciary, can be invested with more authority taken from the representative and accountable branches of government. To the extent that departures from our system of separated powers have become increasingly prevalent—with one branch exercising the powers of another, by "delegations" of constitutional authority,[29] by "hybrid" governmental institutions,[30] and by the withering away of what one justice has described as an antiquated "hermetic division"[31] of powers among the branches—I believe that individual liberties have been diminished and checks on the exercise of governmental power eroded. Nor am I in the market for equally visionary theories by which the power of the federal judiciary can be further amplified in place of that once belonging to state courts and state legislatures.

163

Where the Supreme Court ordains a hitherto undiscovered right to be newly embedded in the Constitution, I will faithfully abide by this direction; however, left to my own devices, I would prefer not to further transform the Constitution and to assert for myself or any of my colleagues on the bench the role of second-guesser-in-chief of those whom the people have selected to establish the most important of all of their laws, those in which the sense of "community [moral] condemnation" has always been foremost—the criminal law.[32]

Random Thought 10—Interpretative Presumptions

Although I do not believe that it is always unconstitutional for the legislature to enact a criminal statute lacking a *mens rea* requirement, I do believe, in the absence of any clear indication that the legislature intends to dispense with such requirement, that *mens rea* must be presumed. A criminal state of mind should be understood as part of any criminal statute in the absence of any clear contrary legislative intent. That is, in the face of silence, the default position should be that a criminal state of mind is required. This strikes me as a reasonable default position because scienter-less crimes were almost completely unknown to the common law, courts from time immemorial have specifically adhered to this default position so that it must be assumed that legislatures by now are well aware of this presumption, and strict-liability crimes remain the exception within a body of criminal law in which crimes are almost always predicated upon a bad state of mind.

In *People v. Tombs*,[33] a decision of the Michigan Supreme Court, the defendant kept several hundred child pornographic images on his employer's lap-top computer. Upon leaving his employment, the defendant returned the computer to his employer with the images "buried inside of what's known as a user profile." The defendant assumed that the employer's standard procedure would be followed and the computer reformatted, thus destroying the image files. But "just to see what was on it," the employer charged with the reformatting decided to look for image files and uncovered the pornographic pictures. While there was no dispute that the defendant could be found guilty of the *possession* of "child sexually abusive materials," the issue before the court was whether he could also be found guilty on *distribution* charges. The latter statute was silent concerning any necessary state of mind.

In a 4-3 decision, in which I was in the majority, the court, citing *Morrisette*, *Staples*, and *X-Citement Video*,[34] held that "offenses not requiring criminal intent are disfavored" and that the defendant could not be convicted of the distribution charge, since it must be presumed, in the face of silence by the legislature, that a criminal *mens rea* was required. The defendant, expecting his computer to be reformatted, lacked any criminal state of mind in returning his computer to his employer. He had demonstrated no intention that any other person be exposed to the images contained on the computer and, therefore, could not be said to have criminally "distributed" such images. Indeed, were it the law that no criminal state of mind is required for the offense of distribution, it would seem to be the case that all other employees handling the computer prior to its reformatting, including those assigned specifically to reformat the computer, could also have been deemed to have committed a crime; indeed, even the police officers who eventually carried away the computer to preserve it as evidence could have been made subject to criminal charges.[35]

In light of this general "disfavoring" of strict-liability crimes, and the judicial presumption that mere legislative silence does not ordinarily obviate the requirement of criminal intent, I believe that Professor Hart's admonition to the courts to develop "an adequate theory of the aims of the criminal law as guides in the interpretation of statutes" has been realized.[36] However, in fact, Professor Hart appears to be seeking significantly more than a mere "interpretative presumption of the court."[37] This is evidenced by his pursuit, specifically, of a presumption "founded on principles and policies rationally related to the ultimate purposes of the social order."[38] By this Kennedy-esque phrase (Anthony, that is, not John), I believe Professor Hart suggests that he is looking to the judiciary for something far grander than a new maxim of interpretation; he is essentially looking to the courts to displace the legislature as the principal definers of the purposes of the criminal justice system.

Random Thought 11—Michigan Criminal Law

Undoubtedly, my attitudes concerning the necessity of a strong criminal justice system to a free society, and the need to ensure that such a system operates effectively to identify and punish criminal perpetrators, are influenced by the nature of criminal jurisdiction within my state, Michigan. I believe that this jurisdiction is essentially reflective of criminal jurisdiction within most of the states.

As with Professor Hart, I can empathize with the federal judge reluctant to express moral sanction concerning many of the criminal offenses to which he must attend.[39] However, while "strict liability" and regulatory crimes of the sort decried by Professor Hart are hardly unknown in the states, their prosecution is far less common than in federal courts. My criminal docket of 150–200 cases each month consists overwhelmingly of crimes that are *malum in se*, what Professor Hart calls "must-nots," such as homicides, arsons, robberies, assaults, and rapes, crimes that have devastated the large cities of our state and that virtually every citizen wishes to see punished severely—crimes largely derived from the common law.[40] With only a few exceptions, Michigan, like most other states, maintains a criminal justice system focused on traditional offenses, with well-understood elements and straightforward and sensible *mens rea* requirements. Where there are interstitial gaps in the law, these tend to be fleshed out through resort to long-established common-law principles, which themselves have evolved glacially. There is little difficulty in either the bench or the public assessing moral blameworthiness with regard to the perpetrators of these crimes.[41]

Moreover, this system is reinforced by the propensity of prosecutors, subject to the constraints both of periodic election and of limited resources, to exercise their considerable discretion in prosecuting crimes most destructive of a peaceable society, those of a traditional character. There is little in the everyday work of the typical prosecutor in any one of Michigan's 83 counties, with the possible exception of drug prosecutions, that would upset most libertarians. Whatever occasional impulse the Michigan legislature may have had to emulate the federal government in the enactment of an increasing array of *malum prohibitum* offenses, and worse, to allow the enactment of such offenses by unelected officials deep within the bureaucracy, and worse still, to allow these same crimes to be investigated and prosecuted outside of the attorney general's office, the broadly decentralized corps of county prosecutors have, with few exceptions, individually exercised judgment to focus the criminal justice process on long-established criminal offenses in which persons and property are directly threatened. Although, as Professor Hart opines, such discretion may raise legitimate questions concerning the transfer of "de facto power" from the legislature to the executive in "determining what the criminal law in action shall be,"[42] its exercise has largely obviated any potential problems concerning the moral underpinnings of criminal jurisdiction in Michigan.

With only a few exceptions, the docket of the Michigan Supreme Court remains focused on the same kinds of offenses that its predecessors were focused on 50 or 100 years ago—crimes in which, to paraphrase Cato Institute Executive Vice President David Boaz, perpetrators have "hit other people, taken other people's stuff, and failed to keep their promises."[43] These are laws that enhance individual freedom and promote domestic tranquility. The people of Michigan are entitled to have these crimes taken seriously by their courts, and, unlike the federal judge described by Professor Hart, I am quite convinced that there is a full measure of moral blameworthiness placed on those who commit these crimes.

Random Thought 12—Constitutional Departures as the Problem, Not the Solution

It is telling, as I have noted, that elected county prosecutors in Michigan, as well I would suspect elsewhere, have, almost without exception, exercised their discretion by a nearly exclusive emphasis on traditional crimes. What this suggests is that the people themselves are not a significant impetus for a criminal justice system unmoored from its historical foundations. Where the people are able to speak most directly concerning the priorities of their criminal justice system, they have focused on the prosecution of common-law crimes. In Michigan, it is not at all uncommon for county prosecutors to be defeated for reelection, and it is, therefore, not merely of academic interest to prosecutors what their constituents believe ought to be the emphasis of the justice system. Thus, the role of the citizenry is, I believe, one very real bulwark against the prosecution of "new" crimes. That Professor Hart recognized this is reflected in his observation that "the criminal law always loses face if things are declared to be crimes which people believe they ought to be free to do even willfully."[44]

This sense of the citizenry is also reflected in the nature of the substantive criminal law initiatives of their representatives in state legislatures. Even today, after decades in which the criminal law trends deplored by Professor Hart have taken hold, when the Michigan legislature enacts new criminal laws, these tend overwhelmingly to involve the imposition of more severe punishments for traditional *malum in se* offenses or the enactment of essentially redundant, but more narrowly focused, criminal statutes, punishing what already is the subject of punishment under existing statutes (for example, a law forbidding the "arson of a school" to supplement a law forbidding the "arson of a public building" to supplement a law forbidding "arson"). Similarly, despite an ever more aggressive reliance on popular referendums, none in Michigan, to the best of my recollection, has sought to extend the criminal law beyond historic boundaries, although several have attempted to introduce a death penalty to a state that has had none since its inception.

Needless to say, this direct communication of public values becomes increasingly attenuated as government becomes more distant. When, for example, a dozen new crimes are considered by the Congress as part of an 850-page health care bill or when new crimes increasingly come to be debated within the pages of the *Federal Register*, rather than on the floor of the Congress and in the *Congressional Record*, much less within the pages of the local *Clarion Ledger*, it is not hard to understand why the voice of the people would become ever more difficult to hear.

Just as states did not run roughshod over individual rights of free speech in the 130 years before the First Amendment was incorporated, and as the states did not routinely disrespect rights of religious conscience in the 150 years before the Free Exercise Clause was incorporated, there is little evidence that the American people, where afforded the practical opportunity to directly influence their criminal justice system, have ever shown any affinity for a criminal law divorced from its common-law roots. Those who believe that rights can be protected only by elevating these to constitutional status, and by conferring decisionmaking on judges, overestimate the role of courts in protecting individual rights and underestimate the role of the people themselves, and their representative bodies, in doing the same.

Thus, despite substantive agreement with Professor Hart, I do not view the solution to the problem of "new crimes" as being the further distortion of constitutional law, with courts asserting authority properly belonging to other institutions of the government.

Instead, I believe that *present* constitutional distortions have contributed significantly to the problem identified by Professor Hart in the first place. As he recognizes, the distortion of what constitutes a crime is disproportionately an aspect of the *federal* criminal justice system, which has been steadily deployed since Professor Hart authored his article in enacting new laws in areas of traditional state authority and in creating an increasingly broad swath of concurrent criminal jurisdiction.[45] Broader understandings of the Commerce Clause and the Enforcement Clauses of the Reconstruction amendments have led the Congress to enact criminal laws in a wide range of areas formerly within the exclusive jurisdiction of the states. Many of the new regulatory and strict-liability crimes tend to fall precisely within this realm of expanded jurisdiction.

As Professor Hart further recognized, the distortion of what constitutes a crime is also disproportionately a function of new regulatory "crimes" created by the Congress and by administrative and executive branch agencies. These crimes are largely a function of the exercise of essentially legislative powers by something other than the legislative branch of government. The Congress enacts a regulatory statute and punishes "whoever violates any provision of this statute or any rule or regulation issued thereunder," and the administering agency proceeds thereafter to issue rules and regulations, each of which is potentially punishable as a crime. In my judgment, this is plainly a distortion of a constitutional system in which *all* legislative power "shall be vested in a Congress of the United States."[46] One need not be a constitutional fundamentalist to question the propriety of an unelected and unaccountable bureaucracy issuing reams of rules and regulations, with each, in turn, becoming subject to punishment by the criminal law.

Instead of urging the restoration of some semblance of constitutional limits on Congress's commerce power,[47] or some greater measure of deference to the traditional criminal authority of the states, or some restored respect for the proposition that the powers of the national government are limited under the Tenth Amendment to those "delegated to the United States" by the Constitution, or some reconsideration of the propriety of Congress according carte blanche authority to bureaucracies to define crimes outside of the legislative process, Professor Hart instead proposes to broaden the authority of the judiciary to intervene in matters until now within the province

169

of legislatures. He, thus, proposes to remedy an existing constitutional imbalance by introducing a new constitutional imbalance. Like too many reformers, he is focused on a single problem and will transform institutions to rectify this problem, whatever the other effects caused by this transformation.

Departures from principles have consequences, and it seems more than serendipity that departures from the Founders' conceptions of federalism, the separation of powers, and limited government have had the particular consequence of dismantling traditional barriers on the creation of new crimes imposed by the sensibilities of the community. It is conceivable that as government grows more distant and complex, and as it becomes less accountable through electoral processes to the oversight of ordinary people possessing an ordinary sense of justice, that the sensibilities of others may become more important—the sensibilities of members of Congress whose vote percentages may vary in good and bad years between the low and high 70s, the sensibilities of interested regulators, the sensibilities of those committed to using the more "efficient" powers of a centralized federal government in place of the dispersed powers of the 50 states, and the sensibilities of congressional and administrative staff determined to leave their own personal legacies.

I would be remiss if I did not also mention one other aspect, in my judgment, of Professor Hart confusing the solution with the problem. It is one theme of his article that, while the legislative branch has a role in the correction of the criminal law, courts in particular must demonstrate greater leadership. What may most immediately strike some contemporary readers of these exhortations is that the Supreme Court has practically become the only institution of government capable of providing "leadership" concerning the American criminal justice system. Over the past 50 years, the American criminal justice system has become increasingly centralized and uniform as a result of Supreme Court decisions constitutionalizing the most important aspects of the criminal justice process. The Michigan Supreme Court, and other state tribunals and legislatures, can do relatively little outside narrow parameters to experiment and innovate with regard to the justice system. Once again, it should not be surprising that departures from traditional constitutional understandings of federalism and the separation of powers should have consequences, in this instance in the stunting of state criminal justice reform. The criminal trial in Kalamazoo has become essentially indistinguishable from the criminal trial in Providence or Fayetteville, the array of criminal punishments and the preconditions for such punishments in Battle Creek have become largely identical to those in Biloxi and Tacoma, and the creativity of the legislative process in Lansing has been dampened by the constitutional standards that apply in all important particulars to Des Moines and Albany in the same fashion. There is simply little room for any judicial institution to exercise a "leadership" role in light of the deadening central direction that the Supreme Court has imposed for the past half-century, the "one-size-fits-all" straitjacket of the Court's criminal justice policies.

Just as *Roe v. Wade* curtailed what was once a vibrant and vigorous debate in the states on abortion, so too has debate (that is, the exercise of self-government) been largely stifled on criminal justice matters by the Supreme Court's constitutionalization of criminal procedure, eroding both judicial federalism and the role of the legislatures.[48] Despite the primary role played by the states since our country's founding in the administration of the criminal law, each session of the Michigan Legislature seems increasingly devoid of serious consideration of consequential criminal justice matters, of bold initiatives, of far-reaching reforms, of experimental and demonstration projects—this despite the devastating impact of violent crime on the quality of life in Michigan's largest cities. The Supreme Court has simply preempted all other public institutions and conferred upon itself exclusive rights to the kind of "leadership" urged by Professor Hart.

Conclusion

Professor Hart raises questions about the criminal law that remain important today. "Why? why? why?" may persons be "convicted of crime under the Constitution of the United States even though they 'may have had no awareness of what the law required or that what they did was wrongdoing?'"[49] The answer may simply be, "Neither the Founders nor subsequent generations thought much about this and it has only lately become a problem," or perhaps, "Neither the Founders nor subsequent generations agreed with Professor Hart that this was much of a problem," or possibly, "Neither the Founders nor subsequent generations thought this was a problem

IN THE NAME OF JUSTICE

of a type that must be resolved by the Constitution." Whatever the correct answer, what seems clear is that, despite Professor Hart's preferences, the Constitution does not appear to say much about the substantive definition of the criminal law. It essentially leaves decisions in this realm, as it does most public policy decisions, to the people acting through their elected legislators. Although there is no doubt that Professor Hart has a great deal that is wise to say about the criminal law, it is the people and their representatives whom he must address, not merely a handful of judges who have already usurped a sufficient portion of the federal and state legislative powers.

Appendix A.

The Federal Prosecutor

Robert H. Jackson*

It would probably be within the range of that exaggeration permitted in Washington to say that assembled in this room is one of the most powerful peacetime forces known to our country. The prosecutor has more control over life, liberty, and reputation than any other person in America. His discretion is tremendous. He can have citizens investigated and, if he is that kind of person, he can have this done to the tune of public statements and veiled or unveiled intimations. Or the prosecutor may choose a more subtle course and simply have a citizen's friends interviewed. The prosecutor can order arrests, present cases to the grand jury in secret session, and, on the basis of his one-sided presentation of the facts, can cause the citizen to be indicted and held for trial. He may dismiss the case before trial, in which case the defense never has a chance to be heard. Or he may go on with a public trial. If he obtains a conviction, the prosecutor can still make recommendations as to sentence, as to whether the prisoner should get probation or a suspended sentence, and after he is put away, as to whether he is a fit subject for parole. While the prosecutor at his best is one of the most beneficent forces in our society, when he acts from malice or other base motives, he is one of the worst.

These powers have been granted to our law-enforcement agencies because it seems necessary that such a power to prosecute be lodged somewhere. This authority has been granted by people who really

* This 1940 address by then-attorney general Robert Jackson, was delivered to the Second Annual Conference of United States Attorneys. Reprinted by special permission of Northwestern University School of Law, *The Journal of Criminal Law and Criminology*.

wanted the right thing done—wanted crime eliminated—but also wanted the best in our American traditions preserved.

Because of this immense power to strike at citizens, not with mere individual strength but with all the force of government itself, the post of federal district attorney from the very beginning has been safeguarded by presidential appointment, requiring confirmation of the Senate of the United States. You are thus required to win an expression of confidence in your character by both the legislative and the executive branches of the government before assuming the responsibilities of a federal prosecutor.

Your responsibility in your several districts for law enforcement and for its methods cannot be wholly surrendered to Washington, and ought not to be assumed by a centralized Department of Justice. It is an unusual and rare instance in which the local district attorney should be superseded in the handling of litigation, except where he requests help of Washington. It is also clear that with his knowledge of local sentiment and opinion, his contact with and intimate knowledge of the views of the court, and his acquaintance with the feelings of the group from which jurors are drawn, it is an unusual case in which his judgment should be overruled.

Experience, however, has demonstrated that some measure of centralized control is necessary. In the absence of it different district attorneys were striving for different interpretations or applications of an act, or were pursuing different conceptions of policy. Also, to put it mildly, there were differences in the degree of diligence and zeal in different districts. To promote uniformity of policy and action, to establish some standards of performance, and to make available specialized help, some degree of centralized administration was found necessary.

Our problem, of course, is to balance these opposing considerations. I desire to avoid any lessening of the prestige and influence of the district attorneys in their districts. At the same time we must proceed in all districts with that uniformity of policy which is necessary to the prestige of federal law.

Nothing better can come out of this meeting of law enforcement officers than a rededication to the spirit of fair play and decency that should animate the federal prosecutor. Your positions are of such independence and importance that while you are being diligent, strict, and vigorous in law enforcement you can also afford to be just. Although the government technically loses its case, it has really won if justice has been done. The lawyer in public office is justified in seeking to leave behind him a good record. But he must remember that his most alert and severe, but just, judges will be the members of his own profession, and that lawyers rest their good opinion of each other not merely on results accomplished but on the quality of the performance. Reputation has been called "the shadow cast by one's daily life." Any prosecutor who risks his day-to-day professional name for fair dealing to build up statistics of success has a perverted sense of practical values, as well as defects of character. Whether one seeks promotion to a judgeship, as many prosecutors rightly do, or whether he returns to private practice, he can have no better asset than to have his profession recognize that his attitude toward those who feel his power has been dispassionate, reasonable, and just.

The federal prosecutor has now been prohibited from engaging in political activities. I am convinced that a good-faith acceptance of the spirit and letter of that doctrine will relieve many district attorneys from the embarrassment of what have heretofore been regarded as legitimate expectations of political service. There can also be no doubt that to be closely identified with the intrigue, the money raising, and the machinery of a particular party or faction may present a prosecuting officer with embarrassing alignments and associations. I think the Hatch Act should be utilized by federal prosecutors as a protection against demands on their time and their prestige to participate in the operation of the machinery of practical politics.

There is a most important reason why the prosecutor should have, as nearly as possible, a detached and impartial view of all groups in his community. Law enforcement is not automatic. It isn't blind. One of the greatest difficulties of the position of prosecutor is that he must pick his cases, because no prosecutor can even investigate all of the cases in which he receives complaints. If the Department of Justice were to make even a pretense of reaching every probable violation of federal law, ten times its present staff would be inadequate. We know that no local police force can strictly enforce the traffic laws, or it would arrest half the driving population on any given morning. What every prosecutor is practically required to do is to select the cases for prosecution and to select those in which the

175

offense is the most flagrant, the public harm the greatest, and the proof the most certain.

If the prosecutor is obliged to choose his cases, it follows that he can choose his defendants. Therein is the most dangerous power of the prosecutor: that he will pick people that he thinks he should get, rather than pick cases that need to be prosecuted. With the law books filled with a great assortment of crimes, a prosecutor stands a fair chance of finding at least a technical violation of some act on the part of almost anyone. In such a case, it is not a question of discovering the commission of a crime and then looking for the man who has committed it, it is a question of picking the man and then searching the law books, or putting investigators to work, to pin some offense on him. It is in this realm—in which the prosecutor picks some person whom he dislikes or desires to embarrass, or selects some group of unpopular persons and then looks for an offense, that the greatest danger of abuse of prosecuting power lies. It is here that law enforcement becomes personal, and the real crime becomes that of being unpopular with the predominant or governing group, being attached to the wrong political views, or being personally obnoxious to or in the way of the prosecutor himself.

In times of fear or hysteria, political, racial, religious, social, and economic groups, often from the best of motives, cry for the scalps of individuals or groups because they do not like their views. Particularly do we need to be dispassionate and courageous in those cases which deal with so-called "subversive activities." They are dangerous to civil liberty because the prosecutor has no definite standards to determine what constitutes a "subversive activity," such as we have for murder or larceny. Activities which seem benevolent and helpful to wage earners, persons on relief, or those who are disadvantaged in the struggle for existence may be regarded as "subversive" by those whose property interests might be burdened or affected thereby. Those who are in office are apt to regard as "subversive" the activities of any of those who would bring about a change of administration. Some of our soundest constitutional doctrines were once punished as subversive. We must not forget that it was not so long ago that both the term "Republican" and the term "Democrat" were epithets with sinister meaning to denote persons of radical tendencies that were "subversive" of the order of things then dominant.

In the enforcement of laws which protect our national integrity and existence, we should prosecute any and every act of violation, but only *overt* acts, not the expression of opinion, or activities such as the holding of meetings, petitioning of Congress, or dissemination of news or opinions. Only by extreme care can we protect the spirit as well as the letter of our civil liberties, and to do so is a responsibility of the federal prosecutor.

Another delicate task is to distinguish between the federal and the local in law-enforcement activities. We must bear in mind that we are concerned only with the prosecution of acts which the Congress has made federal offenses. Those acts we should prosecute regardless of local sentiment, regardless of whether it exposes lax local enforcement, regardless of whether it makes or breaks local politicians.

But outside of federal law each locality has the right under our system of government to fix its own standards of law enforcement and of morals. And the moral climate of the United States is as varied as its physical climate. For example, some states legalize and permit gambling, some states prohibit it legislatively and protect it administratively, and some try to prohibit it entirely. The same variation of attitudes towards other law-enforcement problems exists. The federal government could not enforce one kind of law in one place and another kind elsewhere. It could hardly adopt strict standards for loose states or loose standards for strict states without doing violence to local sentiment. In spite of the temptation to divert our power to local conditions where they have become offensive to our sense of decency, the only long-term policy that will save federal justice from being discredited by entanglements with local politics is that it confine itself to strict and impartial enforcement of federal law, letting the chips fall in the community where they may. Just as there should be no permitting of local considerations to stop federal enforcement, so there should be no striving to enlarge our power over local affairs and no use of federal prosecutions to exert an indirect influence that would be unlawful if exerted directly.

The qualities of a good prosecutor are as elusive and as impossible to define as those which mark a gentleman. And those who need to be told would not understand it anyway. A sensitiveness to fair play and sportsmanship is perhaps the best protection against the abuse of power, and the citizen's safety lies in the prosecutor who tempers zeal with human kindness, who seeks truth and not victims, who serves the law and not factional purposes, and who approaches his task with humility.

Appendix B.

Crime

Milton and Rose Friedman*

Lost is our old simplicity of times,
The world abounds with laws, and teems with crimes.
—Anonymous, "On the Proceedings against America" (1775)

The rising incidence of crime is surely one of the most troubling problems bedeviling American society in recent years. As government has undertaken more and more responsibilities, it has been performing one of its basic functions less and less well. If the first duty of a government is to defend the country against foreign enemies, the second duty is to prevent the coercion of one person by another and to provide security for its citizens and their property.

We are far richer today than in earlier days. We should be better able to secure person and property than we could when fewer resources were available to the nation. Yet the situation is the reverse. Crime has been rising. The average citizen feels less secure than at almost any time in the past hundred years.

We believe that the growth of government in recent decades and the rising incidence of crime in those same decades are largely two sides of the same coin. Crime has risen not *despite* government's growth but largely *because* of government's growth.

The number of violent crimes of all kinds has literally exploded in the past few decades. In 1957—the first year for which we have data—violent crimes of all kinds numbered 199,000. From then to 1980 they multiplied more than sixfold, reaching 1,309,000. Allowing for the increase in population, the rate per 100,000 persons multiplied

---

* This essay is reprinted with permission from *Tyranny of the Status Quo* (Orlando, FL: Harcourt Brace Jovanovich, 1984).

fivefold from 117 to 581. Over the same period, crimes against property increased even more rapidly, the rate per 100,000 persons multiplying more than sevenfold from 719 to 5,319.

Over the same period, public expenditures on law enforcement went from $2.7 billion to $25.9 billion, multiplying nearly tenfold. Since prices rose nearly threefold and population rose by one-third, expenditures on law enforcement per capita rose nearly threefold after allowing for inflation. Clearly, throwing money at the problem has been no more effective in curbing crime than in improving education, or in achieving the fine objectives of the long list of social programs that have been undertaken over those decades. The number of arrests has also risen sharply—from 2 million in 1957 to nearly 10 million in 1980. The rise in the number of arrests simply reflected the rise in the number of crimes committed, not a growing efficiency of law enforcement—the reported number of crimes grew even more rapidly than the number of arrests.

Why the Increase in Crime?

We are not criminologists. Criminologists themselves have no simple and easy explanations of the rapid increase in crime. Nonetheless, some popular explanations can be rejected out of hand, and some partial explanations are highly persuasive.

One popular explanation for crime is poverty and inequality. People are driven to steal, to rob, to murder because they have no other means to avoid hunger and deprivation. Or they are driven to crime because of the spectacle of rich versus poor, a spectacle that feeds a sense of injustice and unfairness, not to speak of the less admirable motive of envy. However plausible this explanation is of why some people turn to crime, it obviously cannot explain the *rise* in crime over recent decades in the United States. As a nation we are wealthier than we were fifty, seventy-five, or a hundred years ago, and that wealth is, if anything, more evenly distributed. Moreover, there is less poverty and less inequality in the United States than in many other countries. Poverty is certainly more prevalent, more degrading, more intolerable in India than in the United States, and unquestionably the spectacle of rich versus poor is more blatant. Yet, there is less chance of being mugged or robbed on the streets of Bombay or Calcutta at night than on the streets of New York or Chicago.

A closely related view is that the actual degree of poverty or the actual degree of inequality is less important than the *perceptions* of potential criminals, and that those perceptions have been greatly affected in the United States by some of the very technological developments that have been most responsible for the increasing well-being of the population at large, notably in communication and transportation—television, radio, and the like. Television programs, it is said, provide a picture of a lifestyle that the poor cannot hope to achieve by honest labor, yet is presented as something that everyone has a right to or that everyone can attain.

No doubt such perceptions do contribute to crime. After all, it would be inconsistent to regard the advertising that television carries for products as effective but ignore as ineffective the advertising that it carries for lifestyles and moral standards. Nonetheless, we find it hard to believe that a change in perceptions is more than a minor contributing cause of the enormous expansion in crime that has occurred in the past few decades.

Two factors seem to us more important. One is the change in the climate of opinion, since the time of the New Deal, about the role of the individual and the role of government. That change shifted emphasis from individual responsibility to societal responsibility. It encouraged the view that people are the creatures of their environment and should not be held responsible for their behavior. In its extreme form, the view is that there is no such thing as "crime," that what is called criminal activity is a form of "illness" that calls for treatment rather than punishment.

If people who are poor hold the view that poverty is not their own fault but the fault of society at large, then it is perfectly understandable that their reaction is "Since society is responsible for my poverty, I have every right to act against society and to take what I need or want." Similarly, if they come to believe that the well-to-do whom they see on TV, or observe in high-income neighborhoods, are well-to-do not because of their own efforts—not because they worked hard or saved or in some way contributed to society—but simply because they happened to draw winning tickets in a social lottery, then it is easy to understand their believing that nothing is wrong in correcting the outcome of that lottery by taking property from others.

A closely associated development has been the change in the character of the family. Statistics on divorce, one-parent families, and illegitimate births demonstrate that the nuclear family is losing its traditional role. The family no longer serves as fully as it once did as an integrative institution, as a vehicle for instilling values and developing standards of behavior. Nothing has taken its place. As a result, an increasing number of our youth grow up without any firm values, with little understanding of "right" and "wrong," with few convictions that will discipline their appetites. This is all the more significant, as criminologists have long emphasized, because crime is disproportionately an activity of the young.

Another development that has unquestionably contributed to the rise in crime is the multiplication of laws and rules and regulations. *These have multiplied the number of actions that are crimes.* It is literally impossible for anyone to obey all the laws, since no one can possibly know what they are. Similarly, it is literally impossible for the legal authorities to enforce all the laws equally and without discrimination. To do so, the whole population would have to be employed to police itself. As a result, enforcement of the laws invariably becomes partly a matter of which laws the authorities choose to enforce and against whom—a situation hardly designed to encourage respect for the majesty of the law. We said in *Free to Choose:*

> When the law contradicts what most people regard as moral and proper, they will break the law—whether the law is enacted in the name of a noble ideal ... or in the naked interest of one group at the expense of another. Only fear of punishment, not a sense of justice and morality, will lead people to obey the law.
>
> When people start to break one set of laws, the lack of respect for the law inevitably spreads to all laws, even those that everyone regards as moral and proper—laws against violence, theft, and vandalism.[1]

What to Do about It

Criminologists and others have made many suggestions for altering procedures for apprehending criminals, for indicting them, convicting them, sentencing them, incarcerating them, and so on. Many have urged controlling guns and other weapons to reduce their availability. We have no competence to discuss these proposed remedies. Instead, we can comment only on those aspects of the problem that are tied to our general theme of the importance of reducing government in order to promote the general welfare.

182

If we are right that the tide is turning, that public opinion is shifting away from a belief in big government and away from the doctrine of social responsibility, then that change will in the course of time tend to alter the circumstances to which we attribute much of the rise in crime. In particular, it will tend to restore a belief in individual responsibility by strengthening the family and reestablishing its traditional role in instilling values in the young.

Moreover, if there is a change in the tide, it will produce some institutional changes that will also contribute to a reduction in crime. In particular, the adoption of vouchers for schooling could have a major effect. It would offer the disadvantaged who now populate the urban slums greater educational opportunities for their children, giving them a wider and more desirable range of alternatives than street crime. However, any such institutional effects will take a long time to yield their fruits—decades, not years.

One set of changes that could yield relatively rapid results is a reduction in the acts that are regarded by the law as crimes. The most promising measure of this kind is with respect to drugs. Most crimes are not committed by people hungry for bread. By far more are committed by people hungry for dope. Should we have learned a lesson from Prohibition? When Prohibition was enacted in 1920, Billy Sunday, the noted evangelist and leading crusader against Demon Rum, greeted it as follows: "The reign of tears is over. The slums will soon be only a memory. We will turn our prisons into factories and our jails into storehouses and corncribs. Men will walk upright now, women will smile, and the children will laugh. Hell will be forever for rent." We know now how tragically wrong he was. New prisons and jails had to be built to house the criminals spawned by converting the drinking of spirits into a crime against the state. Prohibition undermined respect for the law, corrupted the minions of the law, and created a decadent moral climate—and in the end did not stop the consumption of alcohol.

Despite this tragic object lesson, we seem bent on repeating precisely the same mistake in handling drugs. There is no disagreement about some of the facts. Excessive drinking of alcohol harms the drinker; excessive smoking of cigarettes harms the smoker; excessive use of drugs harms the drug user. As among the three, awful as it is to make such comparisons, there is little doubt that smoking and drinking kill far more people than the use of drugs.

All three actions also have adverse effects on people *other than those who drink or smoke or use drugs.* Drunken driving accounts for a large number of all traffic accidents and traffic fatalities. Smoking harms nonsmoking occupants of the same aircraft, the same restaurant, the same public places. Drug users cause accidents when driving or when at work. According to a *Newsweek* article, "employees who use drugs on the job are one-third less productive than straight workers, three times as likely to be injured and absent far more often. . . . Starved, strung-out and coked-up employees affect the morale in the office, scare away customers and hurt the quality of the shirts you wear, the cars you drive and the building you work in."

Whenever we evaluate a government action, we must consider both whether the intended results of that action are ones that it is proper for government to seek to achieve and, further, whether the action will, in fact, achieve these results. The facts about alcohol, tobacco, and drugs raise two very different issues: one of ethics and one of expediency. The ethical question is whether we have the right to use the machinery of government to prevent individuals from drinking, smoking, or using drugs. Almost everyone would answer at least a qualified yes with respect to children. Almost everyone would answer an unqualified yes with respect to preventing users of alcohol or tobacco or drugs from inflicting harm on third parties. But with respect to the addicts themselves, the answer is far less clear. Surely, it is important and appropriate to reason with a potential addict, to tell him the consequences, to pray for, and with, him. But do we have the right to use force directly or indirectly to prevent a fellow adult from drinking, smoking, or using drugs? Our own answer is no. But we readily grant that the ethical issue is a difficult one and that men of goodwill often disagree.

Fortunately, we do not have to resolve the ethical issue to agree on policy because the answer to whether government action *can* prevent addiction is so clear. Prohibition—whether of drinking, smoking, or using drugs—is an attempted cure that in our judgment makes matters worse both for the addict and for the rest of us. Hence, even if you regard government measures to prohibit the taking of drugs as ethically justified, we believe that you will find that considerations of expediency make it unwise to adopt such measures.

Consider first the addict. Legalizing drugs might increase the number of addicts, though it is not certain that it would. Forbidden fruit is attractive, particularly to the young. More important, many persons are deliberately made into drug addicts by pushers, who now give likely prospects their first few doses free. It pays the pusher to do so because, once hooked, the addict is a captive customer. If drugs were legally available, any possible profit from such inhumane activity would largely disappear, since the addict could buy from a cheaper source.

Whatever happens to the total number of addicts—and the possible increase of that number—the *individual* addict would clearly be far better off if drugs were legal. Today, drugs are both extremely expensive and highly uncertain in quality. Addicts are driven to associate with criminals to get the drugs, and they become criminals themselves to finance the habit. They risk constant danger of death and disease.

Consider, next, the rest of us. The harm to us from the addiction of others arises primarily from the fact that drugs are illegal. It has been estimated that from one third to one half of all violent and property crime in the United States is committed either by drug addicts engaged in crime to finance their habit, or by conflicts among competing groups of drug pushers, or in the course of the importation and distribution of illegal drugs. Legalize drugs, and street crime would drop dramatically and immediately. Moreover, addicts and pushers are not the only ones corrupted. Immense sums are at stake. It is inevitable that some relatively low-paid police and other government officials—and some high-paid ones as well—succumb to the temptation to pick up easy money.

The clearest case is marijuana, the use of which has been becoming sufficiently widespread to mimic the pattern that developed under the prohibition of alcohol. In California, marijuana has become either the largest, or second largest, cash crop. In large areas of the state, law enforcement personnel wink at the growers and harvesters of marijuana in much the same way as law enforcement officials did at moonshiners and bootleggers in the 1920s. Special squads must be set up to fly the helicopters that locate marijuana fields and to make the raids that destroy them, just as in the 1920s, special squads were set up to enforce the prohibition of alcohol. And just as bootleggers had to protect themselves in the 1920s from hijackers, so now the marijuana growers must protect their illegal crop themselves. They post armed guards to protect the growing fields. Gun battles inevitably result, as they did under Prohibition.

Under Prohibition, both bootleggers and do-it-yourselfers producing bathtub gin sometimes used wood alcohol or other substances that made the product a powerful poison, leading to the injury and sometimes death of those who drank it. Currently, the same thing is happening in an even more reprehensible fashion. The U.S. government itself has persuaded some foreign governments to use airplanes to spray paraquat—a dangerous poison—on growing marijuana fields. It has itself done so in Georgia. The purpose is to make the marijuana unusable. But there is no way, apparently, to prevent some of the contaminated marijuana from coming on the market and harming those who use it. And there is no certainty that the aim of the helicopter pilots is sufficiently accurate to guarantee that no paraquat falls on plants other than marijuana.

There would be a tremendous outcry if it were known that government officials had deliberately poisoned some of the food eaten by convicted criminals. Surely, it is a far more heinous and utterly unjustifiable practice to spread poison deliberately over crops likely to harm citizens who may or may not be innocent of breaking a law and who have never had their day in court.

Some proponents of the legalization of marijuana have argued that smoking marijuana does not cause harm. We are not competent to judge this much debated issue—though we find persuasive the evidence we have seen that marijuana is a harmful substance. Yet, paradoxical though it may seem, our belief that it is desirable to legalize marijuana and all other drugs does not depend on whether marijuana or other drugs are harmful or harmless. However much harm drugs do to those who use them, it is our considered opinion that seeking to prohibit their use does even more harm both to users of drugs and to the rest of us.

Legalizing drugs would simultaneously reduce the amount of crime and improve law enforcement. It is hard to conceive of any other single measure that would accomplish so much to promote law and order. But, you may say, must we accept defeat? Why not simply end the drug traffic? That is where experience both with Prohibition and, in recent years, with drugs is most relevant. We cannot *end* the drug traffic. We may be able to cut off opium from Turkey—but the opium poppy grows in innumerable other places. With French cooperation, we may be able to make Marseilles an unhealthy place to manufacture heroin—but the simple manufacturing operations can be carried out in innumerable other places. We may be able to persuade Mexico to spray or allow us to spray marijuana fields with paraquat—but marijuana can be grown almost everywhere. We may be able to cooperate with Colombia to reduce the entry of cocaine—but success is not easy to attain in a country where the export is a large factor in the economy. So long as large sums of money are involved—and they are bound to be if drugs are illegal—it is literally impossible to stop the traffic, or even to make a serious reduction in its scope.

In drugs, as in other areas, persuasion and example are likely to be far more effective than the use of force to shape others in our image.

Drug use is not the only area where crime could be reduced by legalizing activities that are now illegal, but it surely is the most obvious and the most important. Our emphasis here is based not only on the growing seriousness of drug-related crimes, but also on the belief that relieving our police and our courts from having to fight losing battles against drugs will enable their energies and facilities to be devoted more fully to combating other forms of crime. We could thus strike a double blow: reduce crime activity directly, and at the same time increase the efficacy of law enforcement and crime prevention.

Appendix C.

An Address to the American Bar Association Annual Meeting

*Anthony M. Kennedy**

Mayor Willie Brown, President Alfred Carlton, President-elect Dennis Archer, and my fellow adherents to the rule of law. Thank you for your gracious welcome and for your friendship.

Since we last met in San Francisco, momentous and tragic events have occurred. Some say these events changed the world. Perhaps it is more accurate to say the world is the same, but we now have a clearer understanding of what the world is. It is a world where in every nation many people seek freedom above all, but where new enemies of freedom vow to attack it. In a sense this is nothing new. In the last century, free societies were attacked from within, attacked by their own citizens, by men such as Stalin, Hitler, and Mussolini. They attacked free institutions because they did not believe an open society, committed to democracy, could provide for the security and welfare of its citizens. In this century, democracy's enemies come from outside the countries they seek to destroy. They, too, see a free and open society as a threat. Once again we face an assault on freedom. Once again we can prevail.

Americans may find the new challenge surprising and disappointing. We tend to think the case has been made that a free society is a stable society, that a free society is the birthright of all people. We do not know why we must make the case all over again when judgment has been given in our favor. History, however, does not acknowledge *res judicata*. History teaches that freedom must make

* This excerpt is from the August 9, 2003, speech by Anthony M. Kennedy, associate justice of the Supreme Court.

its case, again and again, from one generation to the next. The work of freedom is never done.

Embedded in democracy is the idea of progress. Democracy addresses injustice and corrects it. The progress is not automatic. It requires a sustained exercise of political will, and political will is shaped by rational public discourse. One of the ABA's missions is to stimulate that discourse.

The impressive, pluralistic assembly of the American Bar Association reflects many groups and interests in our society. That is fortunate, for a disproportionate share of the responsibility for moving toward progress in public affairs falls, in the first instance at least, on those who are trained in the law. The Bar is an essential catalyst for the discourse we must commence to come closer to a more just society.

The subject of prisons and corrections may tempt some of you to tune out. You may think, "Well, I am not a criminal lawyer. The prison system is not my problem. I might tune in again when he gets to a different subject." In my submission you have the duty to stay tuned. The subject is the concern and responsibility of every member of our profession and of every citizen. This is your justice system; these are your prisons. The Gospel's promise of mitigation at judgment if a convicted felon can say, "I was in prison, and ye came unto me," does not contain an exemption for civil practitioners, or transactional lawyers, or for any other citizen. And, as I will suggest, the energies and diverse talents of the entire Bar are needed to address this matter.

Even those of us who have specific professional responsibilities for the criminal justice system can be neglectful when it comes to the subject of corrections. The focus of the legal profession, perhaps even the obsessive focus, has been on the process for determining guilt or innocence. When someone has been judged guilty and the appellate and collateral review process has ended, the legal profession seems to lose all interest. When the prisoner is taken way, our attention turns to the next case. When the door is locked against the prisoner, we do not think about what is behind it.

We have a greater responsibility. As a profession, and as a people, we should know what happens after the prisoner is taken away. To be sure the prisoner has violated the social contract; to be sure he must be punished to vindicate the law, to acknowledge the suffering of the victim, and to deter future crimes. Still, the prisoner is a person; still, he or she is part of the family of humankind.

Were we to enter the hidden world of punishment, we should be startled by what we see. Consider its remarkable scale. The nationwide inmate population today is about 2.1 million people. In California, even as we meet, this state alone keeps over 160,000 persons behind bars. In countries such as England, Italy, France, and Germany, the incarceration rate is about 1 in 1,000 persons. In the United States it is about 1 in 143.

We must confront another reality. Nationwide, more than 40 percent of the prison population consists of African-American inmates. About 10 percent of African-American men in their mid-to-late 20s are behind bars. In some cities more than 50 percent of young African-American men are under the supervision of the criminal justice system.

While economic costs, defined in simple dollar terms, are secondary to human costs, they do illustrate the scale of the criminal justice system. The cost of housing, feeding, and caring for the inmate population in the United States is over 40 billion dollars per year. In the State of California alone, the cost of maintaining each inmate in the correctional system is about $26,000 per year. And despite the high expenditures in prison, there remain urgent, unmet needs in the prison system.

To compare prison costs with the cost of educating school children is, to some extent, to compare apples with oranges, because the state must assume the full burden of housing, subsistence, and medical care for prisoners. Yet the statistics are troubling. When it costs so much more to incarcerate a prisoner than to educate a child, we should take special care to ensure that we are not incarcerating too many persons for too long.

It requires one with more expertise in the area than I possess to offer a complete analysis, but it does seem justified to say this: Our resources are misspent, our punishments too severe, our sentences too long.

In the federal system the sentencing guidelines are responsible in part for the increase in prison terms. In my view the guidelines were, and are, necessary. Before they were in place, a wide disparity existed among the sentences given by different judges, and even among sentences given by a single judge. As my colleague Justice

Stephen Breyer has pointed out, however, the compromise that led to the guidelines led also to an increase in the length of prison terms. We should revisit this compromise. The Federal Sentencing Guidelines should be revised downward.

By contrast to the guidelines, I can accept neither the necessity nor the wisdom of federal mandatory minimum sentences. In too many cases, mandatory minimum sentences are unwise and unjust.

Consider this case: A young man with no previous serious offense is stopped on the George Washington Memorial Parkway near Washington, D. C., by United States Park Police. He is stopped for not wearing a seatbelt. A search of the car follows and leads to the discovery of just over five grams of crack cocaine in the trunk. The young man is indicted in federal court. He faces a mandatory minimum sentence of five years. If he had taken an exit and left the federal road, his sentence likely would have been measured in terms of months, not years.

United States Marshals can recount the experience of leading a young man away from his family to begin serving his term. His mother says, "How long will my boy be gone?" They say "10 years" or "15 years." Ladies and gentlemen, I submit to you that a 20-year-old does not know how long 10 or 15 years is. One day in prison is longer than almost any day you and I have had to endure. Alexander Solzhenitsyn describes just one day in prison in the literary classic *One Day in the Life of Ivan Denisovich*. Ivan Denisovich had a 10-year sentence. At one point he multiplies the long days in these long years by 10. Here is his final reflection: "The end of an unclouded day. Almost a happy one. Just one of the three thousand six hundred and fifty-three days of his sentence, from bell to bell. The extra three were for leap years."

Under the federal mandatory minimum statutes a sentence can be mitigated by a prosecutorial decision not to charge certain counts. There is debate about this, but in my view a transfer of sentencing discretion from a judge to an assistant U. S. attorney, often not much older than the defendant, is misguided. Often these attorneys try in good faith to be fair in the exercise of discretion. The policy, nonetheless, gives the decision to an assistant prosecutor not trained in the exercise of discretion and takes discretion from the trial judge. The trial judge is the one actor in the system most experienced with exercising discretion in a transparent, open, and reasoned way. Most

192

of the sentencing discretion should be with the judge, not the prosecutors.

Professor James Whitman considers some of these matters in his recent book *Harsh Justice*.[1] He argues that one explanation for severe sentences is the coalescence of two views coming from different parts of the political spectrum. One view warns against being soft on crime; the other urges a rigid, egalitarian approach to sentence uniformity. Both views agree on severe sentences, and both agree on mandatory minimum sentences. Whatever the explanation, it is my hope that after those with experience and expertise in the criminal justice system study the matter, this Association will say to the Congress of the United States: "Please do not say in cases like these the offender must serve 5 or 10 years. Please do not use our courts but then say the judge is incapable of judging. Please, senators and representatives, repeal federal mandatory minimums."

The legislative branch has the obligation to determine whether a policy is wise. It is a grave mistake to retain a policy just because a court finds it constitutional. Courts may conclude the legislature is permitted to choose long sentences, but that does not mean long sentences are wise or just. Few misconceptions about government are more mischievous than the idea that a policy is sound simply because a court finds it permissible. A court decision does not excuse the political branches or the public from the responsibility for unjust laws.

To help those who are serving under the minimums, the ABA should consider a recommendation to reinvigorate the pardon process at the state and federal levels. The pardon process, of late, seems to have been drained of its moral force. Pardons have become infrequent. A people confident in its laws and institutions should not be ashamed of mercy. The greatest of poets reminds us that mercy is "mightiest in the mightiest. It becomes the throned monarch better than his crown."[2] I hope more lawyers involved in the pardon process will say to chief executives, "Mr. President," or "Your Excellency, the Governor, this young man has not served his full sentence, but he has served long enough. Give him what only you can give him. Give him another chance. Give him a priceless gift. Give him liberty."

The debate over the goals of sentencing is a difficult one, but we should not cease to conduct it. Prevention and incapacitation are often legitimate goals. Some classes of criminals commit scores of offenses before they are caught, so one conviction may reflect years of criminal activity. There are realistic limits to efforts at rehabilitation. We must try, however, to bridge the gap between proper skepticism about rehabilitation on the one hand and improper refusal to acknowledge that the more than two million inmates in the United States are human beings whose minds and spirits we must try to reach. We should not ignore the efforts of the countless workers and teachers and counselors who are trying to instill some self-respect and self-reliance and self-discipline in convicted offenders. Credit must be given to the dedicated persons who conduct prison education programs. Over 90 percent of state prisons and 100 percent of federal prisons offer some kind of educational program. And about one in four state prison inmates attains a general equivalency diploma while in prison.

Professor Whitman concludes that the goal of the American corrections system is to degrade and demean the prisoner. That is a grave and serious charge. A purpose to degrade or demean individuals is not acceptable in a society founded on respect for the inalienable rights of the people. No public official should echo the sentiments of the Arizona sheriff who once said with great pride that he "runs a very bad jail."

It is no defense if our current prison system is more the product of neglect than of purpose. Out of sight, out of mind is an unacceptable excuse for a prison system that incarcerates over two million human beings in the United States. To that end, I hope it is not presumptuous of me to suggest that the American Bar Association should ask its president and the president-elect to instruct the appropriate committees to study these matters, and to help start a new public discussion about the prison system. It is the duty of the American people to begin that discussion at once.

In seeking to improve our corrections system, the Bar can use the full diversity of its talents. Those of you in civil practice who have expertise in coordinating groups, finding evidence, and influencing government policies have great potential to help find more just solutions and more humane policies for those who are the least deserving of our citizens, but citizens nonetheless. A decent and free society, founded in respect for the individual, ought not to run a system with a sign at the entrance for inmates saying, "Abandon Hope, All Ye Who Enter Here."

Notes

Introduction

1. See Darryl Fears, "New Criminal Record: 7.2 Million," *Washington Post*, June 12, 2008.

2. See Erik Luna, "The Overcriminalization Phenomenon," *American University Law Review* 54 (2005): 703; Marc Galanter, "The Vanishing Trial: An Examination of Trials and Related Matters in Federal and State Courts," *Journal of Empirical Legal Studies* 1 (2004): 459.

3. Readers interested in a rigorous defense of the first principles discussed are encouraged to study the works cited in the notes to this introduction.

4. Still, the definitional problem remains, as has been noted by Professor Jeffrey S. Parker. See "The Economics of Mens Rea," Virginia Law Review 79 (1993): 741, 753 ("The vast literature that has grown up around [the work of Gary Becker does] not define crime with any rigor at all.")

5. Robert James Bidinotto advances the following definition for "crime": "any intentional non-consensual act entailing the initiation of force, fraud, or coercion against another person or persons." Robert James Bidinotto, "Crime and Moral Retribution," in *Criminal Justice? The Legal System vs. Individual Responsibility* (Irvington-on-Hudson, New York: Foundation for Economic Education, 1994), p. 193. Bidinotto's definition is close to the mark, but two clarifications seem necessary: (1) protections for children from liquor sales, drug sales, and sexual exploitation; and (2) prohibitions against certain acts that can *endanger* innocent bystanders. See Hart, "The Aims of the Criminal Law," pp. 15–22.

6. Hart, "The Aims of the Criminal Law," p. 32.

7. Quoted in Ann Hopkins, "Mens Rea and the Right to Trial by Jury," *California Law Review* 76 (1988): 391, 394 (citation omitted). See also John Calvin Jeffries, Jr. and Paul B. Stephan III, "Defenses, Presumptions, and Burden of Proof in the Criminal Law," *Yale Law Journal* 88 (1979): 1325.

8. *Lambert v. California*, 355 U.S. 225, 228 (1957).

9. Hart, "The Aims of the Criminal Law," p. 32.

10. But see *Apprendi v. New Jersey*, 530 U.S. 466 (2000) (opinion of Thomas, J.).

11. Timothy Lynch, "Ignorance of the Law: Sometimes a Valid Defense," *Legal Times*, April 4, 1994.

12. Hart, "The Aims of the Criminal Law," p. 19.

13. *United States v. Wilson*, 159 F.3d 280 (1998).

14. Ibid., p. 296 (Posner, J., dissenting).

15. Ibid. Relying on principles of statutory interpretation, Judge Posner found it unnecessary to bring in the "heavy artillery" of constitutional principles. In contrast, Hart believed it was a grave mistake for the judiciary to let that artillery remain warehoused. See Hart, "The Aims of the Criminal Law," pp. 30–35.

16. Stephen J. Adler and Wade Lambert, "Common Criminals: Just About Everyone Violates Some Laws, Even Model Citizens," *Wall Street Journal*, March 12, 1993.

17. See, generally, Ronald A. Cass, "Ignorance of the Law: A Maxim Reexamined," *William and Mary Law Review* 17 (1976): 671.

18. *Connally v. General Construction Company*, 269 U.S. 385, 393 (1926) (internal quotation marks omitted).

19. *Papachristou v. City of Jacksonville*, 405 U.S. 156, 162-163 (1972).

20. James Madison, "Federalist Paper 62," in *The Federalist Papers*, ed. Clinton Rossiter (New York: New American Library, 1961), p. 381.

21. See Robert A. Anthony, "Unlegislated Compulsion: How Federal Agency Guidelines Threaten Your Liberty," Cato Institute Policy Analysis no. 312, August 11, 1998.

22. William L. Gardner and Adam H. Steinman, "'Knowing' Remains the Key Word," *National Law Journal*, September 2, 1991, p. 28.

23. Quoted in William P. Kucewicz, "Grime and Punishment," *ECO* (June 1993): 54.

24. Wayne R. LaFave and Austin W. Scott Jr., *Criminal Law*, 2nd. ed. (St. Paul, MN: West Publishing Co., 1986), pp. 193–94.

25. Quoted in *Morissette v. United States*, 342 U.S. 246, 250 n. 4 (1952).

26. *Utah v. Blue*, 53 Pac. 978, 980 (1898).

27. *Morissette v. United States*, 342 U.S. 246, 251 (1952).

28. Richard G. Singer, "The Resurgence of *Mens Rea*: III—The Rise and Fall of Strict Criminal Liability," *Boston College Law Review* 30 (1989): 337. See also *Special Report: Federal Erosion of Business Civil Liberties* (Washington: Washington Legal Foundation, 2008).

29. *Lambert v. California*, 355 U.S. 225, 228 (1957).

30. Professor Herbert Packer argues that the creation of strict liability crimes is both inefficacious and unjust. "It is inefficacious because conduct unaccompanied by an awareness of the factors making it criminal does not mark the actor as one who needs to be subjected to punishment in order to deter him or others from behaving similarly in the future, nor does it single him out as a socially dangerous individual who needs to be incapacitated or reformed. It is unjust because the actor is subjected to the stigma of a criminal conviction without being morally blameworthy. Consequently, on either a preventative or retributive theory of criminal punishment, the criminal sanction is inappropriate in the absence of mens rea." Herbert Packer, "Mens Rea and the Supreme Court," *Supreme Court Review* (1962): 109. See also Jeffrey S. Parker, "The Economics of Mens Rea," *Virginia Law Review* 79 (1993): 741; Craig S. Lerner and Moin A. Yahya, "'Left Behind' After Sarbanes-Oxley," *American Criminal Law Review* 44 (2007): 1383.

31. Hart, "The Aims of the Criminal Law," p. 23. Proponents of strict liability would argue that there is a justification. The deterrent effect of the strict liability law outweighs the cost of stigmatizing innocent persons as "criminals" and sending them to prison. Hart's response is twofold. First, he expresses skepticism. Where, Hart wants to know, is the evidence to support the assertion? Second, even if such evidence can be mustered, Hart says that the policy calculation of sacrificing the innocent would not constitute a "moral justification." Ibid., pp. 23–25.

32. *Thorpe v. Florida*, 377 So.2d 221 (1979).

33. Ibid., p. 223. See also *United States v. Yirkovsky*, 259 F.3d 704 (2001).

34. Judge Richard Posner notes an error in Hart's article with respect to the porter prosecuted for transporting intoxicating liquor (see p. 97). As this book was going

to press, I discovered that it was, in fact, a real case. See *Oregon v. Cox*, 179 P. 575 (1919). Thus, it is safe to assume that Hart's mistake was an innocent one. He simply cited the wrong case.

35. See Wayne R. LaFave and Austin W. Scott Jr., *Criminal Law*, 2nd. ed. (St. Paul, MN: West Publishing Co., 1986), p. 212.

36. Francis Bowes Sayre, "Criminal Responsibility for the Acts of Another," *Harvard Law Review* 43 (1930): 689, 690.

37. Ibid., p. 702.

38. *United States v. Park*, 421 U.S. 658 (1975). Although many state courts have followed the reasoning of the *Park* decision with respect to their own state constitutions, some courts have recoiled from the far-reaching implications of vicarious criminal liability. For example, the Pennsylvania Supreme Court has held that "a man's liberty cannot rest on so frail a reed as whether his employee will commit a mistake in judgment." *Commonwealth v. Koczwara*, 155 A.2d 825, 830 (1959). That Pennsylvania ruling, it must be emphasized, is an aberration. It is a remnant of the common law tradition that virtually every other jurisdiction views as passé.

39. *United States v. Park*, 421 U.S. 658, 666 (1975).

40. Ibid., p. 672.

41. "[T]he willfulness or negligence of the actor [will] be imputed to him by virtue of his position of responsibility." *United States v. Brittain*, 931 F.2d 1413, 1419 (1991). See also *United States v. Johnson & Towers, Inc.*, 741 F.2d 662, 665 n. 3 (1984).

42. See Susan S. Kuo, "A Little Privacy, Please: Should We Punish Parents for Teenage Sex?" *Kentucky Law Journal* 89 (2000): 135.

43. *Bennis v. Michigan*, 516 U.S. 442 (1996).

44. *Department of Housing and Urban Development v. Rucker*, 535 U.S. 125 (2002).

45. Robyn Meredith, "Parents Convicted for a Youth's Misconduct," *New York Times*, May 10, 1996. See also Adam Liptak, "Judging a Mother for Someone Else's Crime," *New York Times*, November 27, 2007.

46. Jeffrey S. Parker, "Doctrine for Destruction: The Case of Corporate Criminal Liability," *Managerial and Decision Economics* 17 (1996): 381, 382. For additional background, see "Symposium: Corporate Criminality: Legal, Ethical, and Managerial Implications," *American Criminal Law Review* 44 (2007): 1269-1552.

47. *New York Central and Hudson River Railroad v. United States*, 212 U.S. 481 (1909).

48. Parker, "Doctrine for Destruction," p. 382.

49. See Vikramaditya S. Khanna, "Politics and Corporate Crime Legislation," *Regulation*, Spring 2004.

50. Parker, "Doctrine for Destruction," p. 393.

51. Ronald G. White and Charles L. Shaw, "'Ionia Mgmt.': Challenge to Corporate Criminal Liability," *New York Law Journal*, November 19, 2008.

52. See Robert Suro, "Rehnquist: Too Many Offenses Are Becoming Federal Crimes," *Washington Post*, January 1, 1999. See also Timothy Lynch, "Dereliction of Duty: The Constitutional Record of President Clinton," *Capital University Law Review* 27 (1999): 783, 832–38.

53. See American Bar Association, *The Federalization of Criminal Law* (Chicago: American Bar Association, 1998); John S. Baker, *Measuring the Explosive Growth of Federal Crime Legislation* (Washington: The Federalist Society for Law and Public Policy Studies, 2005).

54. *United States v. Lopez*, 514 U.S. 549 (1995).

55. Ibid., pp. 657–58 (1995) (Thomas, J., concurring). See also John Baker, "Nationalizing Criminal Law: Does Organized Crime Make It Necessary or Proper?" *Rutgers Law Journal* 16 (1985): 495.

56. See, generally, Lysander Spooner, "Vices Are Not Crimes: A Vindication of Moral Liberty (1875)," in *The Lysander Spooner Reader* (New York: Fox and Wilkes, 1992).

57. Bill Masters, *Drug War Addiction* (Minneapolis, MN: Accurate Press, 2001), p. 107.

58. See Joan Biskupic, Wendy Koch, and John Ritter, "Patients Who Use Marijuana Fear Worst If Forced to Stop," *USA Today*, June 6, 2005. Unlike most of the other first principles discussed in this introduction, the distinction between vices and crimes does not find strong support in American history. Historically, governmental bodies have tried to police vice crimes, such as prostitution, pornography, adultery, gambling, and alcohol and drug consumption. See Lawrence M. Friedman, *Crime and Punishment in American History* (New York: Basic Books, 1993), pp. 324–57.

59. See George McGovern, "Whose Life Is It?" *New York Times*, August 14, 1997.

60. *Olmstead v. United States*, 277 U.S. 438, 479 (1928) (Brandeis, J., dissenting).

61. See Timothy Lynch, "All Locked Up," *Washington Post*, February 20, 2000. See also Milton and Rose Friedman, "Crime," Appendix B, p. 179.

62. See *Lilly v. West Virginia*, 29 F.2d 61 (1928). Note also Tom Jackman, "Fairfax Police Say Shooting Was Accident," *Washington Post*, January 26, 2006 (Sal Culosi, 37, accidentally shot as he was about to be arrested on suspicion of gambling on sports).

63. See Radley Balko, "Overkill: The Rise of Paramilitary Police Raids in America," Cato Institute White Paper, July 17, 2006. See also Mary Anastasia O'Grady, "Innocents Die in the Drug War," *Wall Street Journal*, December 14, 2008.

64. See, generally, James Ostrowski, "The Moral and Practical Case for Drug Legalization," *Hofstra Law Review* 18 (1989): 607; Steven B. Duke and Albert C. Gross, *America's Longest War: Rethinking Our Tragic Crusade Against Drugs* (New York: G. P. Putnam's Sons, 1994).

65. Hart, "The Aims of the Criminal Law," p. 2. Crimes based on the "moral sense of the community" can be very slippery because they often reflect the values of some, but not others. And Lawrence Friedman notes that "values and ideas change over time." Lawrence Friedman, *Crime and Punishment in American History*, pp. 324–57. See also Patricia Sullivan, "Quiet Va. Wife Ended Interracial Marriage Ban," *Washington Post*, May 6, 2008.

66. Hart, "The Aims of the Criminal Law," p. 17.

67. Ibid., note 42. See also Herbert L. Packer, *The Limits of the Criminal Sanction* (Stanford, CA: Stanford University Press, 1968).

68. John H. Langbein, "On the Myth of Written Constitutions: The Disappearance of Criminal Jury Trial," *Harvard Journal of Law and Public Policy* 15 (1992): 119. See also Patrick E. Higginbotham, "So Why Do We Call Them Trial Courts?" *Southern Methodist University Law Review* 55 (2002): 1405.

69. See, generally, George Fisher, *Plea Bargaining's Triumph: A History of Plea Bargaining in America* (Stanford, CA: Stanford University Press, 2003).

70. See *United States v. Booker*, 543 U.S. 220, 273–74 (2005) (Stevens, J., dissenting in part).

71. See Note, "The Unconstitutionality of Plea Bargaining," *Harvard Law Review* 83 (1970): 1387, 1389.

72. See *Bordenkircher v. Hayes*, 434 U.S. 357 (1978). For a critique of that holding, see Timothy Lynch, "An Eerie Efficiency," *Cato Supreme Court Review: 2001–2002* (2002): 171.

73. *Berthoff v. United States*, 140 F.Supp.2d 50, 67–69 (2001). Note also *United States v. Forrest*, 402 F.3d 678 (2005).

74. Ralph Adam Fine, "Plea Bargaining: An *Un*necessary Evil," in *Criminal Justice? The Legal System versus Individual Responsibility* (Irvington-on-Hudson, NY: Foundation for Economic Education, 1994), pp. 84–101.

75. See Alan Finder, "Jailed Until Found Not Guilty," *New York Times*, June 6, 1999.

76. *North Carolina v. Spivey*, 579 S.E.2d 251 (2003). *Spivey* established a legal precedent in North Carolina. A few years later, when a Duke University athlete, Reade Seligmann, was falsely accused of rape, he demanded a speedy trial so that his attorneys could promptly clear his name. "Duke Player Wants Speedy Rape Trial," May 18, 2006, www.cnn.com/2006/LAW/05/18/duke.rape/index.html. The district attorney, Michael Nifong, relied on the *Spivey* precedent to argue for a delay in the case. Months later, the case unraveled and Seligmann was cleared of any wrongdoing. See, generally, Stuart Taylor and KC Johnson, *Until Proven Innocent: Political Correctness and the Shameful Injustices of the Duke Lacrosse Rape Case* (New York: Thomas Dunne Books, 2007).

77. See, generally, Richard A. Nagareda, "Compulsion 'To Be a Witness' and the Resurrection of *Boyd*," *New York University Law Review* 74 (1999): 1575; Thomas Y. Davies, "Farther and Farther from the Original Fifth Amendment: The Recharacterization of the Right Against Self-Incrimination as a 'Trial Right' in *Chavez v. Martinez*," *Tennessee Law Review* 70 (2003): 987.

78. See *Braswell v. United States*, 487 U.S. 99 (1988); *In re: Grand Jury Subpoena*, 21 F.3d 226 (1994).

79. *Shapiro v. United States*, 335 U.S. 1, 70-71 (1948) (Jackson, J., dissenting).

80. Ibid., p. 71.

81. *California v. Byers*, 402 U.S. 424 (1971).

82. See *Wisconsin v. Krajewski*, 648 N.W.2d 385 (2002); *Schmerber v. California*, 384 U.S. 757 (1966).

83. By "abuse," I mean that the police, in their zeal to enforce the law, push the limits of their power. See Christopher Slobogin, "Deceit, Pretext, and Trickery: Investigative Lies by the Police," *Oregon Law Review* 76 (1997): 775, 781 ("Lying meant to effectuate a search or a seizure is routine practice for many police officers. . . . For instance, police may state that they do not need a warrant when they know the law requires they have one, assert they have a warrant when they do not, or state they can get a warrant when in fact they know they cannot.").

84. "NYPD to Use Written Consent Forms for Searches," Associated Press, June 25, 2008; Karin Brulliard, "Police Shootings Shake Austin," *Washington Post*, May 19, 2004.

85. *Jett v. The Commonwealth*, 18 Gratt. (59 Va.) 933, 959 (1867).

86. Daniel A. Braun, "Praying to False Sovereigns: The Rule of Successive Prosecutions in the Age of Cooperative Federalism," *American Journal of Criminal Law* 20 (1992): 4.

87. Ibid., p. 5.

88. *Bartkus v. Illinois*, 359 U.S. 121, 151-55 (1959) (Black, J., dissenting).

89. Conscientious policymakers can undertake such a reform. A number of state governments have, to their credit, restricted their prosecuting officials from initiating

a criminal case against anyone who has already undergone a federal prosecution for any particular incident. See Braun, "Praying to False Sovereigns," p. 5.

90. See, generally, Erik Luna, "Gridland: An Allegorical Critique of Federal Sentencing," *Journal of Criminal Law and Criminology* 96 (2005): 25.

91. See, for example, *United States v. Yirkovsky*, 259 F.3d 704, 707 n. 4 (2001).

92. *United States v. Patillo*, 817 F.Supp. 839, 842 (1993).

93. Hart, "The Aims of the Criminal Law," p. 28. For background on the prerogatives of juries, see Albert W. Alschuler and Andrew G. Deiss, "A Brief History of the Criminal Jury in the United States," *University of Chicago Law Review* 61 (1994): 867; Glenn Harlan Reynolds, "Review Essay: Of Dissent and Discretion," *Cornell Journal of Law and Public Policy* 9 (2000): 685.

94. In Georgia, for example, state officials, including police officers, have been given special privileges that are denied to ordinary citizens. Police officers who have been accused of wrongdoing are allowed to bring their attorneys into the grand jury room when they have been subpoenaed to testify, and the attorneys are permitted to attend all of the grand jury's proceedings in the matter and are even permitted to give a closing statement to the jurors after the prosecutor has presented his case. See Official Code of Georgia, Title 44-11-4.

95. *Mom's, Inc. v. Willman*, 109 Fed.Appx. 629, 636-637 (2004).

96. Quoted in Laurie P. Cohen, "New York Rules Mean It's Tough to Convict Police in Diallo Case," *Wall Street Journal*, April 7, 1999. In some Maryland counties, police officers involved in questionable shootings can decline interviews for 10 days. See Paul Schwartzman, "Weaker Police Law Called Unfair to Pr. George's," *Washington Post*, January 18, 2002.

97. Quoted in David Kravets, "Appeals Panel Hears Ruby Ridge Case," Associated Press, December 20, 2000.

98. *Brady v. Maryland*, 373 U.S. 83 (1963).

99. Bennett L. Gershman, *Prosecutorial Misconduct* (Deerfield, IL: Clark, Boardman, Callaghan, 1991), p. 5-1.

100. Center for Public Integrity, "Harmful Error: Investigating America's Local Prosecutors," Washington, 2003, http://projects.publicintegrity.org/pm/default.aspx?sid=sidebarsa&aid=40.

101. See Andrea Elliot and Benjamin Weiser, "Disciplinary Action Is Rare After Misconduct or Mistakes," *New York Times*, March 21, 2004; Richard A. Rosen, "Disciplinary Sanctions Against Prosecutors for *Brady* Violations: A Paper Tiger," *North Carolina Law Review* 65 (1987): 693.

102. Quoted in Center for Public Integrity, "Harmful Error."

103. This reform can be achieved through a legislative rule or by rethinking the Supreme Court's present "harmless error" approach to violations. See, generally, Vilija Bilaisis, "Harmless Error: Abettor of Courtroom Misconduct," *Journal of Criminal Law and Criminology* 74 (1983): 457.

104. *Armstrong v. United States*, 364 U.S. 40, 49 (1960).

105. *Customer Company v. City of Sacramento*, 895 P.2d 900, 936 (1995) (Baxter, J., dissenting). See also Charles E. Cohen, "Takings Analysis of Police Destruction of Innocent Owners' Property in the Course of Law Enforcement: The View from Five State Supreme Courts," *McGeorge Law Review* 34 (2002): 1.

106. See Timothy Lynch, "The Paper Chase," *Forbes*, January 20, 2003.

107. See, generally, Gary Lawson and Guy Seidman, "Taking Notes: Subpoenas and Just Compensation," *University of Chicago Law Review* 66 (1999): 1081.

108. Richard Willing, "Exonerated Prisoners Are Rarely Paid for Lost Time," *USA Today*, June 18, 2002.

109. Ibid.

110. "State Senate OKs More Cash for Wrongfully Incarcerated," *Houston Chronicle*, April 18, 2001.

111. David W. Simon, "Fighting Back: Remedies for the Wrongfully Prosecuted?" *Wisconsin Lawyer* (September 1998).

112. Frank H. Easterbrook, "Plea Bargaining as Compromise," *Yale Law Journal* 101 (1992): 1969, 1974.

113. See *Moore v. Dempsey*, 261 U.S. 86 (1923).

114. See *Tennessee v. Garner*, 471 U.S. 1 (1985).

Chapter 1

1. Livingston Hall and Sheldon Glueck, *Cases on the Criminal Law and Its Enforcement*, 3d ed. (West Publishing Co., 1958), p. 15.

2. See Herbert Wechsler and Jerome Michael, "A Rationale of the Law of Homicide II," *Columbia Law Review* 37 (1937): 1261, 1262.

3. See "Note on Organized Societies and the Principle of Institutional Settlement," in Henry M. Hart, Jr. and Albert M. Sacks, *The Legal Process: Basic Problems in the Making and Application of Law*, mim. ed. (1957), p. 1.

4. See the discussion of the Italian positivists and their influence in American criminology in Jerome Hall, *General Principles of Criminal Law* (Bobbs-Merrill, 1947), pp. 539–51, especially at p. 549.

5. Cf. Llewellyn, "Law and the Social Sciences—Especially Sociology," *Harvard Law Review* 62 (1949): 1286, 1287: "When I was younger I used to hear smuggish assertions among my sociological friends, such as: 'I take the sociological, *not* the legal, approach to crime'; and I suspect an inquiring reporter could still hear much of the same (perhaps with 'psychiatric' often substituted for 'sociological')—though it is surely somewhat obvious that when you take 'the legal' out, you also take out 'crime'."

6. For a discussion of types of legal duties generally, see Hart and Sacks, 121–23. Account should also be taken of a peculiar type of criminal prohibition, baffling analysis, which purports to forbid not conduct, but certain kinds of personal condition. See Forest W. Lacey, "Vagrancy and Crimes of Personal Condition," *Harvard Law Review* 66 (1953): 1203; Caleb Foote, "Vagrancy-Type Law and Its Administration," *University of Pennsylvania Law Review* 104 (1956): 603. To the extent that these crimes are valid and enforceable, however, it seems that they reduce themselves to prohibitions of the conduct bringing about the condition.

7. See Hart and Sacks, 114–17.

8. Many of the duties of the civil law, of course, are open-ended, the specific nature of what is to be done being privately determined, as in contracts, and wills. In the criminal law, in contrast, officials bear the whole burden of prescribing the details of private conduct. But the same thing is true, for the most part, in the law of torts and other areas of civil law. See ibid., 108–10, 129–31.

9. In many legal systems, moreover, private persons may institute criminal proceedings, as, of course, they could in the English common law and still can in contemporary England.

10. Thus, debtors were once imprisoned. Insane persons, aliens held for deportation, and recalcitrant witnesses still are. Juvenile delinquents are put on probation. A judgment for the payment of money, which objectively considered is all that a fine is, is, of course, the characteristic of civil judgment. And the amount of the civil judgment may be "punitive," and not merely compensatory or restorative.

11. See, e.g., *State v. Dobry*, 217 Iowa 858, 861–62, 250 N.W. 702, 704 (1933): "In finding what shall constitute a crime, the legislature has unlimited power. In other words, they can make it include certain elements or omit certain elements therefrom as in their judgment seems best." See, further, the discussion in part four.

12. See, e.g., in the Constitution of the United States, art. I, § 3, para. 7 (preserving safeguards of criminal trial in matters of impeachment); art. I, § 9, para. 2 (habeas corpus); art. I, § 9, para. 3 (forbidding passage of bills of attainer and ex post facto laws by Congress); art. I, § 10, para. 1, cl. 6 and 7 (forbidding passage of bills of attainder and ex post facto laws by any state); art. III, § 2, para. 3 (jury trial and venue in federal criminal cases); art. III, § 3 (definition and regulation of conviction and punishment for treason); art. IV, § 2, para. 2 (extradition); amendment IV (unreasonable searches and seizures and search warrants); amendment V (indictment by grand jury, double jeopardy, self-incrimination, and due process clauses); amendment VI (rights in criminal cases of speedy and public trial, jury trial, local venue, knowledge of accusation, confrontation of witnesses, compulsory process for obtaining witnesses, and assistance of counsel); amendment VIII (prohibition of excessive bail, excessive fines, and cruel and unusual punishment); amendment XIII (recognition of involuntary servitude as punishment for crime); and amendment XIV (due process and equal protection of the laws in state action).

13. George K. Gardner, "*Bailey v. Richardson* and the Constitution of the United States," *Boston University Law Review* 33 (1953): 176, 193. It is, of course, to be understood that Professor Gardner's statement and the statements in the text do not accurately describe the significance of a criminal conviction under many modern regulatory and other statutes which penalize people who have had no awareness nor reason for awareness of wrongdoing. The central thesis of this paper, to be developed below, is that a sanction which ineradicably imports blame, both traditionally and in most of its current applications, is misused when it is thus applied to conduct which is not blameworthy.

14. Art. I, § 3, para. 7; art. I, § 8, cl. 6; art. I, § 8, cl. 10; art. III, § 3, para. 2; amendment VIII; and amendment XIII.

15. For a convincing statement that the difference does not lie in the necessarily greater gentleness of the treatment administered in the hospital, see Edward de Grazia, "The Distinction of Being Mad," *University of Chicago Law Review* 22 (1955): 339, 348–55. Of course, there are also differences in the legal provisions governing the possibility of release, but these are mostly corollaries of the basic difference in the nature of the judgment directing detention.

16. Hall and Glueck, 19.

17. Is the correlation between describable types of conduct (acts or omissions), on the one hand, and the need for cure and rehabilitation of those who engage in them, on the other hand, so close that the need can be taken as a reliable index of the types of conduct to be forbidden and the differentiation among offenses to be made? These determinations must be made in advance and in general terms. In making them, the extent of the depravity of character characteristically manifested by particular types of behavior ought, of course, to be taken into account so far as it can be. But this is

a factor which is peculiarly difficult to appraise ahead of time by a generalized judgment. Depravity of character and the need of the individual for cure and rehabilitation are essentially personal matters, as the whole modern theory of the individualization of correctional treatment bears witness. A fortiori, the susceptibility of the individual to rehabilitation is personal.

18. For the conclusion that the reformative principle has little that is distinctive to contribute in the substantive differentiation between criminal and noncriminal behavior, see Wechsler and Michael, "A Rationale of the Law of Homicide I," *Columbia Law Review* 37 (1937): 701, 757–61. For a detailed and judicious appraisal of the respective roles of the deterrent and reformative principles in the *treatment* of criminals, including the legislative grading of offenses, see part two of the same article. Ibid., 1261.

19. So, two contemporary advocates of "a rational approach to crime repression" who urge reformation as the central objective in the treatment of criminals are led to follow out the apparent logic of their position by saying that "those who cannot be reformed. . .must be segregated for life—but not necessarily punished—*irrespective of the crimes they have committed.*" (Emphasis added.) Harry E. Barnes and Negley K. Teeters, *New Horizons in Criminology: The American Crime Problem* rev. ed. (Prentice-Hall, 1945), p. 953.

Speaking of the school of positivism which has dominated American criminology in recent years, Professor Jerome Hall says: "Its dogmas biased not only theories concerning prevention but also, combined with its determinism, stigmatized punishment as vengeance—at the same time opening the door to unmitigated cruelty in the name of 'measures of safety'." Hall, 551.

The rash of so-called "sexual psychopath" laws which disgrace the statute books of many states illustrate the possibilities to which this streak of cruelty may lead. See Frederick J. Hacker and Marcel Frym, "The Sexual Psychopath Act in Practice: A Critical Discussion," *California Law Review* 43 (1955): 766; Guttmacher and Weihofen, "Sex Offenses," *Journal of Criminal Law, Criminology, and Police Science* 43 (1952): 153. For the shock of a concrete example of what may happen in the administration of such laws, until the courts correct it, read *In re Maddox*, 88 N.W.2d 470 (Mich. 1958), where the state hospital psychiatrist insisted on assuming the truth of unproved police charges in his treatment of one who had been civilly committed as a "sexual psychopath" and, when his victim kept protesting his innocence, had him transferred to state prison on the ground that this refusal to admit guilt made him "an adamant patient" lacking "the desire to get well" which was necessary to make him amenable to hospital care. Consider also the possibilities implicit in the Maryland Defective Delinquent Law, Md. Ann. Code art. 31B (1951).

20. See, e.g., Advisory Council of Judges, *NPAA Guides for Sentencing* (1957). Almost the whole of what this handbook says about deterrence as a factor in sentencing is contained in the following paragraph:

"In some situations, knowledge of a penalty may deter an individual tempted to violate a law; on the whole, however, the deterrent force of severe penalty alone for major crimes has been highly overrated and belief in its value is unrealistic. A stubborn reliance on deterrence results in making sentences increasingly severe, and excessively severe sentences produce deteriorating effects on prisoners, without corresponding benefits to society." Ibid., 2.

It will be observed that this confuses the question of the efficacy of the threat of criminal condemnation and punishment as a factor in controlling the conduct of the bulk of mankind with the question of the efficacy of severe punishments, a confusion which is not uncommon. Few people will deny that excessively severe sentences are undesirable, and many will agree that a large proportion of the sentences currently meted out *are* excessively severe.

21. Cf. Ranyard West, *Conscience and Society* (Emerson Books, 1945), p. 165: "It is upon the fact of the potential criminal in every man that I would give to law its psychological grounding."

Compare the valuable analysis by a Norwegian scholar, Johs Andenaes, in "General Prevention—Illusion or Reality?" *Journal of Criminal Law, Criminology, and Police Science* 43 (1952): 176, 179–80. Professor Andenaes distinguishes between individual prevention ("the effect of punishment on the punished") and general prevention ("the ability of the criminal law and its enforcement to make citizens law-abiding"). He further distinguishes "three sorts of general-preventive effects": first, a "deterrent" effect (used in the narrow sense of "the mere frightening . . . effect of punishment— the risk of discovery outweighing the temptation to commit the crime"); second, a "moralizing" effect (punishment helping "to form and to strengthen the public's moral code" and so to create "conscious or unconscious inhibitions against committing crime"; and, third, a habit-forming effect (arousing "unconscious inhibitions against committing forbidden acts . . . without appealing to the individual's concepts of morality").

22. See Hart and Sacks, 10–16.

23. Walter Hamilton Moberly, *Responsibility: The Concept in Psychology, in the Law, and in the Christian Faith* (Seabury Press, 1956), p. 23: "Recite a delinquent's disabilities and handicaps in front of him in open court and you are doing something to confirm them; you are impairing that self-respect and sense of responsibility which is the chief incentive to effort. Treat him as sane and responsible and as a whole man and you give him the best chance of rising to this level. In many circumstances to expect and to exact a high standard is the most likely way to get it."

See also the discussion of the problem of growth in responsibility in Wilber G. Katz, "Law, Psychiatry, and Free Will," *University of Chicago Law Review* 22 (1955): 397.

24. See generally Moberly, and especially the opening lecture on "The Concept [of Responsibility] in Psychology and Law."

There are other agencies of social discipline, of course, than the criminal law. But the criminal law is the only one which speaks to the individual formally and solemnly in behalf of the whole society.

In what the criminal law says to the individual, moreover, much more is involved than training simply in the observance of the specific and mostly elementary standards of conduct which the law seeks directly to enforce. Limits of some kind upon the scope of permissible choice perform an indispensable psychological role in the development of personal capacity for successful social adjustment. By fixing even minimal limits, the law thus develops capacities which are transferable to the more complex problems of social existence. This is especially so to the extent that the individual is made conscious of the moral basis and social rationale of the law's commands, for the principles of social living underlying them have far wider relevance than the commands themselves.

25. Laws for the confinement of mentally-ill persons commonly dispense with these requirements, and with many others as well. See Note, "Analysis of Legal and Medical Considerations in Commitment of the Mentally Ill," *Yale Law Journal* 56 (1947): 1178, 1190–96. So also do the "sexual psychopath" laws referred to in note 19.

26. See note 19.

27. Ex post facto clauses are the only important express substantive limitation usually found in American constitutions. It should be noticed, however, that the principles of just punishment implicit in such clauses have relevance in other situations than that only of condemnation under an after-the-fact enactment—a wider relevance than courts have yet recognized.

28. On the special problems of control of reckless and negligent conduct, see subsection B of this part.

29. Compare the illuminating and much more subtle analysis of Jerome Hall in "Ignorance and Mistake in Criminal Law," *Indiana Law Journal* 33 (1957): 1. Professor Hall points out the consideration here stressed: "... namely, that the criminal law represents certain moral principles; to recognize ignorance or mistake of the law as a defense would contradict those values." Ibid., 20. But he is concerned to defend the application of the maxim not only in relation to crimes involving intrinsically wrongful conduct, but in relation to purely regulatory crimes which, if the views hereafter presented are correct, involve no other moral value than that of respect for constituted authority. This leads him into refinements which this paper passes by.

30. See Jerome Hall, "Ignorance and Mistake in Criminal Law," *Indiana Law Journal* 33 (1957): 1, 27–34. Cf. *Morissette v. United States*, 342 U.S. 246 (1952), where the Court invoked the whole broad tradition of criminal intent as a reason for giving a statute a restricted reading, although a reference to the specific doctrine of claim-of-right in theft would have been enough to do the trick.

31. It is important to notice the extent to which the whole doctrine of irresponsibility by reason of mental disease or defect confirms the main thesis of this paper. The doctrine, to be sure, can be understood as a corollary of a coldly utilitarian deterrent theory which simply exculpates nondeterrables. And the *M'Naghten* test, on a narrow and literal reading, may be thought to bear out this view. But if nondeterrability were the sole basis of the doctrine, it would seem to follow that all doubts on that score should be resolved in favor of society. This is not the way in which the test is administered, even by courts which adhere to it most strictly. What the courts actually do, and even more plainly what the critics of the courts say, is eloquent testimony to the general understanding that something more is involved than a cold-blooded estimate of deterrability. The "something more" surely is not the defendant's personal need for cure and rehabilitation, for the greater the insanity, the greater the need. Nor can susceptibility to cure and rehabilitation be taken as the touchstone consistently with general principle, or else the more hardened the criminal, the better would be his claim to irresponsibility. What seems to be involved in general understanding, and certainly in any adequate analysis of the problem, is a reaching for criteria which will avoid attaching moral blame where blame cannot justly be attached, while, at the same time, avoiding a denial of moral responsibility where the denial would be personally and socially debilitating.

32. Through use of the doctrine of conspiracy, attempt, and solicitation, and in other ways, the criminal law often condemns the deliberate planning of a blameworthy harm, even though no harm actually results. But even where it punishes the inadvertent creation of a risk which actually causes harm, Anglo-American law, wisely or unwisely, has developed no general principle condemning the same kind of risk-creating conduct in cases in which, by good fortune, no ultimate harm eventuates. Of course, however, there are a good many *ad hoc* statutes declaring specific forms of such conduct, such as speeding, to be criminal, regardless of their consequences.

33. See *Commonwealth v. Pierce*, 138 Mass. 165 (1884).

34. See *Regina v. Benge*, 4 F. & F. 504 (Kent Summer Assizes 1865).

35. See *Commonwealth v. Welansky*, 316 Mass. 383, 55 N.E.2d 902 (1944).

36. See MODEL PENAL CODE § 2.02(2)(c) and (d) (Tent. Draft No. 4, 1955):

"(c) Recklessly.

"A person acts recklessly with respect to a material element of an offense when he consciously disregards a substantial and unjustifiable risk that the material element exists or will result from his conduct. The risk must be of such a nature and degree that, considering the nature and purpose of the actor's conduct and the circumstances known to him, its disregard involves culpability of high degree. [Alternative: its disregard involves a gross deviation from proper standards of conduct.]

"(d) Negligently.

"A person acts negligently with respect to a material element of an offense when he should be aware of a substantial and unjustifiable risk that the material element exists or will result from his conduct. The risk must be of such a nature and degree that the actor's failure to perceive it, considering the nature and purpose of his conduct, the circumstances known to him and the care that would be exercised by a reasonable person in his situation, involves substantial culpability. [Alternative: considering the nature and purpose of his conduct and the circumstances known to him, involves a substantial deviation from the standard of care that would be exercised by a reasonable man in his situation.]"

37. See pp. 13–14.

38. For a valuable general discussion of problems of criminal negligence, see Jerome Hall, *General Principles of Criminal Law*, Chapter 9 (Bobbs-Merrill, 1947).

39. See generally Mr. Justice Jackson's review of the development in *Morissette v. United States*, 342 U.S. 246 (1952); Francis Bowes Sayre, "Public Welfare Offenses," *Columbia Law Review* 33 (1933): 55; Jerome Hall, *General Principles of Criminal Law*, Chapter 10 (Bobbs-Merrill, 1947).

40. Obviously, the courts must have a share, whether it is desirable or not, in the interpretation of such enactments. See Hall, pp. 435–36.

41. See *United States v. Murdock*, 290 U.S. 389 (1933); *Spies v. United States*, 317 U.S. 492, 497–98 (1943); Herbert Wechsler, "The American Law Institute: Some Observations on Its Model Penal Code," *American Bar Association Journal* 42 (1956): 321, 324.

42. The dominant objective of public education in the obligations of responsible citizenship is prejudiced if the public mind is confused by assertion of too many obligations. The force of the threat of criminal condemnation and punishment, moreover, is weakened if serious enforcement is impracticable, and there are, and seemingly must inevitably be, severe limitations upon the load which the machinery of criminal law enforcement can carry. See part four. Finally, the criminal law always loses face if things are declared to be crimes which people believe they ought to be free to do, even willfully.

43. See note 29.

44. Cf. Graham Hughes, "Criminal Omissions," *Yale Law Journal* 67 (1958): 590, 603: "The conventional analyses of *mens rea* in omissions suffer either from a complete neglect of the aspect of ignorance of the law or a tendency to confuse the two separate issues of ignorance of the duty and ignorance of the circumstances which triggered the duty."

45. Hughes, 636.

46. See the discussion of the Supreme Court's recent decision in *Lambert v. California*, 355 U.S. 225, 433–34 (1957).

47. Roscoe Pound, "Sources and Forms of Law," *Notre Dame Lawyer* 22 (1946): 1, 76.

48. The devices have generally dealt only with the extreme situation in which the defendant was misled by some form of official advice that his conduct was lawful. See, e.g., *State v. Jones*, 44 N.M. 623, 107 P.2d 324 (1940), overruling a prior judicial interpretation of a statute now regarded as erroneous "with prospective effect only." See Hart and Sacks, note 3, at 661–64. Cf. *Long v. State*, 44 Del. (5 Ter.) 462, 65 A.2d 489 (1949), allowing a defendant in a bigamy prosecution to show that he had acted in reliance on an attorney's advice that a prior divorce was valid.

49. MODEL PENAL CODE § 2.04(3) and (4) (Tent. Draft. No. 4, 1955):

"(3) A reasonable belief that conduct does not legally constitute an offense is a defense to a prosecution for that offense based upon such conduct, when:

(a) the statute or other enactment defining the offense is not known to the actor and has not been published or otherwise reasonably made available to him prior to the conduct alleged; or

(b) he acts in reasonable reliance upon an official statement of the law, afterward determined to be invalid or erroneous, contained in (i) a statute or other enactment; (ii) a judicial decision, opinion or judgment; (iii) an administrative order or grant of permission; or (iv) an official interpretation of the public officer or body charged by law with responsibility for the interpretation, administration or enforcement of the law defining the offense.

"(4) A defense arising under paragraph (3) of this section constitutes an affirmative defense which the defendant is required to prove by a preponderance of evidence. The reasonableness of the belief claimed to constitute the defense shall be determined as a question of law by the Court."

50. See paragraph (4) of the Model Penal Code provision in note 49.

51. See subheading B of this part.

52. Cf. *Commonwealth v. Mixer*, 207 Mass. 141, 93 N.E. 249 (1910). [Ed. note: See p. 196 n. 34].

53. *State v. Dobry*, 217 Iowa 858, 250 N.W. 702 (1933).

54. *United States v. Dotterweich*, 320 U.S. 277 (1943).

55. See *City of Hays v. Schueler*, 107 Kan. 635, 193 Pac. 311 (1920).

56. There are more strict liability and other criminal statutes on the books than investigators and prosecutors, with their existing staffs, can hope to enforce. See part four. Nor is there any pretense that most of them are seriously enforced. Even with statutes which a genuine effort is made to enforce, only a relatively few cases of violation are selected for prosecution, and these are commonly chosen in accordance with standards quite different from the strict liability standards laid down by the legislature or judicially attributed to it. See, e.g., L.B. Schwartz, "Federal Criminal Jurisdiction and Prosecutors' Discretion," *Law & Contemporary Problems* 13 (1948): 64, 83–84; Developments in the Law, "The Federal Food, Drug, and Cosmetic Act," *Harvard Law Review* 67 (1954): 632, 694–97.

57. Think, for example, about the implications of the language of an English court in rejecting as preposterous the suggestion that the defense of ignorance and good faith should be allowed in a prosecution for criminal conspiracy: "We demur to the notion that there is anything particularly wicked attached to the word 'conspiracy.' No doubt in common speech 'conspiracy' has a melodramatic and sinister implication, but it has been pointed out that it carries no such implications in law. . . . It does not

207

matter how prosaic the unlawful act may be or how ignorant the conspirators may be of the fact that the act is prohibited by the statutory provision." *Rex v. Clayton* (Ct. Cr. App. 1943, unreported), reported in footnote to *Rex v. Percy Dalton*, 33 Cr. App. Rep. 102, 119 (1949). "There, there," says the court to the once sturdy-minded yeomen of old England, "no matter what your mothers and fathers may have told you, there is really nothing particularly wrong about being a criminal." The same overtones, though usually less baldly expressed, run through countless American opinions. See, e.g., Mr. Justice Frankfurter, in *United States v. Dotterweich*, 320 U.S. 277, 280–81 (1943); and in *Lambert v. California*, 355 U.S. 225, 230–31 (1957).

58. See note 56.

59. See, e.g., the unconscionable proposal sanctioned by a commission of the American Bar Association, the leading association of lawyers in the United States, that in a Model Anti-Gambling Act, all forms of gambling, even purely social gambling, should be declared to be criminal, even while recognizing "that it is unrealistic to promulgate a law literally aimed at making a criminal offense of the friendly election bet, the private, social card game among friends, etc." The commission's reason for being thus "unrealistic" was that "it is imperative to confront the professional gambler with a statutory façade that is wholly devoid of loopholes." Its report indicated that pressure from prosecutors accounted for the proposal and that it was relying on prosecutors' discretion to avoid abuses. Approval of the proposition was mitigated by the fact that the commission, evidently uneasy about what it was doing, also reported an "optional" provision giving the social gambler a limited statutory protection. But the report gave no hint of awareness that basic issues of public morality were involved. ABA Commission on Organized Crime, *Organized Crime and Law Enforcement* 2 (1953): 74–78.

60. See Felix Frankfurter and Thomas G. Corcoran, "Petty Federal Offenses and the Constitutional Guarantee of Trial by Jury," *Harvard Law Review* 39 (1926): 917; *Callan v. Wilson*, 127 U.S. 540 (1888); *Schick v. United States*, 195 U.S. 65 (1904); *District of Columbia v. Clawans*, 300 U.S. 617 (1937). By the standards laid down in these cases, it will be seen, hosts of strict liability offenses are plainly not "petty."

61. See *Ex parte* Wilson, 114 U.S. 417 (1885); *In re Claasen*, 140 U.S. 200 (1891); *United States v. Moreland*, 258 U.S. 433 (1922); Oppenheimer, "Infamous Crimes and the *Moreland* Case," *Harvard Law Review* 36 (1923): 299. By the standards of these cases, it will be seen, many a conviction for a strict liability offense carries infamy.

62. The Model Penal Code, as tentatively drafted, recognizes, in large part, the moral indefensibility of strict liability and the lack of any real public necessity for it. See MODEL PENAL CODE § 2.05 (Tent. Draft No. 4, 1955). The draftsman's "comment" on this section, *id.* at 140, explains it as follows:

"1. This section makes a frontal attack on absolute or strict liability in penal law, whenever the offense carries a possibility of sentence of imprisonment. The method used is not to abrogate such liability but to provide that when conviction rests upon that basis, the grade of the offense is reduced to a violation, which is not a "crime" and under Sections 1.04(5) and 6.02 may result in no other sentence than a fine or fine and forfeiture or other civil penalty. If, on the other hand, the culpable commission of the offense has been established, the reduction in grade does not occur. Negligence is, however, treated as sufficient culpability in cases of this kind.

"This position is affirmed not only with respect to offenses defined by the Penal Code; it is superimposed on the entire corpus of the law, so far as penal sanctions are involved. Since most strict liability offenses are involved in special, regulatory legislation, this superimposition is essential if the problem is to be attacked. We have no doubt that the attempt is one that should be made. The liabilities involved are indefensible in principle, unless reduced to terms that insulate conviction from the type of moral condemnation that is and ought to be implicit when a sentence of imprisonment may be imposed. In the absence of minimal culpability, the law has neither a deterrent nor corrective nor an incapacitative function to perform.

"It has been argued, and the argument undoubtedly will be repeated, that absolute liability is necessary for enforcement in a number of the areas where it obtains. But if practical enforcement cannot undertake to litigate the culpability of alleged deviation from legal requirements, we do not see how the enforcers rightly can demand the use of penal sanctions for the purpose. Crime does and should mean condemnation and no court should have to pass that judgment unless it can declare that the defendant's act was wrong. This is too fundamental to be compromised. The law goes far enough if it permits the imposition of a monetary penalty in cases where strict liability has been imposed."

The only shortcoming of the draft is that strict liability so far as concerns ignorance or mistake with respect to the existence or meaning of the applicable law is retained, subject only to the narrowly limited exceptions set forth in note 49. In view of the magnitude of the reform actually urged by the Code, however, the decision to restrict the proposal reflects an understandable counsel of prudence.

63. Notable exceptions, of course, are the mandatory death sentence and the mandatory life term for recidivists, both of which, however, have fallen into widespread disrepute and, one may hope, are on the way to complete abandonment.

64. See note 19.

65. See note 59 and accompanying text.

66. See note 56.

67. See note 41 and accompanying text.

68. The bellwether case is *Regina v. Prince*, L.R. 2 Cr. Cas. Res. 154 (1875).

69. On this issue, Massachusetts led the way in *Commonwealth v. Mash*, 48 Mass. (7 Metc.) 472 (1844). A majority of the English judges, recoiling from *Regina v. Prince*, note 68, went the other way. *Regina v. Tolson*, 23 Q.B.D. 168 (1889).

70. A possible exception is Mr. Justice Jackson's spread-eagle dissertation in *Morissette v. United States*, 342 U.S. 246 (1952), involving the question whether a defendant charged with having "knowingly converted" government property consisting of rusty bomb casings dumped on a remote Air Force practice bombing range (which the defendant had openly appropriated and sold for junk) should have been allowed the defense that he believed in good faith that the casings had been abandoned. However, the opinion, which held the defense available, seems open to the objections indicated in the following imaginary concurring opinion, which is here reproduced to illustrate the main theme of the text of the importance of interpretative presumptions.

"Mr. Justice TENTHJUDGE, concurring in result.

"While I have an emotional sympathy with most of what is said in my brother Jackson's engaging opinion in this case, I should not wish to be understood as expressing judicial agreement with any part of it, except the very limited part which is necessary for decision of the narrow issue before us.

"We ought to refrain from writing discursive essays on the law, if only to spare law students the burden of reading them and law professors the pain of deciding whether to reproduce them in their casebooks. But there is a still more compelling reason for restraint. We cannot possibly apply our minds to all the considerations which are relevant to all the propositions which the Court's opinion advances. We cannot possibly be sure, therefore, that each proposition will stand up when it is tested in the crucible of a litigation squarely involving it. Thus, to the peccadillo of announcing too much law in this case, we add the cardinal sin of announcing law of dubious reliability.

"We have to deal here with a typical modern statute consolidating—with typical looseness of draftsmanship—the various forms of theft, so far as these crimes are of concern to the United States as a governmental entity. With respect to all these forms of theft—not only those which are of judicial origin, like trespassory larceny and larceny by trick, but those which have their origin in statutes, like obtaining property by false pretenses and embezzlement—a 'claim of right' has traditionally been a defense. Morissette's claim falls comfortably within the types of claims which have traditionally been recognized as affording this defense. E.g., *People v. Shaunding*, 268 Mich. 218, 255 N.W. 770 (1934); *People v. Lapique*, 120 Cal. 25, 52 Pac. 40 (1898); *cf. Commonwealth v. Althause*, 207 Mass. 32, 51, 93 N.E. 202 (1910). See generally Rollin M. Perkins, *Criminal Law* (1957): 223.

"Hence the simple question before us is whether the vague and general language of the 'knowingly converts' clause of 62 STAT. 725 (1948), 18 U.S.C. § 641 (1952) should be read as incorporating this established element of the crime of theft or as eliminating it.

"There are a plethora of good reasons for the narrower reading.

"Statutes, generally, should be read in the light of the common law, save where they make plain a purpose to depart from it.

"This is doubly true of statutes defining crimes, which ancient learning tells us should be strictly construed, if a strict construction is sensible. *McBoyle v. United States*, 283 U.S. 25 (1931); *United States v. Wiltberger*, 18 U.S. (5 Wheat.) 76, 95–96 (1820).

"It is trebly true of statutes defining federal crimes, which are not readily to be given an expansive interpretation overlapping the criminal prohibitions of the states.

"It is quadruply true of a section which the statutory revisers tell us simply 'consolidates' previous provisions of the code, which provisions, as we know, had never been held to dispense with the common law defense.

"It is quintuply true when the section in question is contained in a recodification which, as the Court's opinion tells us (note 28), was generally 'not intended to create new crimes, but to recodify those then in existence.'

"It is sextuply true when the recodification in question—why not come right out and say it?—is one for which the spadework was done by the hired hands of three commercial law-book publishers, on delegation from a congressional committee desirous of escaping the responsibility of hiring and supervising its own staff.

"In these circumstances, the case against finding a major change of public policy in the interstices of this slovenly enactment is overwhelming.

"If the Court's opinion had chosen merely to add as a seventh reason that it is a general principle of our law that criminal condemnation imports moral blameworthiness and that the legislature ought not lightly to be taken as wishing to weaken this principle, I should have had no objection; indeed, I should have applauded.

"But I see no occasion for examination and labored distinction of the notorious instances in which Congress and this Court have sanctioned blatant defiance of this principle. In particular, whether *United States v. Balint*, 258 U.S. 250 (1922), *United States v. Behrman*, 258 U.S. 280 (1922), and *United States v. Dotterweich*, 320 U.S. 277 (1943), were soundly decided on their facts, and what, if any, the ramifications of their reasoning may be are questions which, I think, we ought to leave to the riper wisdom of another day.

"As an example of the need for such wisdom, it may not be inappropriate to call attention to the paradox in which my brother Jackson's ratiocinations have involved him.

"In relation to offenses of a traditional type, the Court's opinion seems to be saying, we must be much slower to dispense with a basis for genuine blameworthiness in criminal intent than in relation to modern regulatory offenses. But it is precisely in the area of traditional crimes that the nature of the act itself commonly gives some warning that there may be a problem about its propriety and so affords, without more, at least some slight basis of condemnation for doing it. Thus, Morissette knew perfectly well that he was taking property which, at least up to the moment of caption, did not belong to him.

"In the area of regulatory crimes, on the other hand, the moral quality of the act is often neutral; and on occasion, the offense may consist not of any act at all, but simply of an intrinsically innocent omission, so that there is no basis for moral condemnation whatever. Thus, in *Dotterweich*, the Court upheld a conviction of the president and general manager of a corporation doing a reputable business merely because the corporation had happened to ship an adulterated and misbranded drug in interstate commerce and Dotterweich happened to be its responsible executive.

"I think the Court is right in holding that Morissette should have been allowed to go to the jury on the question of his consciousness of wrongdoing. But it will take something more than the lucubrations of the present opinion to convince me that Morissette had a better title to do so than Dotterweich."

71. The earliest discussion seems to be the elaborate and much cited dictum in *Shevlin-Carpenter Co. v. Minnesota*, 218 U.S. 57, 67–69 (1910). The case was a *civil* action for damages against a lumber company for trespass in cutting timber on state land after a permit to do so had expired. The state court had entered judgment for double damages against the company on the ground that the trespass was "wilful." Among the grounds of the company's appeal was the claim that the statute also made a "casual and involuntary trespasser" liable to the state in double damages, and that it included also a severe criminal penalty, "'and that declaring his act a felony violates the Fourteenth Amendment,' because those provisions 'eliminate altogether the question of intent,' and that the 'elimination of intent as an element of an offense is contrary to the requirements of due process of law.'" The Court's opinion made the obvious rejoinders that the company was in no position to advance this complaint, first, because its action had been found to be "wilful" and, second, because in any event, the provisions for a criminal penalty were separable. But then, with impatience, and corresponding lack of hard thinking, it went on to say broadly that the argument with respect to the necessity of criminal intent was not any good anyway. It cited no authority whatever. Manifestly, the company had no claim of surprised innocence sufficiently plausible to draw the Court's real attention to the question.

Mr. Justice McKenna's *Shevlin-Carpenter* dictum was followed the next year by a dictum of Mr. Justice Holmes in *United States v. Johnson*, 221 U.S. 488, 497–98 (1911)—again, wholly nude of supporting authority. The case held that false claims of being a cure for cancer on the labels of plaintiff's patent medicine bottles did not make the bottles "misbranded" within the meaning of the Food and Drugs Act of 1906, because they constituted simply innocent puffing, rather than misstatements about the identity of the contents. For this shockingly narrow and distorting interpretation, the opinion gave the ironical reason that "the article may be misbranded without any conscious fraud at all," and that while "it was natural enough to throw this risk on shippers with regard to the identity of their wares," it was "a very different and unlikely step to make them answerable for mistaken praise." Morality and rationality alike, it is submitted, could hardly be more completely inverted.

72. *United States v. Balint*, 258 U.S. 250 (1922); *United States v. Behrman*, 258 U.S. 280 (1922), both decided on the same black Monday. Both cases involved facts which, one may surmise, would have permitted conviction on orthodox principles. But Mr. Justice Holmes, dissenting in the *Behrman* case (although not in *Balint)*, said that the indictment there had been framed "for the very purpose of raising the issue that divides the Court"; and the same thing seems to have been true of the *Balint* indictment. The *Balint* case held that a physician could be convicted of selling a certain opium derivative without the use of a required form, under a statute carrying a maximum penalty of five years imprisonment and a fine of $2,000, even though he had been without knowledge of the contents of the drug. The *Behrman* case made a similar holding with reference to the prescription of drugs.

Chief Justice Taft's *Balint* opinion said that the objection "that punishment of a person for an act in violation of law when ignorant of the facts making it so" had been "considered and overruled" in *Shevlin-Carpenter Co. v. Minnesota*, 218 U.S. 57 (1910), note 71, a manifestly cavalier use of dictum as controlling authority. For further authority, the opinion cited only some state court cases, some lower federal court cases, and two English cases. Mr. Justice Day's *Behrman* opinion cited only *Balint* and some lower federal court cases.

Chief Justice Taft said that the statute had the "manifest purpose" of requiring "every person dealing in drugs to ascertain, at his peril, whether that which he sells comes within the inhibition of the statute." It expressed its reasons for approving this in two sentences: "Congress weighed the possible injustice of subjecting an innocent seller to a penalty against the evil of exposing innocent purchasers to danger from the drug, and concluded that the latter was the result preferably to be avoided. Doubtless considerations as to the opportunity of the seller to find out the fact and the difficulty of proof of knowledge contributed to this conclusion." Exactly how the desired end of protecting innocent purchasers was served by convicting innocent sellers the opinion did not explain. Nor did it explore any of the other relevant considerations.

73. *United States v. Dotterweich*, 320 U.S. 277 (1943). See the discussion of the case in note 70. Mr. Justice Frankfurter's opinion disposes of the problem in a curt half paragraph, citing only the *Balint* case, note 72, and Holmes' dictum in *United States v. Johnson*, 221 U.S. 48 (1911), note 71. It pays no attention to the differences between the possibilities of protecting themselves which sellers of drugs have and those which corporation presidents have.

74. 355 U.S. 225 (1957).

75. For the possibilities of such an analysis, see Hughes, note 44.

76. The cases, as the Court said, "involved only property interests in civil litigation."

77. The analysis by Hughes, note 44, recognizes how crucial the question of the bearing of this doctrine is and comes to intellectual grips with it.

78. It is true that the problem in *Lambert* was one of constitutionality under the fourteenth amendment and, so, of a kind which raises for Mr. Justice Frankfurter the ultimate problem of judicial self-restraint in the interpretation of the Constitution. That this is so, however, serves only to emphasize the casual way in which in *United*

States v. Dotterweich, 320 U.S. 277 (1943), note 70, he disposed of an issue which was simply one of the just interpretation of a federal statute.

79. See Book Review, *Harvard Law Review* 67 (1954): 1456, 1485–86. See also the opinion in note 70.

80. The protection of society by disabling offenders who are likely to offend again is conventionally said to be one of the functions of the criminal law, and the statement in the text may be thought to be mistaken in ignoring this purpose. It is suggested, however, that there is serious danger in admitting so speculative a factor as a criterion in the exercise of general sentencing discretion. The existence of a special need for disablement of particularly dangerous individuals seems better taken into account either (1) by parole authorities, in the light of prison experience, in deciding whether to release a prisoner before his maximum term has expired; or (2) through statutory provisions for extended terms laying down carefully-stated criteria to be applied by the judge on the basis of special findings of fact. See Model Penal Code § 7.03 and accompanying comment (Tent. Draft No. 2, 1955).

81. As just suggested in subdivision A of this part, the judge has an important discretion also in deciding just what kind of ceremony he will make of the formal pronouncement of the judgment of conviction. In addition, the Model Penal Code, as presently drafted, proposes that he should have a discretion to reduce the grade of the offense for which the defendant is convicted in order to deal justly with those cases in which there are special ameliorating circumstances not taken into account in the general statutory definition of the crime. See ibid. § 6.11.

82. See pp. 26–27.

83. See pp. 27–28.

84. The Model Penal Code proposes that the trial judge should be given the authority to fix a minimum prison term of not less than one year—the theory of the one-year minimum for the judicially-fixed minimum term being that it is "an institutional necessity" for effective treatment. See Model Penal Code § 6.06 and accompanying comment (Tent. Draft No. 3, 1955).

85. For an alternative form of power to give this recognition, see note 81.

86. See pp. 27–28.

87. The Model Penal Code denies the judge the power to fix an individualized maximum term which is less than the statutory term, except in the special case where sentence for an extended term is imposed. See Model Penal Code § 6.06 and accompanying comment (Tent. Draft. No. 2, 1955).

88. The provisions of the Model Penal Code (Tent. Draft No. 2, 1954) which the italicized paragraphs (a) and (b) replace are as follows:

"(a) To forbid and prevent conduct that unjustifiably and inexcusably inflicts or threatens substantial harm to individual and public interests;

"(b) To subject to public control persons whose conduct indicates that they are disposed to commit crimes";
In the suggested revision, the latter paragraph is transferred to subsection (2) of the section dealing with sentencing and treatment.

89. The words "not blameworthy" are substituted for "without fault."

90. The language is substituted for the clause, "To prevent the commission of offenses."

91. See note 88.

Chapter 2

1. "Duty Owed By Citizens," *New York Times*, September 6, 1895, p. 8.

2. Robert H. Jackson, "The Federal Prosecutor," *Journal of the American Judicature Society* 24 (1940): 18–20, reprinted herein, see Appendix A, p. 173.

3. Hart, "The Aims of the Criminal Law," pp. 5–6.

4. John S. Baker, Jr., *Measuring the Explosive Growth of Federal Crime Legislation* (Washington: The Federalist Society for Law and Public Policy Studies, 2004); John C. Coffee, Jr., "Does 'Unlawful' Mean 'Criminal'?: Reflections on the Disappearing Tort/Crime Distinction in American Law," *Boston University Law Review* 71 (1991): 216.

5. *United States v. Hoflin*, 880 F.2d 1033, 1036–39 (9th Cir. 1989).

6. *United States v. International Minerals & Chemical Corp.*, 402 U.S. 558, 569 (1971) (Stewart, J., dissenting).

7. *United States v. Hanousek*, 176 F.3d 1116, 1119–22 (9th Cir. 1999).

8. 18 U.S.C. § 1346; *United States v. Rybicki*, 354 F.3d 124, 133 (2nd Cir. 2003) (en banc).

9. *United States v. Bronston*, 658 F.2d 920, 921–28 (2nd Cir. 1981); ibid. at 930–31 (Van Graafeiland, J., dissenting).

10. *Rybicki*, 354 F.3d at 145; ibid. at 162 (Jacobs, J., dissenting).

11. Ibid. at 161 (Jacobs, J., dissenting).

12. Executive Office of the President, Office of National Drug Control Policy, "Drug Use Trends," Drug Policy Information Clearinghouse Factsheet, October 2002, p. 7.

13. Sentencing Commission, "Sourcebook of Federal Sentencing Statistics," 2007, tables 14, 33, www.ussc.gov/ANNRPT/2007/SBTOC07.htm.

14. Steven D. Levitt and Stephen J. Dubner, *Freakonomics: A Rogue Economist Explores the Hidden Side of Everything* (New York: Harper-Collins, 2005), p. 25.

15. 26 U.S.C. § 7201.

16. 18 U.S.C. § 1001(a)(2).

17. *United States v. Leo*, 941 F.2d 181, 190 (3rd Cir. 1991).

18. *Brogan v. United States*, 522 U.S. 398 (1998); ibid. at 411 (Ginsburg, J., concurring in judgment).

19. *United States v. McNab*, 331 F.3d 1228 (11th Cir. 2003); Ellen S. Podgor and Paul Rosenzweig, "Bum Lobster Rap," *Washington Times*, January 6, 2004, p. A14.

20. 18 U.S.C. § § 1956, 1957; *United States v. Hill*, 167 F.3d 1055, 1066 (6th Cir. 1999); *United States v. Allen*, 129 F.3d 1159, 1165 (10th Cir. 1997).

21. Todd R. Russell and O. Carter Snead, "Federal Criminal Conspiracy," *American Criminal Law Review* 35 (1998): 741–42, 764–66.

22. Kathleen M. Olivares, Velmer S. Burton, Jr., and Francis T. Cullen, "The Collateral Consequences of a Felony Conviction: A National Study of State Legal Codes 10 Years Later," *Federal Probation* 60 (1996): 10, 11–14.

23. John R. Lott, Jr., *Freedomnomics: Why the Free Market Works and Other Half-Baked Theories Don't* (Washington: Regnery, 2007), pp. 72–78.

24. Hart, "The Aims of the Criminal Law," pp. 24–25.

25. Ibid., pp. 28–29.

26. Jackson, "The Federal Prosecutor," See Appendix A., p. 173.

27. Rick Shepherd, Letter to the Editor, "Spitzer, FBI Both Cut from Same Power-Abusing Cloth," *Palm Beach Post*, March 27, 2008, p. 17A.

28. C. J. Chivers and Erin E. Arvedlund, "Russia Tycoon Given 9 Years on Tax Charge," *New York Times*, June 1, 2005, p. A1; C. J. Chivers, "New Charges in Russia

214

Against Oil Executives," *New York Times*, February 6, 2007, p. A10; Sabrina Tavernise, "As Tycoons Slip Overseas, Putin Appears to Lay Siege," *New York Times*, November 5, 2003, p. A12.

29. Hart, "The Aims of the Criminal Law," pp. 10–11.

Chapter 3

1. Graeme Newman, *Comparative Deviance: Perception and the Law in Six Cultures* (New York: Elsevier, 1976), table 4.

2. J. E. Scott and F. Al-Thakeb, "Perceptions of Deviance Cross-Culturally," in *Crime and Deviance*, ed. Graeme Newman (Beverly Hills, CA: Sage, 1980), p. 64.

3. Alfred Blumstein, Jacqueline Cohen, and Daniel Nagin, eds., *Deterrence and Incapacitation* (Washington: National Academy of Sciences, 1978).

4. Steven D. Levitt, "Deterrence," *Crime: Public Policies for Crime Control*, ed. James Q. Wilson and Joan Petersilia (Oakland, CA: ICS Press, 2002), pp. 435–50.

5. David Rowe and D. W. Osgood, "Sociological Theories of Delinquency and Heredity: A Reconsideration," *American Sociological Review* 49 (1984): 526–540; James Q. Wilson and Richard J. Herrnstein, *Crime and Human Nature* (New York: Simon & Schuster, 1985), ch. 3; Adrian Raine, "The Biological Bases of Crime," in *Crime: Public Policies for Crime Control*, ed. James Q. Wilson and Joan Petersilia (Oakland, CA: ICS Press, 2002), pp. 43–74.

6. William Spelman, "The Limited Importance of Prison Expansion," in *The Crime Drop in America*, ed. Alfred Blumstein and Joel Wallman (Cambridge, U.K.: Cambridge University Press, 2000), pp. 97–129.

7. Robert J. Blendon and John T. Young, "The Public and the War on Illicit Drugs," *Journal of the American Medical Association* 279 (March 18, 1998): 827.

8. Pew Research Center on the People and the Press, "Interdiction and Incarceration Still Top Remedies," Survey Report, March 21, 2001.

9. Charles F. Manski, John V. Pepper, and Carol V. Petrie, eds., *Informing America's Policy on Illegal Drugs* (Washington: National Academy Press, 2001), pp. 192–93.

10. Tom R. Tyler, Jay D. Caspar, and B. Fisher, "Maintaining Allegiance Toward Political Authorities," *American Journal of Political Science* 33 (1989): 629–52; E. Allen Lind and Tom R. Tyler, *The Social Psychology of Procedural Justice* (New York: Plenum, 1988).

11. Craig A. McEwen and Richard J. Maiman, "Mediation in Small Claims Courts," *Law and Society Review* 18 (1984): 11–49.

12. Alfred Blumstein, Jacqueline Cohen, Susan E. Martin, and Michael Tonry, eds., *Research on Sentencing* (Washington: National Academy Press, 1983), p. 10. See also Brian Forst, "Prosecution," in *Crime: Public Policies for Crime Control*, ed. Wilson and Petersilia (Oakland, CA: ICS Press, 2002), p. 514.

Chapter 4

1. Hart, "The Aims of the Criminal Law," pp. 1–42, 17.
2. Ibid., p. 17.
3. Ibid., pp. 18–19.
4. Ibid., p. 41.
5. Ibid., p. 20.
6. 11 U.S. 32 (1812).

7. *Dowling v. United States*, 473 U.S. 207, 213 (1985) (citing *Liparota v. United States*, 471 U.S. 419, 424 (1985)).

8. Hart, "The Aims of the Criminal Law," p. 21.

9. Ibid., p. 41. Emphasis in original. Hart recommends that the two italicized words be substituted instead of the words "without fault," which appear in the original American Law Institute draft.

10. Ibid., p. 41.

11. Ibid., pp. 40–41.

12. Paul H. Robinson, "Reforming the Federal Criminal Code and the Model Penal Code: A Top Ten List," *Buffalo Criminal Law Review* 225 (1997): Available at SSRN, http://ssrn.com/abstract=10237 or DOI: 10.2139/ssrn.10.2139/ssrn.10237

13. *Morissette v. United States*, 342 U.S. 246 (1952). Many of the facts of the case that I recite here are taken from the Supreme Court's opinion at 247–50. Further details were gleaned from the majority and dissenting opinions of the Court of Appeals panel that affirmed Morissette's conviction by a vote of 2-1. See *Morissette v. United States*, 187 F.2d 427 (6th Cir. 1951).

14. See, for example, Ford W. Hall, "The Common Law: An Account of Its Reception in the United States," *Vanderbilt Law Review* 4 (1951): 791.

15. Justice William O. Douglas concurred in the result without signing onto Justice Jackson's opinion, and Justice Sherman Minton took no part in the decision of the case.

16. According to the Bureau of Justice Statistics, "cases were terminated against 83,391 defendants during 2004. Most (90%) defendants were convicted. Of the 74,782 defendants convicted, 72,152 (or 96%) pleaded guilty or no-contest." See Bureau of Justice Statistics, "Federal Justice Statistics, Sentencing," December 20, 2007, www.ojp.usdoj.gov/bjs/fed.htm#Sentencing.

17. Andrew Good and I were long-time law partners in the firm of Silverglate & Good. In July 2003, I withdrew from the firm and became "of counsel" to the successor firm of Good & Cormier, an arrangement that currently continues.

18. *Konop v. Hawaiian Airlines, Inc.*, 302 F.3d 868 (9th Cir. 2002).

19. *United States v. Councilman*, 245 F. Supp. 2d 319 (D. Mass. 2003).

20. A different issue is presented when a statute or regulation gives specialized meaning to a word, in which case the dictionary or common meaning goes out the window. However, *Councilman* was not such a case.

21. Carrie Johnson, "Charge Against KPMG Dropped: Firm Cooperated Over Tax Shelters, Prosecutors Say," *WashingtonPost.com*, January 4, 2007; and Lynnley Browning, "Ernst & Young Won't Face Criminal Charges," *New York Times*, May 31, 2007.

22. Malcolm Gladwell, "Open Secrets: Enron, Intelligence, and the Perils of Too Much Information," *The New Yorker*, January 8, 2007, www.newyorker.com/reporting/2007/01/08/070108fa_fact_gladwell.

23. The nation's top international accounting firms—the ones large enough to conduct audits of even the largest corporations—were, not so many years ago, dubbed "the Big Eight." In 2002, after various mergers, they became "the Big Five." They were Arthur Andersen, Deloitte & Touche, KPMG, Ernst & Young, and Pricewaterhouse Coopers.

24. Robert A. Mintz, "Too Late for Arthur Andersen," *Legal Times*, June 6, 2005. At the time, Mintz was the head of the securities litigation, government investigations, and white collar criminal defense practice group at McCarter & English law firm in Newark, New Jersey.

25. Ibid.

26. This lack of opposition "usually indicates," wrote the *New York Times'* savvy Supreme Court analyst Linda Greenhouse, in reporting the unexpected grant of the petition, that "the government considers an appeal to be frivolous or inconsequential." See Linda Greenhouse, "Supreme Court Will Review Conviction of Arthur Andersen," *New York Times*, January 8, 2005.

27. See, for example, 18 U.S.C. § 1512.

28. *Arthur Andersen LLP v. United States*, 544 U.S. 696, 706 (2005).

29. 18 U.S.C. § § 1512(b)(2)(A) and (B).

30. In this context, such a charge against earnings is a nonrecurring charge-off made by the company that reduces its earnings for the reportable period, but does not indicate a recurring or regular pattern. In other words, the reader is supposed to assume that while some event caused this particular charge, it would not necessarily be a regular or recurring event. It might well be a one-time charge. In contrast, normal expenses of doing business are expected to recur in each reporting period. Corporations are thought to have an incentive to classify charges as nonrecurring, where possible, to make current financial results seem more positive or, at least, indicative of a more positive future. Enron was thought to have classified many normal costs of doing business as one-time nonrecurring charges, thereby overstating the company's financial health.

31. Tony Mauro, "One Little E-Mail, One Big Legal Issue," *National Law Journal*, April 25, 2005, p. 7.

32. The jury's role is to determine the facts. The judge instructs the jury as to the legal principles that govern the case. The jury, once instructed on the law, then proceeds to decide how the facts fit within the legal framework and whether the case requires a verdict of guilty or not guilty.

33. Quoted in Jess Bravin, "Supreme Court Hints at Curbing Strategy on White-Collar Crime," *Wall Street Journal*, April 28, 2005.

34. The Hurwitz case is told in Tina Rosenberg's article, "Doctor or Drug Pusher," *New York Times Magazine*, June 17, 2007. Likewise, John Tierney reported the case for the *New York Times*, "At Trial, Pain Has a Witness," April 24, 2007. Jacob Sullum has an excellent discussion, "Chilling Conviction," *Washington Times*, December 26, 2004. For a more general discussion, see Ronald T. Libby, "Treating Doctors as Drug Dealers: The DEA's War on Prescription Painkillers," Cato Institute Policy Analysis no. 545, June 16, 2005.

35. *United States v. Prigmore*, 243 F.3d 1 (1st Cir. 2001).

36. Daniel Fischel, *Payback: The Conspiracy to Destroy Michael Milken and His Financial Revolution* (New York: HarperBusiness, 1995).

37. In fact, Michael Milken pleaded guilty not because he believed the "scheme" to be unlawful, but because the government indicted his younger brother, Lowell, and agreed to dismiss the charges if Michael would plead guilty, which he did. The story is skillfully told by Daniel Fischel, *Payback*, pp. 157–67.

38. *United States v. Singleton*, 165 F.3d 1297 (10th Cir. 1999) (en banc).

39. 18 U.S.C. § 1001.

Chapter 5

1. Hart, "The Aims of the Criminal Law," p. 1.

2. Ibid., p. 2.

3. Ibid., p. 4.

4. Ibid., p. 5.
5. Ibid.
6. See, for example, Sheldon Glueck, "Predictive Devices and the Individualization of Justice," *Law and Contemporary Problems* 23 (1958): 461.
7. Hart, "The Aims of the Criminal Law," p. 11.
8. Ibid., p. 17.
9. Ibid., p. 38.
10. Ibid.
11. Ibid., pp. 27–28.
12. Ibid., p. 26.
13. Ibid., p. 12 (emphasis in original).
14. Ibid., p. 13 (footnote omitted). See also ibid. p. 18.
15. Ibid., p. 16.
16. Ibid., p. 16 n. 36, p. 21.
17. Ibid., pp. 31–32.
18. Ibid., p. 22, citing *Commonwealth v. Mixer*, 93 N.E. 249 (Mass. 1910).
19. *Commonwealth v. Mixer*, note 18, 93 N.E. at 251–52:

> The Legislature may say with respect to transportation of liquors that ordinarily common carriers do not transport them without either knowing or having reasonable ground to suspect their nature, or that usually packages containing them give some evidence of their contents to those reasonably alert to detect it, or that directly or indirectly some information generally is conveyed to the carrier as to their character. . . . Moreover railroads and street railways, common carriers which do not deliver merchandise to houses or places of business, are exempted from the operation of the statute, although they are subject to the provisions of Rev. Laws, c. 100, § 49, as are all shippers of intoxicating liquor, whether by railroad, railway or other carrier. This circumstance tends to emphasize its application to those carriers who deliver goods in such a way as to make especially difficult of detection violations of the law. Evasion of laws of this kind is well known to be more likely to be practiced when small quantities are involved. Taking into account the magnitude of the evils arising from the use of intoxicating liquors and the manifest struggle of the Legislature by successive enactments to regulate its transportation so that secrecy may be prevented, and so that those municipalities which have voted 'no license' may be protected from furtive and slyly clandestine efforts to override the popular desire for freedom from its illicit traffic, an exemption ought not to be read into the statute contrary to what seems to be a deliberate legislative purpose based upon grounds of public policy. It follows from what has been said that the carrier has a right to use any reasonable efforts, by the establishment and publication of general rules, by specific inquiry, or in proper cases by the inspection of packages, or otherwise, to ascertain whether intoxicating liquors constitute any part of the goods offered for transportation, and to refuse to take any as to which this right is denied, in order to protect himself against committing the crime created by the statute.

20. Hart, "The Aims of the Criminal Law," p. 31.

21. See, for example, Paul H. Robinson and John M. Darley, "The Utility of Desert," *Northwestern University Law Review* 91 (1997): 453. For some experimental evidence, see Janice Nadler, "Flouting the Law," *Texas Law Review* 83 (2005): 1399.

22. Herbert Wechsler and Jerome Michael, "A Rationale of the Law of Homicide: I," *Columbia Law Review* 37 (1937): 701, 750–51.

23. Hart, "The Aims of the Criminal Law," p. 36.

24. For sophisticated treatments, see Nathan Hanna, "Say What? A Critique of Expressive Retributivism," *Law and Philosophy* 27 (2008): 123; Dan M. Kahan, "What Do Alternative Sanctions Mean?" *University of Chicago Law Review* 63 (1996): 591.

25. James Fitzjames Stephen, *A History of the Criminal Law of England*, vol. 2 (London: William S. Hein & Co., 1883), p. 81.

26. Ibid., p. 82.

27. I assume a case of pure vengeance rather than one in which the motivation for going after one's oppressor is to prevent him from doing further injury, to recover property, or to obtain any other benefit or reward—except the satisfaction of satisfying one's desire for vengeance. On the criminal law's roots in vengeance, see Richard A. Posner, *Law and Literature*, rev. and enlarged ed. (Cambridge, MA, and London: Harvard University Press, 1998), pp. 49–60.

28. As when he said, "No one can fail to be touched when he sees a judge, who has reached the bench by an unusual combination of power, industry and good fortune, bending the whole force of his mind to understand the confused, bewildered, wearisome, and half-articulate mixture of question and statement which some wretched clown pours out in the agony of his terror and confusion." James Fitzjames Stephen, *A General View of the Criminal Law of England* (London and Cambridge, U.K.: Macmillan and Co., 1863), p. 232.

29. James Fitzjames Stephen, *Liberty, Equality, Fraternity* (Chicago and Oxford, U.K.: University of Chicago Press, 1992 [1872]), p. 152.

30. Andrew Oldenquist, "An Explanation of Retribution," *Journal of Philosophy* 85 (1988): 464.

31. Stephen, *Liberty, Equality, Fraternity*, p. 151.

32. See, for example, Bernard Williams, "Moral Luck," in *Moral Luck: Philosophical Papers 1973–1980*, ed. Bernard Williams (Cambridge, U.K.: Cambridge University Press, 1981), p. 20.

33. Not that there weren't exceptions. I mentioned the Herbert Wechsler and Jerome Michael article in note 22. Another example is Thurman W. Arnold, "Criminal Attempts: The Rise and Fall of an Abstraction," *Yale Law Journal* 40 (1930): 53, an exemplary work of legal realism.

34. Jeremy Bentham, *Introduction to the Principles of Morals and Legislation*, ed. J. H. Burns and H. L. A. Hart (Oxford, U.K.: Oxford University Press, 1996 [1780]), parts XII–XVII.

35. See Jillisa Brittan and Richard A. Posner, "Classic Revisited: Penal Theory in *Paradise Lost*," *Michigan Law Review* 105 (2007): 1049.

36. See, for example, Gary S. Becker, "Crime and Punishment: An Economic Approach," *Journal of Political Economy* 76 (1968): 169; Richard A. Posner, "An Economic Theory of the Criminal Law," *Columbia Law Review* 85 (1985): 1193; Steven Shavell, "Criminal Law and the Optimal Use of Nonmonetary Sanctions as a Deterrent," *Columbia Law Review* 85 (1985): 1232; and discussion and other citations in Richard A. Posner, *Economic Analysis of Law*, 7th ed. (New York: Aspen Publishers, 2007), pp. 215–47.

Chapter 6

1. Hart, "The Aims of the Criminal Law," p. 1.

2. Here, I am not speaking of scientific truth, which may well be singular and uniform (though always subject to challenge and reformulation), but rather of moral truth, which is not nearly as objective.

3. Alan M. Dershowitz, *Preemption: A Knife That Cuts Both Ways (Issues of Our Time)* (New York: W.W. Norton Inc., 2006), pp. 193–94.

4. Hart, "The Aims of the Criminal Law," pp. 40–41:

> (a) To foster the development of personal capacity for responsible decision to the end that every individual may realize his potentialities as a participating and contributing member of his community:
>
> (b) To declare the obligation of every competent person to comply with (1) those standards of behavior which a responsible individual should know are imposed by the conditions of community life if the benefits of community living are to be realized, and (2) those further obligations of conduct, specially declared by the legislature, which the individual either in fact knows or has good reason to know he is supposed to comply with, and to prevent violations of these basic obligations of good citizenship by providing for public condemnation of the violations and appropriate treatment of the violators;
>
> (c) To safeguard conduct that is not blameworthy from condemnation as criminal;
>
> (d) To give fair warning of the nature of the conduct declared to constitute an offense; and
>
> (e) To differentiate on reasonable grounds between serious crimes and minor offenses.
>
> (2) The general purposes of the provisions governing the conviction, sentencing, and treatment of offenders are:
>
> (a) To further the purposes of the provisions governing the definition of offenses;
>
> (b) To promote the correction and rehabilitation of offenders;
>
> (c) To subject to a special public control those persons whose conduct indicates that they are disposed to commit crimes.

5. Hart uses the following terms: "A formal and solemn pronouncement of the moral condemnation of the community. . . . At least under existing law, there is a vital difference between the situation of a patient who has been committed to a mental hospital and the situation of an inmate of a state penitentiary. The core of the difference is precisely that the patient has not incurred the moral condemnation of his community, whereas the convict has." (Ibid., pp. 5–6).

6. "The danger to the individual is that he will be punished, or treated, for what he is or is believed to be, rather than for what he has done. If his offense is minor but the possibility of his reformation is thought to be slight, the other side of the coin of mercy can become cruelty." (Ibid., pp. 7–8).

7. Ibid., p. 9.

8. Ibid., pp. 9–10.

9. Ibid., p. 41.

10. Ibid., p. 10.

11. Ibid., pp. 40, 10.

12. Suicide terrorists might be deterred by the threat that their family and friends will be killed if they engage in acts of suicide terrorism. But this approach to deterrence—called "sippenhaft" by the Nazis—is unacceptable to civilized nations.

13. Hart, "The Aims of the Criminal Law," p. 41.

14. O. W. Holmes, Jr., *The Common Law* (Boston: Little, Brown, and Company, 1881), pp. 43, 46.

15. William Blackstone, *Commentaries on the Laws of England: Book the Fourth* (Oxford, U.K.: Clarendon Press, 1769), p. 249.

16. Francis Wharton, *A Treatise on Criminal Law*, 8th ed. (Philadelphia: Kay and Brother, 1880), p. 2.

17. Cesare Beccaria, *Essays on Crimes and Punishments*, trans. M. de Voltaire (New York: Gould & Van Winkle, 1809), pp. 41–42.

18. Immanuel Kant, *Metaphysical Elements of Justice: The Complete Text of the Metaphysics of Morals Part I*, 2nd ed., trans. John Ladd (Indianapolis: Hackett Publishing, 1999), p. 138.

19. Francis Wharton, *A Treatise on Criminal Law*, 8th ed. (Philadelphia: Kay and Brother, 1880), p. 2.

20. O. W. Holmes, Jr., *The Common Law* (Boston: Little, Brown, and Company, 1881), p. 46.

21. William Blackstone, *Commentaries on the Laws of England: Book the Fourth* (Oxford, U.K.: Clarendon Press, 1769), p. 249.

22. Frederick Pollock and Frederic William Maitland, *The History of English Law*, vol. 2 (Cambridge, U.K.: Cambridge University Press, 1898), p. 475.

23. Code of Hammurabi, section 116, 209–10, and 229–30, www.wsu.edu/~dee/MESO/CODE.HTM.

24. Payment of this bot could, under certain circumstances and for "emendable" crimes, satisfy the victims and the state. It was also somewhat preventive, insofar as any painful response is preventive, in that it made crime expensive and, thus, presumably reduced its frequency.

25. Pollock and Maitland, *The History of English Law*, p. 478. This practice was described as follows:

> Though we must not speculate about a time in which there was no law, the evidence which comes to us from England and elsewhere invites us to think of a time when law was weak, and its weakness was displayed by a ready recourse to outlawry. It could not measure its blows; he who defied it was outside its sphere; he was outlaw. He who breaks the law has gone to war with the community; the community goes to war with him. It is the right and duty of every man to pursue him, to ravage his land, to burn his house, to hunt him down like a wild beast and slay him; for a wild beast he is; not merely is he a "friendless man," he is a wolf. Even in the thirteenth century, when outlawry had lost its exterminating character and had become an engine for compelling the contumacious to abide the judgment of the courts, this old state of things was not forgotten; *Caput great lupinum*—in these words the court decreed outlawry.

Ibid., p. 449.

26. This argument has been repeatedly offered against efforts to construct a jurisprudence of torture. See, for example, Richard H. Weisberg, "Loose Professionalism,

or Why Lawyers Take the Lead on Torture," in *Torture: A Collection*, ed. Sanford Levinson (Oxford, U.K.: Oxford University Press, 2004), pp. 299–305.

27. Hart, "The Aims of the Criminal Law," pp. 10–11.

28. Ibid., p. 11.

29. Ibid., p. 7. "The danger to the individual is that he will be punished, or treated, for what he is or is believed to be, rather than for what he has done. If his offense is minor but the possibility of his reformation is thought to be slight, the other side of the coin of mercy can become cruelty." Ibid., pp. 7–8.

30. Ibid., p. 24.

31. Alan M. Dershowitz, *Preemption: A Knife That Cuts Both Ways*, pp. 249–50.

Chapter 7

1. See Dan M. Kahan, "What Do Alternative Sanctions Mean?" *University of Chicago Law Review* 63 (1996): 591, 631–32; Dan M. Kahan, "Reciprocity, Collective Action, and Community Policing," *California Law Review* 90 (2002): 1513, 1528.

2. Dan M. Kahan, "What Do Alternative Sanctions Mean?"

3. Chicago Police Department, "CLEARpath," www.chicagopolice.org/ps/list.aspx.

4. Jeff Mosier and Holly Yan, "New Tools in Prostitution Crackdown Arlington: Police Posting Arrestees' Photos on City Web Site, Postcards," *Dallas Morning News*, June 7, 2007, p. 15B.

5. Fort Worth Police Department, "Prostitution and Indecent Exposure Arrests," www.fortworthpd.com/johntvarrests.htm.

6. Stop DUI AZ, www.stopduiaz.com.

7. Orlando Police Department, "Prescription Fraud Unit," www.cityoforlando.net/police/Rx/Rx.htm.

8. Maricopa County Sheriff's Office, "Mugshots," www.mcso.org/index.php?a = GetModule&mn = Mugshot.

9. Maricopa County Sheriff's Office, "Deadbeat Parents," www.mcso.org/index.php?a = GetModule&mn = Deadbeat_Parents.

10. John Braithwaite, *Crime, Shame and Reintegration* (Cambridge, U.K.: Cambridge University Press, 1989), p. 8.

11. Ibid.

12. Dan Kahan calls "stigmatizing publicity" the most straightforward type of shaming in which the penalty "attempt[s] to magnify the humiliation inherent in conviction by communicating the offender's status to a wider audience." Dan M. Kahan, "What Do Alternative Sanctions Mean?" Kahan identifies three other types of shaming sanctions: literal stigmatization, self-debasement, and contrition.

13. "Kansas Criminal History Records" now available at www.accesskansas.org, Business Wire, May 12, 2004, http://findarticles.com/p/articles/mi_m0EIN/is_2004_May_12/ai_n6023367.

14. A $17.50 fee is required to obtain an individual's criminal record.

15. Kansas Bureau of Investigation, "Requesting Someone Else's Criminal History Record," www.accesskansas.org/kbi/criminalhistory/request_public.shtml (last visited Dec. 27, 2007).

16. Ibid.

17. "Kansas Criminal History Records."

18. See SEARCH, National Consortium for Justice Information and Statistics, "National Task Force on the Criminal Backgrounding of America," (2005), p. 1, www.search.org/files/pdf/ReportofNTFCBA.pdf.

Chapter 8

1. Hart, "The Aims of the Criminal Law," pp. 1–41.

2. Fourth Amendment (prohibiting "unreasonable searches and seizures"); Fifth Amendment (prohibiting double jeopardy, self-incrimination); Sixth Amendment (requiring a "speedy and public trial, by an impartial jury," the right to confront witnesses, and the right to counsel); Seventh Amendment (right to trial by jury); Eighth Amendment (prohibiting "cruel and unusual punishments").

3. Hart, "The Aims of the Criminal Law," p. 9.

4. See Ariz. Rev. Stat. § § 36-3701 to -3717 (effective July 1, 1996); Calif. Welf. & Inst. Code § § 6600–6609.3 (effective October 11, 1995); D.C. Code § § 22-3803–3811 (effective May 21, 1994); Fla. Stat. § § 394.910–.931 (effective January 1, 1999); 725 Ill. Comp. Stat. 207/1–/99 (effective January 1, 1998); Iowa Code § § 229A.1–.16 (effective May 6, 1998); Kan. Stat. Ann. § § 59-29a01 to -29a21 (effective July 1, 1994); Mass. Gen. Laws ch. 123A, § § 1–16 (effective January 14, 1994); Minn. Stat. § § 253B.01–.23 (effective May 22, 1997); Mo. Stat. § § 632.480–.513 (effective January 1, 1999); N.J. Stat. § § 30:4-27.24 to .38 (effective August 12, 1999); N D. Cent. Code § § 25-03.1-01 to -46 (effective April 8, 1997); S.C. Code § § 44- 48-10 to -170 (effective June 5, 1998); Texas Health & Safety Code § § 841.001–.147 (effective September 1, 1999); Va. Code § § 37.1-70.1 to .19 (effective January 1, 2003); Wash. Rev. Code § § 71.09.010–.902 (effective July 1, 1990); Wis. Stat. § § 980.01–.13 (effective June 2, 1994).

5. See David Boerner, "Confronting Violence: In the Act and in the Word," *University of Puget Sound Law Review* 15 (1992): 525 (providing a first-person account of the enactment of Washington's Sexually Violent Predator law).

6. *Tacoma News Tribune*, Front page, May 24, 1989.

7. *Spokane Spokesman Review*, Front page, May 24, 1989.

8. *Seattle Post-Intelligencer*, Editorial, May 24, 1989.

9. Letter from Governor, *Seattle Post-Intelligencer*, May 26, 1989.

10. For example, see *Korematsu v. United States*, 323 U.S. 214 (1944) (upholding the internment of Japanese-Americans in the western United States during·World War II); see also *The Federalist* No. 8 (Alexander Hamilton) (November 20, 1787) ("The violent destruction of life and property incident to war, the continual effort and alarm attendant on a state of continual danger, will compel nations the most attached to liberty to resort for repose and security to institutions which have a tendency to destroy their civil and political rights. To be more safe, they at length become willing to run the risk of being less free.").

11. Washington's march to enact SVP laws was not unique. Kansas enacted its SVP law following a similar scenario involving the rape and murder of Stephanie Schmidt by a paroled rapist. See Steven I. Friedland, "Treatment, Punishment and Civil Commitment of Sex Offenders," *University of Colorado Law Review* 70 (1999): 94.

12. "Deterrence ... ought not to be thought of as the overriding and ultimate purpose of the criminal law." Hart, "The Aims of the Criminal Law," p. 9.

13. See, for example, Wash. Rev. Code § 71.09.020(16) (defining a "sexually violent predator" as "any person who has been *convicted of or charged with* a crime of sexual violence and who suffers from a mental abnormality or personality disorder which

makes the person likely to engage in predatory acts of sexual violence if not confined in a secure facility" (emphasis added)).

14. See D.C. Code § § 22-3810.

15. See Mo. Stat. § 632-486.

16. Wash. Rev. Code 71.09.030. What constitutes a "recent overt act" is hotly debated in Washington courts.

17. See, for example, Wash. Rev. Code § 71.09.060.

18. The U.S. Supreme Court has held that the clear and convincing evidentiary standard of civil commitment is the constitutional minimum. See *Addington v. Texas*, 441 U.S. 418 (1979).

19. *In re Detention of Young*, 857 P.2d 989 (1993).

20. See, for example, Wash. Rev. Code § 71.09.070.

21. Hart, "The Aims of the Criminal Law," p. 11.

22. Ibid.

23. The fundamental difference between general civil commitment of the mentally ill and SVP civil commitment is that general civil commitment of the mentally ill is grounded in the state's *parens patriae* power, where the state confines the individual to protect the individual from him or herself. See, for example, *Hawaii v. Standard Oil Co.*, 405 U.S. 251, 257 (1972) (stating the *parens patriae* power includes the duty to protect "persons under legal disabilities to act for themselves"). Whereas, SVP civil commitment is grounded in the state's police power to confine individuals to protect society. See *Kansas v. Hendricks*, 521 U.S. 346 (1997); *Kansas v. Crane*, 534 U.S. 407 (2002). This distinction is explicit in the separate statutory schemes. Compare, for example, Wash. Rev. Code § 71.05 et seq. (mental health civil commitment) with Wash. Rev. Code § 71.09 et seq. (SVP civil commitment).

24. 309 U.S. 270 (1940).

25. Twenty-six states and the District of Columbia had "sexual psychopath" laws by 1960 in addition to other procedures of civil commitment of the mentally ill. Raquel Blacher, "Historical Perspective of the Sex Psychopath Statute: From the Revolutionary Era to the Present Federal Crime Bill," *Mercer Law Review* 46 (1995): 903. Hart lamented this "rash of so-called 'sexual psychopath' laws which disgrace the statute books of many states." Hart, "The Aims of the Criminal Law," p. 8 n.19.

26. Hart commented on this distinction. "The core of the difference is precisely that the patient has not incurred the moral condemnation of his community, whereas the convict has." Hart, "The Aims of the Criminal Law," p. 6.

27. See Barbara K. Schwartz, "The Case Against Involuntary Commitment," in *The Sexual Predator*, ed. Anita Schlank and Fred Cohen (Kingston, N.J.: Civic Research Institute, 1999), pp. 3–4; see also Blacher, "Historical Perspective of the Sex Psychopath Statute," pp. 906–7.

28. See Aman Ahluwalia, "Civil Commitment of Sexually Violent Predators: The Search for a Limiting Principle" *Cardozo Public Law, Policy & Ethics Journal* 4 (2006): 490.

29. Eric Janus, "Civil Commitment as Social Control: Managing the Risk of Sexual Violence," in *Dangerous Offenders: Punishment and Social Order*, ed. Mark Brown and John Pratt (New York: Routledge, 2000), p. 74.

30. Hart, "The Aims of the Criminal Law," pp. 36–40.

31. Ibid. For a convincing argument limiting SVP commitment to only sexually violent undeterrable recidivists, see Christopher Slobogin, "A Jurisprudence of Dangerousness," *Northwestern University Law Review* 98 (2003): 1–62.

32. Notably, courts who weigh those factors fail to consider the harm caused to the Constitution when the government detains those who have long paid for their crimes.

33. Hart, "The Aims of the Criminal Law," pp. 7–8.

34. 422 U.S. 563 (1975).

35. Ibid. at 568.

36. Ibid. at 575; see also *Jackson v. Indiana*, 406 U.S. 715, 738 (1972). ("[D]ue process requires that the nature and duration of commitment bear some reasonable relation to the purpose for which the individual is committed.")

37. 481 U.S. 739 (1987).

38. 18 U.S.C. § 3142(e).

39. *Salerno* at 750.

40. Ibid. at 747.

41. But compare *Foucha v. Louisiana*, 504 U.S. 71, 81 (1992) (distinguishing *Salerno* on the fact of "pretrial detention") with *Kansas v. Hendricks*, 521 U.S. 346, 363 (1996) (relying on *Salerno* to hold civil commitment of SVPs as nonpunitive).

42. 504 U.S. 71 (1992).

43. Immediately one should ask: How can a person be insane, but not mentally ill? Foucha's legal insanity resulted from a temporary drug induced psychosis but otherwise Foucha was not mentally ill. See *Foucha* at 74–75. This highlights the "interstitiality" of criminal law. See Eric Janus, "Preventing Sexual Violence: Setting Principled Constitutional Boundaries on Sex Offender Commitment" *Indiana Law Journal* 72 (1996): 161–62. Under the doctrine of interstitiality the criminal law is the primary mechanism in which society vindicates its interest in the prohibited conduct; the state may only resort to the civil system if the person's mental capacity has diminished his ability to comply with the law to such an extent the state can no longer vindicate its interests through the criminal law.

Hart explicitly recognized the first half of the doctrine—see Hart, "The Aims of the Criminal Law," pp. 5–6 (noting the difference between a patient and a prisoner as "the patient has not incurred the moral condemnation of his community, whereas the convict has")—and implicitly recognized the second half, see Ibid., p. 14 n. 31 (noting the problem as "reaching for criteria which will avoid attaching moral blame where blame cannot justly be attached, while, at the same time, avoiding a denial of moral responsibility where the denial would be personally and socially debilitating").

44. *Foucha* at 75.

45. Ibid. at 77 (citing *Jones v. United States*, 463 U.S. 354 (1983) (holding that an acquittee—by reason of insanity—may be committed without satisfying the burden of proving mental illness and dangerousness)).

46. Ibid. at 77 (quoting *Jones*, 463 U.S. at 368).

47. Ibid. at 77 n. 4 (noting the dissent "would permit the indefinite detention"); ibid. at 82 (noting the detention permitted under *Salerno* "was strictly limited in duration"); ibid. at 83 n. 6 (noting the dissent "embraces the view that the State may indefinitely hold an insanity acquittee who is found by a court to have been cured of his mental illness and who is unable to prove that he would not be dangerous").

48. Ibid. at 78–79 (quoting *Vitek v. Jones*, 445 U.S. 480, 492 (1980)).

49. Ibid. at 82.

50. Ibid. at 82–83.

51. Hart, "The Aims of the Criminal Law," p. 5.

52. *Foucha* at 88 (O'Connor, J., concurring).

53. Ibid. at 82–83.

54. *Kansas v. Hendricks*, 521 U.S. 346, 353–54 (1997). Hendricks has been called the ideal person to determine the constitutionality of SVP commitment; he was in his 60s and had spent half his adult life in jail for sexual offenses involving young children. Jeffery R. Glovan, "I Don't Think We're in Kansas Anymore Leroy: *Kansas v. Hendricks* and the Tragedy of Judicial Restraint," *McGeorge Law Review* 30 (1999): 337–39.

55. Ibid., p. 354.

56. Ibid.

57. Ibid.

58. Ibid., p. 355.

59. Ibid., p. 355 n. 2.

60. Ibid., p. 355.

61. Ibid., p. 356.

62. Ibid.

63. Ibid., p. 358 (citing *Heller v. Doe*, 509 U.S. 312, 314–15 (1993) (upholding a Kentucky statute permitting commitment of "mentally retarded" or "mentally ill" and dangerous individuals); *Allen v. Illinois*, 478 U.S. 364, 366 (1986) (upholding an Illinois statute permitting commitment of "mentally ill" and dangerous individuals); *Pearson*, 309 U.S. 271–72 (1940)).

64. *Hendricks* at 359.

65. Ibid.

66. Ibid. at 360. The importance of this should not be understated; it renders the mental illness prerequisite to civil commitment a mere formality. In effect, the U.S. Supreme Court gives carte blanche to state legislatures to commit its citizenry based on dangerousness alone. As one commentator notes, "By denying the distinction between mental illness and mental abnormality [the *Hendricks* opinion] precludes a discussion ... of whether the diluted mental abnormality standard satisfies due process." Ahluwalia, "Civil Commitment of Sexually Violent Predators," p. 512.

67. See *Foucha*, 504 U.S. at 82–83. Unlike *Hendricks*, however, the record in *Foucha* did not contain *any* testimony of Foucha having a mental illness. *Foucha* at 79 ("Here, according to the testimony given at the hearing in the trial court, Foucha is not suffering from a mental disease or illness.").

68. For a deeper discussion on the shortcomings of *Hendricks*, see Mara Lynn Krongard, "A Population at Risk: Civil Commitment of Substance Abusers after *Kansas v. Hendricks*," *California Law Review* 90 (2002): 130–33.

69. *Hendricks* at 366 (quoting *In re Hendricks* 912 P.2d at 136). The Court ignored the obvious import of this segregation; civil commitment of criminal recidivists is "prejudice against discrete and insular minorities," which supposedly calls for "a correspondingly more searching judicial inquiry." *United States v. Carolene Products Co.*, 304 U.S. 144, 153 n.4 (1938). The Court's failure to invoke its higher level of review is surprising when one considers the majority of states that disenfranchise convicted felons. For example, article V, section 2 of the Kansas State Constitution permits the legislature to disenfranchise the mentally ill or incarcerated individuals until "restored to [their] civil rights." For a civilly committed SVP, this would arguably be forever. We suppose the Court may choose which "discrete and insular minorities" it wishes to bestow judicial favor on.

70. Hart, "The Aims of the Criminal Law," p. 4.

71. Hart, "The Aims of the Criminal Law," p. 5.

72. John C. Coffee, Jr., "Paradigms Lost: The Blurring of the Criminal and Civil Law Models—and What Can Be Done About It," *Yale Law Journal* 101 (1992): 1884.

73. Ibid., p. 1882.

74. Ibid., p. 1883.

75. Ibid., p. 1884.

76. Randy E. Barnett, *Restoring the Lost Constitution: The Presumption of Liberty* (Princeton, N.J.: Princeton University Press, 2004).

77. Ibid., p. 38.

78. Ibid., p. 44 (emphasis in original). See also Friedrich Hayek, *The Constitution of Liberty* (Chicago: University of Chicago Press, 1960), p. 21 (positing the government's monopoly on coercive power may only be properly exercised to protect the rights of its citizens).

79. Barnett, *Restoring the Lost Constitution*, p. 59 ("Make any list of liberty rights you care to and one can always add twenty or thirty more.").

80. Ibid., p. 53 ("These commands would nevertheless carry with them a duty of obedience, even without consent, if there is a procedural assurance that they do not violate the rights of the persons on whom they are imposed and that their requirements are necessary to protect the rights of others.").

81. As Chief Judge David Bazelon noted:

> when a determination of 'dangerousness' will result in a deprivation of liberty, no court can afford to ignore the very real constitutional problems surrounding incarceration predicated only upon a supposed propensity to commit criminal acts. Incarceration may not seem 'punishment' to the jailors, but it is punishment to the jailed. Incarceration for a mere propensity is punishment not for acts, but for status, and punishment for status is hardly favored in our society. In essence, detention for status is preventive detention. . . . It may be that in some circumstances preventive detention is in fact permissible. If so, such detention would have to be based on a record that clearly documented a high probability of serious harm, and circumscribed by procedural protections as comprehensive as those afforded criminal suspects.

Cross v. Harris, 418 F.2d 1095, 1101–02 (D.C. Cir. 1969) (footnotes omitted).

82. As Hart ventures, "what distinguishes a criminal from a civil sanction and all that distinguishes it . . . is the judgment of community condemnation which accompanies and justifies its imposition." Hart, "The Aims of the Criminal Law," p. 4.

83. As Justice Robert Jackson stated in *Williamson v. United States*, 184 F.2d 280, 282 (2nd Cir. 1950), "Imprisonment to protect society from predicted but unconsummated offenses is so unprecedented in this country and so fraught with danger of excesses and injustice that I am loath to resort to it."

84. Hart, "The Aims of the Criminal Law," p. 10.

85. See Slobogin, "A Jurisprudence of Dangerousness," pp. 29–30.

86. *In re Detention of Campbell*, 986 P.2d 771, 786 (Wash. 1999) (Sanders, J., dissenting).

87. Hart, "The Aims of the Criminal Law," p. 9.

88. *Hendricks* at 375–77.

89. American Psychiatric Association, *Diagnostic and Statistical Manual of Mental Disorders*, 4th ed. (Arlington, VA: American Psychiatric Association, 1994), p. xxiii (emphasis added) (hereinafter referred to as "*DSM-IV*").

90. *Kansas v. Crane*, 534 U.S. 407, 413 (2002).
91. See, for example, *In re Detention of Young*, 857 P.2d 989 (Wash. 1993).
92. Hart, "The Aims of the Criminal Law," p. 7.
93. In fact, earlier editions of the *DSM* classified homosexuality as a mental disorder until 1974, but no one would seriously suggest detaining homosexuals as mentally ill simply on the basis of this classification. For an argument applying civil detention to substance abusers, see Krongard, "A Population at Risk," pp. 142–54.
94. Indeed, the *DSM-IV* contains countless diagnosable conditions an expert could use to diagnose a mental illness. For example, the *DSM-IV* includes antisocial personality disorder, alcohol induced sleep disorder, and nicotine use disorder—to name a few. See *DSM-IV*, pp. 243, 603, 645.
95. For example, the recidivism rate for burglary is 31.9 percent, four times higher than that of rape. See David P. Bryden and Roger C. Park, "'Other Crimes' Evidence in Sex Offense Cases," *Minnesota Law Review* 78 (1994): 572.
96. As one commentator observes, "[t]he logic of the predator commitment law can be applied to people who drive while under the influence of alcohol, who assault their domestic partners or children, who use crack cocaine, or who commit whatever the new 'crime-of-the-month' happens to be." John Q. LaFond, "Washington's Sexually Violent Predator Law: A Deliberate Misuse of the Therapeutic State for Social Control," *University of Puget Sound Law Review* 15 (1992): 698–99.
97. On reliability and validity, see John Monahan and Laurens Walker, *Social Science in Law*, 6th ed. (Westbury, N.Y.: Foundation Press, 2006), pp. 57–58. Reliability is the extent to which different examiners, assessing the same individual, will assign the same diagnosis. Validity is the extent to which diagnostic criteria identify a supposed mental disorder within the stated purpose of civil commitment. In other words, it is how well an examiner discriminates between sex offenders subject to civil commitment and those not subject to civil commitment.
98. As the Washington State Psychiatric Association pointed out in its amicus brief to the Washington State Supreme Court in *In re Detention of Young*, "[b]ecause the concept of 'abnormality' has such diverse meaning . . . there is no way to assure with reasonable medical certainty that it will be applied accurately and uniformly." Amicus brief of the Washington State Psychiatric Association, *In re Detention of Young*, 122 Wn.2d 1 (1993), pp. 3–4.
99. "Occasionally sex offending arises as a result of mental illness but more commonly it comes about through a complex mixture of influences which include social attitudes and individual training, level of personal morality and respect for others, the strength of sexual drives and directions in which these drives have developed, the ability to acquire legitimate sexual partners, and the presence of anxiety—or anger—laden emotional responses in ordinary sexual interactions." Adarsh Kaul, "Sex Offenders—Cure or Management?" *Medical Science and Law* 33 (1993): 208.
100. *Hendricks* at 357–58 (requiring proof of dangerousness "coupled . . . with the proof of some additional factor, such as a 'mental illness' or 'mental abnormality.'").
101. 534 U.S. 407 (2002). In *Crane*, the Court recognized that "there must be proof of serious difficulty in controlling behavior" sufficient to "distinguish the dangerous sexual offender whose serious mental illness, abnormality, or disorder subjects him to civil commitment from the dangerous but typical recidivist convicted to an ordinary case." Ibid. at 413. The factor distinguishing the criminal recidivist from the sexual predator is the mental illness that causes dangerousness. This causal link is also explicit in the statutory scheme. See Wash. Rev. Code § 71.09.020(16) (defining a SVP

as "any person who has been convicted of or charged with a crime of sexual violence and who suffers from a mental abnormality or personality disorder *which makes* the person likely to engage in predatory acts of sexual violence if not confined in a secure facility." (emphasis added)).

102. *DSM-IV*, p. xxiii.

103. As one commentator notes, given the prevalence of sex crimes in our society, this tautological reasoning could result in a sizeable proportion of the population being subject to civil commitment. Brett C. Trowbridge and Jay Adams, "Sexually Violent Predator Assessment Issues," *The Trowbridge Foundation Report* 8/9 (Fall 2006–Winter 2007): 6.

104. As the Washington State Psychiatric Association stated, "sexual predation in and of itself does not define a mental illness. It defines criminal conduct . . . it is inappropriate to make broad generalizations as to a causal connection between sexual offenses in general and any particular psychiatric condition." Amicus brief of the Washington State Psychiatric Association, *In re Detention of Young*, 857 P.2d 989 (Wash. 1993), pp. 3–4. "Moreover, mental health professionals do not consider sex offenders to be suffering from a personality disorder which causes an individual to commit a sex offense." Ibid., p. 5. In fact, when the proposal to include a rape-related mental disorder was raised during a prior revision of the *DSM*, it was rejected. Trowbridge and Adams, "Sexually Violent Predator Assessment Issues," n. 103, p. 7 (citing Sari Staver, "APA Reaches Compromise on Diagnosis" *American Medical News*, July 18, 1986, p. 41).

105. Hart, "The Aims of the Criminal Law," p. 7.

106. *In re Detention of Young*, 857 P.2d 989, 1008 (Wash. 1993).

107. See, for example, *In re Linehan*, 557 N.W.2d 171, 181 (Minn. 1996) (The Minnesota Supreme Court requires proof that dangerousness is "highly likely.").

108. R. Karl Hanson, "What Do We Know About Risk Assessment?" in *The Sexual Predator*, ed. Anita Schlank and Fred Cohen (Kingston, N.J.: Civic Research Institute, 1999), pp. 4–8.

109. For example, all currently developed actuarial instruments include some element of incest recidivism. See Trowbridge and Adams, "Sexually Violent Predator Assessment Issues," n. 103, p. 10. Because a "predatory" sex offense is generally defined as a sex offense directed toward a stranger, any use of these actuarial instruments is inappropriate. See Wash. Rev. Code § 71.09.020(9) (defining "predatory" as an act "directed towards: (a) strangers; (b) individuals with whom a relationship has been established or promoted for the primary purpose of victimization; or (c) persons of casual acquaintance with whom no substantial personal relationship exists.").

110. See Trowbridge and Adams, "Sexually Violent Predator Assessment Issues," n. 103, p. 10 (concluding "forensic psychologists familiar with the research readily acknowledge that clinical judgments of dangerousness must be regarded with considerable caution.").

111. *In re Linehan*, 518 N.W.2d 609, 616 (Minn. 1994) (Coyne, J., dissenting).

112. John Q. LaFond, "Washington's Sexually Violent Predator Law," n. 96, p. 699.

113. *Frye v. United States*, 293 F. 1013 (D.C. Cir. 1923); *Daubert v. Merrel Dow Pharmaceuticals Inc.*, 509 U.S. 579 (1993).

114. *Frye* at 1014.

115. *Daubert* at 590.

116. Amicus brief of the American Psychiatric Association, *Tarasoff v. Regents of the Univ. of California*, 17 Cal.3d 425 (1976), p. 6.

117. Christopher Slobogin, "Dangerousness and Expertise," *University of Pennsylvania Law Review* 133 (1984): 100–11.

118. "[T]he research literature shows that mental health professionals can generally make sound expert predictions of violence only as matters of probabilities, which are 'rarely above 50%' and often substantially less." See amicus brief of the American Psychiatric Association, *Kansas v. Hendricks*, 521 U.S. 346 (1997), p. 18 (quoting Grisso and Appelbaum, "Is It Unethical to Offer Predictions of Future Violence?" *Law and Human Behavior* 16 (1992): 626).

119. Eric Janus and Paul Meehl, "Assessing the Legal Standard for Prediction of Dangerousness in Sex Offender Commitment Proceedings," *Psychology, Public Policy & Law* 3 (1997): 37.

120. Randy K. Otto, "On the Ability of Mental Health Professionals to 'Predict Dangerousness': A Commentary on Interpretations of the 'Dangerousness' Literature," *Law & Psychology Review* 18 (1994): 67–68.

121. See *In re Detention of Young*, 857 P.2d 989, 1017 (Wash. 1993) ("The sciences of psychiatry and psychology are not novel; they have been an integral part of the American legal system since its inception."); see also *People v. Ward*, 71 Cal.App.4th 368 (1999); *Westerheide v. State*, 767 So.2d 637 (Fla. 5th Dist. 2000).

122. See *In re Detention of Holtz*, 653 N.W.2d 613 (Iowa Ct. App. 2002); *In re Commitment of Lalor*, 661 N.W. 2d 898 (Wis. App. 2003); *In re Commitment of Burton*, 884 So.2d 1112 (Fla. 2nd Dist. 2004).

123. See *Daubert v. Merrell Dow Pharmaceuticals, Inc.*, 509 U.S. 579, 591–92 (1993).

124. *In re Detention of Harris* at 111.

125. See amicus brief of the American Psychiatric Association, *Kansas v. Hendricks*, 521 U.S. 346 (1997), pp. 18–19.

126. Hart, "The Aims of the Criminal Law," p. 10.

127. Ibid., p. 39.

128. See Vernon L. Quinsey, "Review of the Washington State Special Commitment Center Program for Sexually Violent Predators," *University of Puget Sound Law Review* 15 (1992): 705–7.

129. Hart, "The Aims of the Criminal Law," p. 39.

130. "Research on motivation suggests that . . . labeling [a person a 'predator'] might become a self-fulfilling prophecy. The individual shunted into the 'predator' system will come to believe that, unlike those who are punished as volitional actors, he in incapable of acting differently." Slobogin, "A Jurisprudence of Dangerousness," p. 30.

131. See *Eirhart v. Libbey-Owens-Ford Co.*, 996 F.2d 837, 841 n.5 (7th Cir. 1993).

132. Stephen J. Schulhofer, "Two Systems of Social Protection: Comments on the Civil-Criminal Distinction with Particular Reference to Sexually Violent Predator Laws," *Journal of Contemporary Legal Issues* 7 (1996): 78–79.

Chapter 9

1. Hart, "The Aims of the Criminal Law," pp. 1, 29.

2. Hart, "The Aims of the Criminal Law," p. 4. Indeed, I am inclined to believe that such detail argues against the very conclusions drawn by Professor Hart that there are specific and unstated substantive limits on the definition of a "crime."

3. Ibid.

4. Ibid., p. 2.

5. See, generally, the series of studies done under my supervision by the U.S. Department of Justice's Office of Legal Policy from 1985–89 on the subject of "Truth in Criminal Justice," *University of Michigan Journal of Law Reform* 22 (1989).

6. This discussion is not intended to suggest that there are not other "aims of the criminal justice system" that may regularly come into play in the appellate process. One of those aims, for example, is the need in sentencing to properly balance consideration of the crime and consideration of the criminal. In my judgment, federal and state sentencing guidelines have proven extraordinarily successful in achieving a reasonable equilibrium in this regard. Although Hart recognizes that the "very ideal of justice is offended by seriously unequal penalties for substantially similar crimes," his general extolling of judicial discretion suggests that he might have been lukewarm specifically about the virtues of guidelines, as he is about mandatory minimum sentences, given that the principal purpose of both has been to limit judicial discretion. Hart, "The Aims of the Criminal Law," p. 39.

7. *Mapp v. Ohio*, 367 U.S. 483 (1961); *Miranda v. Arizona*, 384 U.S. 436 (1966); *Roe v. Wade*, 410 U.S. 113 (1973); *Baker v. Carr*, 369 U.S. 186 (1962); *Garcia v. San Antonio Metropolitan Transit Authority*, 469 U.S. 528 (1985); *Fay v. Noia*, 372 U.S. 391 (1963); *Katzenbach v. Morgan*, 384 U.S. 641 (1966); *South Dakota v. Dole*, 483 U.S. 203 (1987); *Heart of Atlanta Motel v. United States*, 379 U.S. 241 (1964); *Lemon v. Kurzman*, 403 U.S. 602 (1971); *Shapiro v. Thompson*, 394 U.S. 618 (1969); *Dunn v. Blumstein*, 405 U.S. 330 (1972).

8. Hart, "The Aims of the Criminal Law," p. 2.

9. Ibid., pp. 30–31.

10. Ibid., p. 35.

11. Ibid.

12. Ibid., p. 4.

13. Ibid., p. 17.

14. Ibid., p. 36.

15. Ibid., p. 30.

16. For example, *Kelo v. City of New London*, 545 U.S. 469 (2005); *Garcia v. San Antonio Metropolitan Transit Authority*, 469 U.S. 528 (1985); *Morrison v. Olson*, 487 U.S. 654 (1988).

17. For example, *Rasul v. Bush*, 542 U.S. 466 (2004); *Miranda v. Arizona*, 384 U.S. 436 (1966).

18. United States Constitution, art. III, § 1; Constitution of 1963 of Michigan, art. VI, § 1.

19. Hart, "The Aims of the Criminal Law," p. 18.

20. See *Stanford v. Kentucky*, 492 U.S. 361, 379 (1989) (This Court "limited [the Eighth] Amendment's extension to those practices contrary to the 'evolving *standards of decency* that mark the progress of a maturing *society*.' It has never been thought that this was a shorthand reference to the preferences of a majority of this Court.")

21. Hart, "The Aims of the Criminal Law," p. 15.

22. Ibid., p. 5.

23. *Grannis v. Ordean*, 234 U.S. 385, 394 (1914).

24. *Ingraham v. Wright*, 360 U.S. 474, 507–08 (1959).

25. Hart would certainly be disappointed that Justice Felix Frankfurter, in his dissent in *Lambert v. California*, 355 U.S. 225, 245 (1957), has largely been proven right that "the present decision will turn out to be an isolated deviation from the strong current of precedents—a derelict on the waters of the law."

26. "[I]f this decision were to be given its relevant scope, a whole volume of the United States Reports would be required to document in detail the legislation in this country that would fall or be impaired." *Lambert* at 245 (dissent of Frankfurter, J., describing the potential impact of the majority's decision).

27. Barbara Wooten, *Crime and the Criminal Law* (Andover, U.K.: Stevens & Sons 1963), p. 55.

28. Ibid., pp. 55–56.

29. See *Immigration & Naturalization Service v. Chadha*, 462 U.S. 919 (1983).

30. *Mistretta v. United States*, 488 U.S. 361, 411 (1989).

31. Ibid. at 381.

32. Hart, "The Aims of the Criminal Law," pp. 4, 11.

33. 472 Mich. 446, 697 N.W.2d 494 (2005).

34. *Morrisette v. United States*, 342 U.S. 246 (1952); *Staples v. United States*, 511 U.S. 600 (1994); *United States v. X-Citement Video*, 513 U.S. 64 (1994).

35. Although I do not believe that "strict liability" crimes can ordinarily be described as producing "absurd results," at least not in the narrow legal sense of something that no legislature could possibly have intended, such crimes would seem far more susceptible than ordinary crimes to specific applications, such as described in the text, that might easily rise to the level of producing a genuinely "absurd result." See, for example, *K Mart Corp v. Cartier, Inc.*, 486 U.S. 281, 324 n. 2 (1988) (Scalia, A., concurring in part and dissenting in part) ("it is a venerable principle that a law will not be interpreted to produce absurd results."); *Public Citizen v. United States Dept. of Justice*, 491 U.S. 440, 470 (1989) ("absurd results" rule "demonstrates a respect for the coequal Legislative Branch, which we assume would not act in an absurd way.")

36. Hart, "The Aims of the Criminal Law," p. 31.

37. Ibid., p. 35.

38. Ibid.

39. Ibid., p. 36.

40. It must be said, of course, that there are a not insignificant number of drug and narcotics prosecutions in Michigan, as in most other states. Although I am not oblivious to the continuing debate concerning the merits of these laws, drug offenses are obviously not strict liability crimes. Their rationale is grounded in part in the arguably close connection between the proscribed conduct and genuinely *malum in se* offenses, such as robbery, theft, and assault, as well as in their perceived connection with such undisputed social ills as domestic abuse, impaired driving, and delinquency.

41. Indeed, under state sentencing guidelines, it has become increasingly incumbent on sentencing judges in order to exceed the guideline range in a particular case to articulate the special or distinctive blameworthiness of a defendant.

42. Hart, "The Aims of the Criminal Law," pp. 24, 28.

43. See David Boaz, *The Politics of Freedom* (Washington: Cato Institute, 2007), pp. xv–xvi.

44. Hart, "The Aims of the Criminal Law," p. 19 n. 42.

45. Such expansion has already diminished the import of the federal "double jeopardy" clause by enabling consecutive state–federal prosecutions on the grounds that these constitute separate "sovereigns." See *Bartkus v. Illinois*, 359 U.S. 121 (1959).

232

46. United States Constitution, art. I, § 1. For background, see *Industrial Union Department v. American Petroleum Institute*, 448 U.S. 607 (1980) (Rehnquist, J., concurring); and Gary Lawson, "Who Legislates?" in *The Public Interest Law Review*, ed. Roger Clegg and Leonard Leo (Durham, NC: Carolina Academic Press, 1995), p. 147.

47. Cf. *United States v. Morrison*, 529 U.S. 598 (2000); *United States v. Lopez*, 514 U.S. 549 (1995) (Thomas, J., concurring opinion).

48. *Roe v. Wade*, 410 U.S. 113 (1973). We may well see as one of the next great criminal justice frontiers the increasing constitutionalization of substantive criminal punishments pursuant to the "proportionality" doctrine of *Harmelin v. Michigan*, 501 U.S. 957 (1991).

49. Hart, "The Aims of the Criminal Law," p. 33.

Appendix B

1. Friedman, Milton, and Rose Friedman. *Free to Choose: A Personal Statement* (Orlando, FL: Harcourt Brace Jovanovich, 1980), p. 145.

Appendix C

1. James Q. Whitman, *Harsh Justice: Criminal Punishment and the Widening Divide between America and Europe* (Oxford, U.K.: Oxford University Press, 2003).

2. William Shakespeare, *The Merchant of Venice*.

Recommended Bibliography

Books:

American Bar Association, Criminal Justice Section, Task Force on Federalization of Criminal Law. *The Federalization of Criminal Law*. Chicago: American Bar Association, 1998.

Ayoob, Massad F. *The Truth about Self Protection*. New York: Bantam Books, 1983.

Barnett, Randy E., and John Hagel, eds. *Assessing the Criminal: Restitution, Retribution, and the Legal Process*. Pensacola, FL: Ballinger Publishing, 1977.

Benson, Bruce. *To Serve and Protect: Privatization and Community in Criminal Justice*. New York: New York University Press, 1998.

Bidinotto, Robert James, ed. *Criminal Justice?: The Legal System versus Individual Responsibility*. Irvington-on-Hudson, NY: Foundation for Economic Education, 1994.

Bogira, Steve. *Courtroom 302: A Year Behind the Scenes in an American Criminal Courthouse*. New York: Knopf, 2005.

Bovard, James. *Freedom in Chains: The Rise of the State and the Demise of the Citizen*. New York: St. Martin's Press, 1999.

Conrad, Clay S. *Jury Nullification: The Evolution of a Doctrine*. Durham, NC: Carolina Academic Press, 1999.

Dershowitz, Alan M. *The Best Defense*. New York: Random House, 1983.

Duke, Steven B., and Albert C. Gross. *America's Longest War: Rethinking Our Tragic Crusade Against Drugs*. New York: G. P. Putnam's Sons, 1994.

Dwyer, Jim, Peter Neufeld, and Barry Scheck. *Actual Innocence: When Justice Goes Wrong and How to Make It Right*. New York: Penguin Group, 2001.

Fine, Ralph Adam. *Escape of the Guilty: A Trial Judge Speaks Out Against Crime*. New York: Dodd Mead, 1986.

Green, Thomas Andrew. *Verdict According to Conscience: Perspectives on the English Criminal Trial Jury, 1200–1800*. Chicago: University of Chicago Press, 1985.

Hasnas, John. *Trapped: When Acting Ethically Is Against the Law*. Washington, DC: Cato Institute, 2006.

Healy, Gene, ed. *Go Directly to Jail: The Criminalization of Almost Everything*. Washington, DC: Cato Institute, 2004.

Jacobs, James B., and Kimberly Potter. *Hate Crimes: Criminal Law and Identity Politics*. Oxford, U.K.: Oxford University Press, 1998.

Klinger, David. *Into the Kill Zone: A Cop's Eye View of Deadly Force*. Hoboken, NJ: Jossey-Bass, 2004.

Kopel, David B., ed. *Guns: Who Should Have Them?* Amherst, MA: Prometheus Books, 1995.

Kopel, David B., and Paul H. Blackman. *No More Wacos: What's Wrong with Federal Law Enforcement and How to Fix It*. Amherst, MA: Prometheus Books, 1997.

Lynch, Timothy, ed. *After Prohibition: An Adult Approach to Drug Policies in the 21st Century*. Washington, DC: Cato Institute, 2000.

Masters, Sheriff Bill. *Drug War Addiction*. Minneapolis, MN: Accurate Press, 2001.

Murray, Charles A. *Losing Ground: American Social Policy, 1950–1980*. New York: Basic Books, 1984.

Packer, Herbert L. *The Limits of the Criminal Sanction*. Stanford, CA: Stanford University Press, 1968.

Roberts, Paul Craig, and Lawrence M. Stratton. *The Tyranny of Good Intentions: How Prosecutors and Bureaucrats Are Trampling the Constitution in the Name of Justice*. Roseville, CA: Prima Publishing, 2000.

Skolnick, Jerome H., and James J. Fyfe. *Above the Law: Police and the Excessive Use of Force*. New York: Maxwell Macmillan International, 1993.

Snyder, Jeffrey R. *A Nation of Cowards: Essays on the Ethics of Gun Control*. Minneapolis, MN: Accurate Press, 2001.

Stamper, Norm. *Breaking Rank: A Top Cop's Exposé of the Dark Side of American Policing*. New York: Nation Books, 2006.

Taylor, Stuart, and KC Johnson. *Until Proven Innocent: Political Correctness and the Shameful Injustices of the Duke Lacrosse Rape Case*. New York: Thomas Dunne Books, 2007.

Walker, Samuel. *The New World of Police Accountability*. Thousand Oaks, CA: Sage Publications, 2005.

Articles:

Baker, John. "Measuring the Explosive Growth of Federal Crime Legislation." The Federalist Society for Law and Public Policy Studies (May 2004).

———. "Nationalizing Criminal Law: Does Organized Crime Make It Necessary or Proper?" *Rutgers Law Journal* 16 (1985): 495.

———. "Reforming Corporations through Threats of Federal Prosecution." *Cornell Law Review* 89 (2004): 310.

Balko, Radley. "Overkill: The Rise of Paramilitary Police Raids in America." Cato Institute White Paper, July 17, 2006.

Blue, Jon C. "High Noon Revisited: Commands of Assistance by Peace Officers in the Age of the Fourth Amendment." *Yale Law Journal* 101 (1992): 1475–90.

Blumenson, Eric D., and Eva S. Nilsen. "Policing for Profit: The Drug War's Hidden Economic Agenda." *University of Chicago Law Review* 65 (1998): 35.

Boaz, David. "A Drug-Free America—Or a Free America." *University of California Davis Law Review* 24 (1991): 617.

Chevigny, Paul G. "The Right to Resist an Unlawful Arrest." *Yale Law Journal* 78 (1969): 1128–50.

Davies, Thomas Y. "Recovering the Original Fourth Amendment." *Michigan Law Review* 98 (1999): 547–750.

Dillard, W. Thomas, Stephen R. Johnson, and Timothy Lynch. "A Grand Façade: How the Grand Jury Was Captured by Government," Cato Institute Policy Analysis no. 476, May 13, 2003.

Fine, Ralph Adam. "Plea Bargaining: An Unnecessary Evil." *Criminal Justice? The Legal System versus Individual Responsibility* (1994): 84–101.

Janis, N. Richard. "Deputizing Company Counsel as Agents of the Federal Government." Cato Institute White Paper, July 14, 2008.

Lear, Elizabeth T. "Is Conviction Irrelevant?" *University of California Los Angeles Law Review* 40 (1993): 1179–1239.

236

Luna, Erik. "Drug Exceptionalism." *Villanova Law Review* 47 (2002): 753.

_____ . "The Overcriminalization Phenomenon." *American University Law Review* 54 (2005): 703.

_____ . "Traces of a Libertarian Theory of Punishment." *Marquette Law Review* 91 (2007): 263.

Lynch, Timothy. "In Defense of the Exclusionary Rule." *Harvard Journal of Law and Public Policy* 23 (1999): 711.

_____ . "No Confidence: An Unofficial Account of the Waco Incident." Cato Institute Policy Analysis no. 395, April 9, 2001.

_____ . "Polluting Our Principles: Environmental Prosecutions and the Bill of Rights." Cato Institute Policy Analysis no. 223, April 20, 1995.

_____ . "The Case against Plea Bargaining." *Regulation* 26 (2003): 24–27.

Murray, Charles. "The Coming of Custodial Democracy." *Commentary* (September 1988): 19–24.

Ostrowski, James. "The Moral and Practical Case for Drug Legalization." *Hofstra Law Review* 18 (1989): 607.

Parker, Jeffrey S. "Doctrine for Destruction: The Case of Corporate Criminal Liability." *Managerial & Decision Economics* 17 (1996): 381.

Pilon, Roger. "Criminal Remedies: Restitution, Punishment, or Both?" *Ethics* 88 (1978): 384.

Polsby, Daniel D. "The False Promise of Gun Control." *Atlantic Monthly* (March 1994): 57–60.

Reynolds, Glenn Harlan. "Of Dissent and Discretion." *Cornell Journal of Law and Public Policy* 9 (2000): 685.

Roots, Roger. "Are Cops Constitutional?" *Seton Hall Constitutional Law Journal* 11 (2001): 685.

Spooner, Lysander. "Vices Are Not Crimes: A Vindication of Moral Liberty." *The Lysander Spooner Reader*. New York: Fox and Wilkes, 1992.

Stuntz, William J. "The Pathological Politics of Criminal Law." *Michigan Law Review* 100 (2001): 505.

Whitehead, Barbara Dafoe. "Dan Quayle Was Right." *Atlantic Monthly* (April 1993): 47–84.

Contributors

Alan M. Dershowitz is the Felix Frankfurter Professor of Law at Harvard University.

Henry M. Hart (1904–1969) was Dane Professor of Law at Harvard University.

James B. Jacobs is the director of the Center for Research in Crime and Justice at the New York University School of Law.

Alex Kozinski is a judge on the U.S. Court of Appeals for the Ninth Circuit.

Timothy Lynch is the director of the Project on Criminal Justice at the Cato Institute.

Stephen J. Markman is a justice on the Michigan Supreme Court.

Richard A. Posner is a judge on the U.S. Court of Appeals for the Seventh Circuit.

Richard B. Sanders is a justice on the Washington Supreme Court.

Harvey A. Silverglate is Of Counsel to the Boston law firm of Good & Cormier. He specializes in criminal defense, civil liberties, academic freedom, and student rights law.

James Q. Wilson is the Ronald Reagan Professor of Public Policy at Pepperdine University.

Index

241

246

About the Editor

Timothy Lynch is the director of the Cato Institute's Project on Criminal Justice. His research interests include overcriminalization, terrorism, the drug war, the militarization of police tactics, and gun control. In 2000, he served on the National Committee to Prevent Wrongful Executions. Lynch has also filed several amicus briefs in the U.S. Supreme Court in cases involving constitutional rights. He is the editor of *After Prohibition: An Adult Approach to Drug Policies in the 21st Century*. Since joining Cato in 1991, Lynch has published articles in the *New York Times*, the *Washington Post*, the *Wall Street Journal*, and the *National Law Journal*. He has appeared on PBS's *The NewsHour with Jim Lehrer*, Fox's *The O'Reilly Factor*, and C-SPAN's *Washington Journal*, among other venues. Lynch is a member of the Wisconsin, District of Columbia, and Supreme Court bars. He earned both a BS and a JD from Marquette University.

Cato Institute

Founded in 1977, the Cato Institute is a public policy research foundation dedicated to broadening the parameters of policy debate to allow consideration of more options that are consistent with the traditional American principles of limited government, individual liberty, and peace. To that end, the Institute strives to achieve greater involvement of the intelligent, concerned lay public in questions of policy and the proper role of government.

The Institute is named for *Cato's Letters*, libertarian pamphlets that were widely read in the American Colonies in the early 18th century and played a major role in laying the philosophical foundation for the American Revolution.

Despite the achievement of the nation's Founders, today virtually no aspect of life is free from government encroachment. A pervasive intolerance for individual rights is shown by government's arbitrary intrusions into private economic transactions and its disregard for civil liberties.

To counter that trend, the Cato Institute undertakes an extensive publications program that addresses the complete spectrum of policy issues. Books, monographs, and shorter studies are commissioned to examine the federal budget, Social Security, regulation, military spending, international trade, and myriad other issues. Major policy conferences are held throughout the year, from which papers are published thrice yearly in the *Cato Journal*. The Institute also publishes the quarterly magazine *Regulation*.

To maintain its independence, the Cato Institute accepts no government funding. Contributions are received from foundations, corporations, and individuals, and other revenue is generated from the sale of publications. The Institute is a nonprofit, tax-exempt, educational foundation under Section 501(c)3 of the Internal Revenue Code.

CATO INSTITUTE
1000 Massachusetts Ave., N.W.
Washington, DC 20001
www.cato.org